About the Author

Richard N. Potter directs the social work department at a liberal arts college in Nebraska, where he has taught innovative sources in dream analysis and the individual transformative journey. Raised in a family of mystics, Richard was initiated into the Sufi Order of the West and now pursues a deeper realization of his own unique path.

SPIRITUALITY

The Direct Path to Consciousness

Richard N. Potter

2004
Llewellyn Publications
St. Paul, Minnesota 55164-0383, U.S.A.

First Edition
First Printing, 2004

Book design and editing by Michael Maupin
Cover image © 2003 by Brand X
Cover design by Gavin Dayton Duffy

Library of Congress Cataloging-in-Publication Data
Potter, Richard N., 1945–
    Authentic spirituality : the direct path to consciousness / Richard N. Potter.
        p. cm.
    Includes bibliographical references and index.
    ISBN 0-7387-0442-3
        1. Spiritual life. I. Title.

    BL624.P668 2004
    204—dc22   2003069478

Llewellyn Worldwide does not participate in, endorse, or have any authority or responsibility concerning private business transactions between our authors and the public.
    All mail addressed to the author is forwarded but the publisher cannot, unless specifically instructed by the author, give out an address or phone number.
    Any Internet references contained in this work are current at publication time, but the publisher cannot guarantee that a specific location will continue to be maintained. Please refer to the publisher's website for links to authors' websites and other sources.

Llewellyn Publications
A Division of Llewellyn Worldwide, Ltd.
P.O. Box 64383, Dept. 0-7387-0442-3
St. Paul, MN 55164-0383, U.S.A.
www.llewellyn.com

Printed in the United States of America

To Jan, my spiritual partner and muse.

Contents

PART THREE
Spiritual Practices and the Development of Consciousness

PREFACE

I BEGAN WRITING this book almost two years before the events of September 11, 2001, brought fundamentalism to the forefront of the Western mind. Before this pivotal event there seemed to be a cultural blind spot where fundamentalism was concerned. Since September 11, Americans have been much more attuned to the chasm between fundamentalist religion and modernity. There is a dim realization that some people in this world do not respect the viewpoint that we hold. Our freedom to think for ourselves and to voice our opinions is not seen as positive, but rather as a sign of having lost our spiritual base. Our individualism is seen by many in the world as a loss rather than as a gain. In short, we are regarded as being lost in our materialistic culture and unable to uphold the moral and spiritual dictates of our ancestors.

What we still don't sufficiently understand is that the Muslim fundamentalists that we have cast as being against our way of life are just the tip of a very large iceberg. There is indeed a vast chasm between Muslim, Jewish, and Christian fundamentalism and the scientific materialism that dominates Western society, especially in the United States. There is also a very real disconnection between worldviews of conservative, patriarchal, literalist segments of society and liberal, equalitarian, well-educated segments. The growing ethnic diversity in most Western societies brings together highly divergent perspectives on religion, politics, morality, and gender. How can such societies survive if each of the diverse subgroups believes that the others are misguided, morally bankrupt, or damned to eternal hell? If we are to live together and get along, it is becoming apparent that we need perspectives that unite us, not divide us.

Religion and spirituality form the roots of most cultures. Even our modern materialistic culture has its roots in European Protestantism. If spirituality continues to be associated with history and culture, there can be no end to ethnic hostilities, religious hatred, and cultural exploitation. Recognition of the common human spiritual experiences related to consciousness development can do much to bridge the divide between cultures. It may also deprive those who would breed distrust and hatred among people for political or economic reasons the use of religion to further their aims.

Consciousness does not belong to any one race, gender, or ethnic group. Consciousness belongs to all human beings and is a force that could bind us together rather than separate us. A spirituality that focuses on transforming consciousness can promote harmony among people, religions, and nations. We have moved beyond the point where we can tolerate hate and hostility based upon religious doctrine. The world is too small and our destructive capabilities too great to continue to tolerate the modern equivalent of tribal religious warfare.

I hope that the *authentic spirituality of consciousness* presented in these pages will contribute to a change in viewpoint regarding what is at the core of spirituality and what is culturally inflected. We need to begin to understand better what it means to "render unto Caesar what belongs to Caesar, and to God what belongs to God." Caesar represents history, culture, and politics, which comprise the bulk of religious doctrine, and God can be understood to represent the evolution of consciousness. The latter is the focus of this book.

INTRODUCTION

Culture and Consciousness

LIVING IN TWO worlds is not easy. One world tells us that we should study, learn, evaluate, and assimilate knowledge. It insists that we need to be hardheaded and critical of fuzzy thinking or claims that have nothing to back them up. The other world exhorts us to faith. We need to suspend critical judgment and accept what we can't prove through normal means. Many people seem to have no trouble with this polarity, at least outwardly. Some people seem to be able to develop "cognitive exceptions," which allow them to ignore reason in certain "exceptional" cases, such as their religious beliefs. The tension between these two worlds has always troubled me.

I have spent a large part of my life studying spirituality. I was not simply following the lead of many in my generation who had sought "truth" or "wisdom" in mystical traditions of East or West. Although I was part of that cultural phenomenon, I was born into this stuff. My grandmother, who had a great impact on shaping my life, had been a healer, spiritualist, seeker, and most of all a truly saintly soul. My grandfather had been a Rosicrucian and had also spent much time with Native Americans in northern Wisconsin. My stepfather was initiated in a shamanic Buddhist ceremony in Korea. Even though I was an army kid and grew up moving quite often, my grandmother's house was home base. So between moves and for periods of time when my stepfather was stationed in places where we could not go, my mother, brother, and I lived with my grandmother and grandfather. It is the sights and smells and feel of my grandmother's house that I, in my adulthood, have come to associate with the joy and safety of childhood. I can remember being a five-year-old sitting quietly in my grandmother's house, listening to adult conversation about "spirits," "the afterlife," or some equally fascinating topic. I grew up with a mystical perspective.

After that kind of a beginning, it was rather disconcerting to find myself apparently back at square one, not sure what to believe anymore, less than a decade ago. I'd gone on an ardent search for "Truth," culminating in nearly twenty years as an initiate and guide in an esoteric school. I had learned and experienced so much. Finally my questions started to penetrate places where belief cannot go, places where intellect, insight, and discernment are needed to illuminate hidden realities. I began to see that much of what I was learning involved buying into a cultural viewpoint rather than liberation into transcendent knowledge. My spiritual guides were beautiful people, but what at first had seemed like enlightenment started to look more like cultural affectations wrapped around knowledge of human behavior and consciousness development. It was clear that the guides were very helpful and brought healing, joy, and spiritual growth to their students, which is no small task in today's world. But that was not enough for me. I was a bit too much like Jelaludin Rumi, who said, "enough of myth and metaphor, I want burning." I wanted Truth with a capital *T,* and nothing short of that would do.

It took me a while to realize how much I had already learned. Although it seemed that I was overturning everything I had thought I knew, I really wasn't. Those years of study had had a very profound impact on my consciousness. I needed to learn, as I subsequently have, that it was the transformation of my consciousness that was the real journey and not the limited cultural truths that I at first thought I had found and then thought I had lost. Once I began to realize that it was the transformation of consciousness that was the goal all along and not necessarily the cultural and psychological content, I began to better understand all the wise and kind people who had guided me in that process. I began to remember how often a guide had pointed out that the words were simply an excuse to be together and that I should not get hung up on them. I remembered the vastness of their consciousness and how it had helped me to glimpse the vastness of my own. As is typical of those on spiritual paths, I had gotten inflated by my realizations and had not fully understood the process. A little time and perspective has given me a deeper understanding of spiritual paths and spiritual guidance.

This book is an outgrowth of this spiritual crisis. In some ways my crisis reflects the spiritual crisis of our postmodern world. In addition to being a lifelong mystic, I am also a professor in a liberal arts college. That role has initiated me into the myths of modernity, with their reliance on science and linear knowledge. Being unwilling to abandon either perspective, I reflect the cultural struggle between spirit and matter, outer and inner, head and heart, linear and holistic.

I refuse to accept that these paradigms cannot be reconciled. I am convinced that if truth is found anywhere it is when we can reconcile those things that seem irreconcilable. (My old teacher Pir Vilayat Inayat Khan has been known for his insistence that "one must learn to reconcile the irreconcilables.") The North African Christian theologian Tertullian (160–220 C.E.) stated that Athens and Jerusalem (symbolizing rationality and belief) can never be reconciled; I believe that Athens and Jerusalem *can* be reconciled, and I believe that mystics of a certain ilk have always found the way to do it.

Consciousness needs to be placed at the center of spirituality, and doctrine needs to take its rightful place as culture, history, and myth. *Culture* is the container that carries the wisdom that human beings have developed over millennia. It is not a denigration of doctrine to equate it with culture, since doctrine may (or may not) be the wisdom of our ancestors and needs the container of culture in order to be maintained from one generation to the next. Culture is also what helps us live together in communities and therefore must involve developing structure and rules. Much religious doctrine fits this category.

The historical aspect of doctrine helps us to understand our world and ourselves by understanding our past. Despite its importance, history generally has been written by the winners of the wars, both cultural and actual, and therefore cannot always be viewed as fact. Much of what constitutes religious doctrine is the mythologized history of the people who hold their religion dear and have been able to emerge victorious in their wars with neighbors.

The third aspect of doctrine involves the mythic stories that provide guidance regarding the inner and outer patterns of life. Wisdom regarding ways to live a meaningful life is saved within the myths and stories of a culture and can be deciphered, layer-by-layer, as consciousness awakens and develops in the individual. Myths and stories can be potent tools in unlocking inner doors to the depths of understanding. I have come to see these three components—culture, history, and myth—as belonging to the *spirituality of culture* as opposed to the *spirituality of consciousness* that we will soon explore.

We need not give up the beauty of a mysterious and magical world in order to acknowledge the place of science. Mystery and magic belong to the domain of consciousness, while science is related to the material world. The two need not conflict. Spirituality, the awakening and developing of consciousness within the individual, can function side by side with both religion and science. Religion and science serve as the vessels in which wisdom is stored and from which wisdom can be extracted, and consciousness serves as the active principle that discovers and discerns. It is the job of the spirituality of consciousness, what I also call "authentic spirituality," to train the individual consciousness to be able to sift through the cultural content and glean the wisdom that connects with the highest (or deepest) understanding that the individual can assimilate. This becomes an ever-evolving process. Cultures differ in their ability to provide for individuals' growing consciousness, but it is this perennial process that has fed the evolution of humanity.

The Direct Path and the Balanced Path

There is a type of mysticism that goes beyond the religious and cultural roots in which it grows. It seems to be related to a temperament that some spiritual seekers have and others don't. These are the audacious souls who "shatter" their cultural viewpoints, even their most cherished religious concepts, and go only for truth. Sufis call this path

Zat as opposed to *Sifat,* the Arabic words for the knower and the known. I call these the *direct* path and the *balanced* path. I am not making an exact correlation between the Arabic words and my words, because the Arabic words have many layers of meaning not intended here. The *direct* inclination may be compared to the flight of the moth that flies directly into the flame, extinguishing itself in the fire. The *balanced* inclination is like the path of the moths that circle the flame, drawn and held fast to its light but not entering the flame.

From my experience, it would seem that the vast majority of spiritual seekers are temperamentally best suited for the *balanced* path. They are comfortable staying within the boundaries of a tradition, and even though they seek well beyond the normal ranges of spiritual knowledge and experience, they remain wedded to the fundamentals of the cultural path. For instance, Christian mystics follow the teachings of Jesus as filtered through the Christian Bible, and Muslim mystics recite the Qur'an and observe the Shariat. Some of these mystics attain realization that takes them well beyond the cultural paradigm, but they continue to accept the need for the cultural observances and often teach students within the prevailing paradigm.

Then there are those mystics who like myself find themselves drawn to the *direct* path. We feel uncomfortable with the cultural paradigms that surround our paths and seek to go beyond the forms that have kept us safe and provide meaning and guidance for those around us. A few years ago I began to realize that I am not alone in this predisposition. There is an entire lineage of *direct* mystics like myself. They come from a multitude of traditions around the world. I began to feel heartened by their teachings and just the fact that they lived and left some record of their discoveries.

Many of the people I will discuss or quote in this book fall into the *direct* lineage. They come from virtually all traditions. Buddhist teachers like Padma Sambhava and Tilopa, Sufis like Jelaludin Rumi and Rabia, and Christians like some of the early desert fathers could be considered to be kindred souls in this regard. Western mystics like Carl Jung and Joseph Campbell (although I'm not sure that either would be willing to wear the label), and most recently Joe Miller, are individuals who also have found and taught truths beyond the prevailing paradigms of their day. They have taken the perilous journey into the oneness and returned with access to new realities.

It is what I call *direct mysticism* that I believe contains the seeds of a new perspective that can heal the vast chasms between the modern materialistic paradigm, the traditional religious paradigm, and the fractious and dangerous rush to fundamentalism we see everywhere around us today. Direct mysticism relates specifically to transforming consciousness, and forms the basis of what I view as an authentic spirituality for our time. With this perspective, the world becomes one. All religions serve to help humans make sense of life. All cultures arise to provide the context for human life, and all gods become the highest ideal that can be imagined by the consciousness of individuals within their cultures. (What of God with a capital *G*? We will discuss that thorny subject in the chapter 2.) It is the consciousness of the individual that emerges as the mediator of reality and the focus of spirituality. All else, including science and religion, become the servants of individual consciousness and the emerging group consciousness, which is from a certain perspective, God.

Consciousness

We have been talking about consciousness at length, which means we have need for some common understanding about what this means. There is much philosophical debate about what consciousness is and where its origin might be. The debate ranges from those who see it as completely related and dependent upon the functioning of the brain to those who see consciousness as result of something beyond a mechanical process. I choose to stay out of this philosophical debate, and will simply describe the phenomenon to which I refer. The perspective I bring to the discussion is one of mysticism balanced with reason; I believe that the range of reality is far vaster than the territory acknowledged by empiricists.

The consciousness to which I refer is the faculty for awareness. It is the primary dualism, where self becomes aware of that which is other than self. One can surmise that anything that is aware of its surroundings as different from itself has consciousness. It appears that, as far as we know, human beings have the most evolved consciousness on the planet. This evolution allows human beings to reflect upon their selves, their feelings, their thoughts, and their cultures. We humans seek and create meaning in life because of our unique ability for reflection upon our awareness. Another way to say the same thing would be that consciousness is our capacity for knowing.

The Prophet Mohammed is quoted in a religious Hadith as saying: "I was a hidden treasure that desired to be known." (He was speaking in a God-conscious state.) Carl Jung said that the emerging myth for future generations was that "the purpose of human life is the creation of consciousness" (Edinger 1983:17). These two statements uttered almost fifteen hundred years apart seem to me to say the same thing. For Mohammed, God is saying that human purpose is to become conscious of the hidden treasure within, which is the very being of God. For Jung, making what is unconscious, conscious, is the guiding myth of our time. Is not the part of our beings of which we are not conscious at least one very large aspect of the "hidden treasure"?

Consciousness, in its knowing capacity, is the central function of human beings (along with reproduction). Consciousness depends greatly upon what we choose to notice. That, to which we choose to attune ourselves, both internally and externally, becomes what fills our consciousness. Knowing this helps us understand that we create our own reality. It also helps us understand how consciousness can evolve, transform, and grow into its rightful heritage, an understanding that is far deeper and richer than most of us would ever guess.

Changing and refining consciousness is the purpose of spiritual practice. Experiences of ecstasy, exaltation, awe, love, longing, and many others work upon consciousness in predictable ways. The beginner experiences brief states of consciousness that go beyond the norm, and continual work with these states over time creates a changed level of awareness. The individual's consciousness is opened to wider horizons, made more sensitive to self and others, becomes more penetrating of illusion, and more capable of probing the depths of the psyche. Through spiritual practice, individual awareness is cleared of its blinders and given power.

Spiritual practice is not the only means of developing consciousness. Education, falling in love, spending time in nature, exercising mastery in the workplace, and many more activities develop consciousness. Indeed, consciousness is greatly enhanced as the natural outcome of a life well lived. Spiritual practice is simply a methodical approach to a natural process and an attempt to speed and ensure the growth. We generally expect that those who both lead their life well and also engage in spiritual practice will attain more profound levels of consciousness.

It is from this viewpoint that we can talk about levels of consciousness. The concept of higher and lower levels of consciousness is an approximation of what is typically a gradual opening of horizons as well as a deepening of insight that is the natural human inheritance. Unfortunately, this inheritance is often stifled or oppressed by our cultural environment, and we—like Prometheus—must steal back this fire from the gods. We too often have the idea that consciousness descends from above, as a gift from the gods. We need to remember that Prometheus had to steal fire (consciousness) from the gods and paid a heavy price. Higher consciousness is born out of the crucible of life. The metaphor of the sea (the vast unknowing force of life) meeting the shore (matter and existence), creating the foam of consciousness, is an apt one. Higher consciousness is born of this continual pounding, called life. The work of a true spiritual path intensifies the process.

Postmodernism and Spirituality

The most important questions I have asked myself when deciding to write about spirituality relate to whether there is a need for this book. This book calls into question the beliefs of most religious people, who see the content of their faith as being all-important and are likely to have little interest in viewing that content as culture. Even though I affirm the premise that all cultures and religions contain within them the seeds of wisdom that can be discerned by the awakening consciousness, this is not likely to satisfy those who feel their religious doctrine is the "Truth." This book also challenges the modern scientific perspective that often sees spiritual perspectives as at least irrelevant, if not pathological. So, why write this book if people are comfortable with the worldview they have? It is a difficult question, and one I struggle with every day.

The answer that has kept me working is that many people are not satisfied. The dual pathologies of materialism and fundamentalism are creating a world devoid of heart and soul. While these two pathologies may be seen as polar opposites, they are really cut from the same cloth. Fundamentalism, ironically, is materialistic religion. Fundamentalism replaces myth, mystery, and consciousness with reading a book, and its doctrines often promote gender, ethnic, and racial inequality, not to mention warfare and genocide. On the positive side, fundamentalism is a response to dissatisfaction with materialism and indicates a longing for a deeper relationship with spirit and the transforming of consciousness. Fundamentalists have simply chosen a flawed vessel in which to carry their disillusionment and desire.

I also fear the trivialization of life that comes with the mechanistic, reductionistic, and compartmentalized view that pervades modernity. Modernity's emphasis on individualism and progress has led much of the world to a never-before imagined level of freedom, prosperity, and knowledge. Science, which is at the heart of modernity, has helped humankind to understand, predict, and control larger and larger portions of our physical environment. Science and modernity also bring with them alienation from ourselves, degradation of the natural world, and in many cases robotic lives in dehumanizing institutions. George Ritzer, who writes of the "McDonaldization of society," calls this the "irrationality of rationality"(1993:121).

Postmodernism has begun to question the assumptions of the rational modern world. It generally accepts the contributions of science and recognizes the usefulness of modern concepts such as individual freedom, but it calls into question the utopian myth of progress and the idea that modernity is the "best" and "most advanced" way of life. Postmodern thinkers place science and modernity as one perspective amidst many, all of which deserve understanding and respect. The stance of postmodernism may upset not only scientists and proponents of modernity's virtues, but also those who believe their religion is the only one worthy of praise. My perspective shares some similarities with postmodernism, as it calls into question the claim to absolute truth of both science and religion and places them side by side in the service of consciousness. My perspective differs from many postmodern writers in that it argues for an ultimate ideal, the development of human consciousness.

In answer to my earlier question about whether there is a need for this book, I continue to believe the answer is a resounding yes. Both materialistic modernism and religion are being called into question today. People's attempts to cope with these flawed worldviews are creating toxic manifestations from fundamentalism to addiction, from terrorism to "shop 'til you drop." What is needed is a unifying perspective that makes sense, but also contains the promise of spiritual growth. One way to accomplish this is to turn current paradigms on their heads by viewing content (i.e., belief systems) as being secondary to consciousness.

When dogma, either religious or scientific, stands in the way of wisdom, it is time to reconsider the usefulness of the dogma. When consciousness, which in our experience feels like a *process* but in actuality is a *capacity*, is made the central focus of spirituality, the content of religion and science becomes useful again. Content can be studied, meditated upon, contemplated, struggled with, integrated or discarded. Traditions can change and grow. Religions can meet the spiritual and social needs of societies. Science and technology can help humanity to understand and improve our physical world. The difference is only one of focus.

Consciousness has evolved since the time of our ancestors. We have, for better or worse, left the tribal mentality of our ancestors behind. Human beings in modern societies, especially those with more education, have a hard time understanding the group consciousness of previous eras. I believe that this change is an evolutionary one. We have reached that point when we can probe the "hidden treasure" of our own beings and follow Carl Jung's myth for the future by becoming "creators of consciousness." This is the *authentic spirituality* that will be explored more deeply in the following chapters.

We will begin by looking at the current need to transform old rigid cultural forms into dynamic renewed paths. The chapters in part two will decipher the core work required of seekers on any spiritual path. In the third section I will share some of the practices that need to be included in any path that seeks to transform human consciousness. In the final chapter, we will explore what authentic spirituality, as presented here, may mean for the future.

Our highest ideal (called "God" by many) is the vanguard of our evolving consciousness. When we can conceive of and yearn for more profound wisdom, clearer insight, deeper love, and a more harmonious world, it is sure to follow in time. A new understanding of the centrality of consciousness provides us a means by which we can move beyond ideals that can take us no further. We need to "shatter our ideals on the rock of Truth" (Khan, 1978:115).

PART ONE

Transforming Old Habits

WE MUST FACE head-on the lack of a central myth in today's postmodern world. What can we look to when meaning is drained from our world? It is time to look closely at the mythology, cosmology, and morality that try to make sense of the great mystery that is life and ask ourselves some very basic questions. Can our present religious and scientific perspectives make sense of our world and bring meaning to our lives, or are rationality and meaning mutually exclusive? A new world cannot be born until the old world has been put to rest. The time is ripe to re-evaluate our too literal and too limited perspectives on the nature of reality.

1

ONE

Stories and Myths

ALONG WITH LANGUAGE, myths, and stories are the bones of culture. Myths and stories tell us who we are, why we live the way we do, and how to handle life's difficulties. Today we do not have a central myth, except possibly for science, and without a commonly accepted mythological foundation, Western technological culture flounders in a sea of competing ideologies and moralities. Stories, too, have lost much of their ability to inform us about how to meet life's challenges and crises, because the prevailing worldview sees them as stories, nothing more. If myths and stories are the bones upon which the fullness of a culture is built, then trouble with those bones will show up in all aspects of a culture.

Just as the physical body provides a vehicle in which human mind, emotion, personality, and consciousness can function in this world, culture provides a body in which groups of individuals can function. Human beings create their cultures but do so in slow, mostly unconscious ways over long periods of time. Cultures are all-pervasive and provide the basic template as well as the material for all interaction, understanding, motivation, and meaning in the lives of their members. Cultures persist by being constantly reinforced in everyday life. For example, if the myth of a people tells them that they are God's chosen people, all community events are interpreted in the light of that belief,

3

reinforcing the belief, and it will be obvious to everyone in the community that they are God's chosen ones. Culture is like the air we breathe, and often it is just as invisible.

Language is also at the heart of culture. Language determines what can and cannot be said—even what can and cannot be thought. Language reinforces cultural realities when it provides many choices of words, phrases, and idioms in relationship to experiences that are central to the culture. By providing few or no words for those experiences that are outside of the cultural perspective, language discourages our considering alternative realities. Those who speak several languages know that some languages are better for expressing emotions such as love, while others are better for conducting business. Language shapes us but is also shaped by us, in one of life's many circles.

Language is also inextricably tied to the stories of a culture. Stories are the way in which cultural ideals have always been transmitted. Language is the medium not only of story but also of much of the communication that serves the function of socializing people into their cultures. Just as it limits people's perspectives to the prevailing cultural perspective, language limits what can happen in stories. Stories are greatly influenced by the richness of their language in describing particular situations, emotions, and subtle worlds.

Cultures that are closely related to nature have a lot of interest in the natural world and have many words about natural phenomena. These cultures often produce far more rich and complex stories using animals, places, and weather than do societies where most people are somewhat distanced from nature. Societies that stress human actors and minimize the natural world generally have languages that are much more attuned to complicated family and emotional interactions and are less descriptive of nature. Some groups, such as many North American First Nations, have developed languages that are rich in words related both to nature and to human relationships. Even though the stories of some types of culture tend to focus on more limited topics most suited to their interest and language, their stories still need to meet the needs of individuals going about their daily lives. Basic human questions like "Why do I exist?" "What happens when I die?"

4

and "Why do humans suffer?" will still need to be addressed, but each language and culture will vary the answer based upon its available strengths and unique perspectives.

Few individuals go very far beyond the boundaries of their cultures. Some hardy persons do venture out beyond the limitations of their societies' geographical boundaries and cultural perspectives and succeed in developing uniquely broad and deep personalities. Occasionally individuals who explore the regions beyond the cultural perimeters without adequate guidance may become psychologically unstable. Some mystics and sages have the ego strength to go beyond cultural limitations and later return to their societies to widen perspectives of others, but this is even rare among the wise.

The fascinating challenge of today's global culture is that cultures are losing their hold on more and more individuals, which creates the potential for both psychopathology and enlightenment. We no longer need to be global adventurers or seekers of spiritual truths in order to find ourselves ripped out of our cultural encapsulation; it can happen through a multitude of ways. Even though culture is powerful and holds most of us in a vice-like grip, breaking the cultural trance requires inner motivation combined with experiences like extensive travel, emersion in scientific or social scientific education, disillusionment, or other forms of social marginalization. And then what? Once outside of the boundaries how are we to function?

I have known several returned Peace Corps volunteers who, upon returning to their own cultures, have experienced difficulties building meaningful lives in their former social contexts. I have also known people who experienced great loss when their conservative religious views crumbled during the process of postgraduate education. Some of the social activists of the 1960s became so disillusioned that they found ways to "drop out" and exist outside of the mainstream culture.

There are, however, important positives associated with emerging from the cocoon of one's culture. Many of the returned Peace Corps volunteers who experienced some degree of alienation from their own cultures went on to become dynamic and creative individuals, sought after by business and governmental groups. Some of the disillusioned

5

1960s activists returned to work within organizations to create positive change. Some of those who lost their conservative religious convictions went on to develop rich spiritual lives. How did these people manage to overcome their alienation?

 Stepping outside of our cultures can prepare us to approach Sophia, the goddess of wisdom, as an empty vessel waiting to receive the nectar of illumination. Creativity often requires some degree of alienation in order to give the creative person perspective. It all depends upon our readiness for the experience. In other words, it depends upon the degree to which our consciousness has been developed.

There is a Sufi story that addresses this question. David Less, a spiritual mentor and friend, tells this story best, and it has always been one of my favorites. This is my version.

A Tavern Story

There is a tavern that is occupied by everyone you know and everyone I know (it is a pretty big tavern). Like most taverns, it is dark, smoky, and full of a lot of activity. Most of the activity occurs near the bar where the bartender, a rather magnetic fellow, serves the various drinks to the patrons. For one person, he pours from a bottle with the word "depression" written on it; for another, he finds a bottle with the label "hate." There are many bottles, and he pours from them such exotic concoctions as greed, pettiness, gluttony—well, you get the picture.

Imagine that you take your particular drink (related to your current propensity) and settle in at your table at the back of the tavern. After a while you become restless, maybe feeling as the old song goes, "Is this all there is?" You begin to explore the more remote recesses of this large tavern. Suddenly you notice light filtering in from a window with curtains drawn, and, fascinated, you walk over to the window. You pull the curtain back and are blinded by the light. You quickly turn away and return to the bar for another drink.

A little later your curiosity draws you back to the window. This time you are prepared for the shock of the light so you turn your head a bit and allow yourself to get used to the light, so you eventually are

6

able to look out of the tavern window. You are amazed by what you
see! There is another world out there in the bright light, a world
whose existence you had never imagined. There are flowers and trees
and grass and an incredible sun overhead. You stand mesmerized for
what seems like an eternity. Then you decide that, whatever the cost,
you must find a way to get out of the tavern and into this strange and
beautiful new land you are seeing.

You look around the room, but cannot find a door. You become
mighty thirsty. You feel a compulsion to return to the bar for another
drink, but your fascination with finding a way out keeps you occupied
enough to tolerate your thirst. Now you devise a plan. You figure that if
you circumambulate the perimeter wall of the tavern you should be
able to find an opening to the outside. Slowly you make your way
around the tavern wall until you discover a door frame and door knob.
You open the door slowly and again are blinded by dazzling light.

You step outside and stand there for a while until you are able to
see. Even before your eyes are completely accustomed to the sunlight
you feel warmed by the sun. Sweet fragrances drift in on a light breeze
and lift your spirits. You look around and see flowers, trees, plants and
animals, all living in natural splendor. It vaguely reminds you of
another time and another place that you just can't quite remember. You
feel happier and more contented than you are capable of comprehending, and you just wander in this scene for a while.

Suddenly you feel the presence of another being. You feel a tap on
your shoulder. You turn around to behold a person who appears kind
and gentle, and who says that you must make a choice. It is not possible
to remain outside of the tavern and live. You are welcome to remain in
this land, but in order to do so you must cease to exist. If you wish to
remain alive, you must return to the tavern. The kind person suggests
that there are those in the tavern that need you and are depending on
you. Your heart sinks! Never before have you known such beauty, clarity, and freedom. Never before have you been sober and free of the
weight of your stupor. You realize that what you had thought was life
was really a sort of sleepwalking brought about by imbibing the various
intoxicants served to you in the tavern. The messenger smiles, nods, and

says, "The gift that you take back with you is to remember." So you take a deep breath of the fragrant air of freedom and return to the tavern armed with the "gift of remembering."

Once inside you realize how thirsty you are. You remember that no one can remain within the tavern and not drink, so you return to the bar and ask for a drink. The bartender starts to pour you a glass of "anger," and you say, "No, thank you." Everything becomes hushed; it's not normal to refuse what the bartender offers. He reaches for a bottle marked "depression" and you say, "No, thank you." Now things are getting a bit tense—everyone is looking to see what will happen next. The bartender is getting upset and growls back at you, "So what *do* you want?"

You peer over the top of the bar and see some old, dusty bottles on the bottom shelf. "What's in those?" you ask. He picks one up, blows off some dust and replies, "Hmmm, I haven't seen this one in a long time—it's kindness." "Yes, I'll have some of that," you say. A soft sense of well-being fills your chest, and you realize that *you did it*—you remembered! From this day forward, you will remember. Every time you approach the bar you will remember that world outside, and that will give you the freedom to *choose* what you wish to drink in this tavern of life.

This story shows us that a spiritual discipline bestows upon the brave soul who chooses to step outside of his or her culture two gifts: the knowledge that one cannot live as a human being without participation in a culture, and the freedom to choose *how* to participate. Without knowledge, self-discipline, and love (all key elements in the story), the choices are grim. Without these qualities, people can become depressed, angry, or cynical and withdraw from society or even worse. Some may experience emotional and mental disorders that are the result of losing a sense of order and meaning in life. With the requisite knowledge, self-discipline, and love, the wise can participate in the game of life, while remembering that every thought, word, and deed is a choice. It is possible to make these choices out of love for the dear ones that populate this earth. This perspective is similar to the Buddhist concept of the bodhisattva, the one who has achieved Union with the One Mind, and yet chooses to continue incarnating to serve others.

As we leave behind our cultural blinders, we have to choose the stories and myths that will provide the patterns that guide our lives. When the central myth of a culture can no longer bring meaning and purpose to our daily life pursuits, how might we find the stories that could help us? We are fortunate in this global community to have access to stories from around the world. Some of these stories can help us to understand and even to recreate the cultural stories that were changed, suppressed, and lost as the dominant Judeo-Christian myth rose to prominence.

As the Christian story spread across Europe and the Americas, its missionaries were quick to merge local stories into Christian stories. Many of the birth and miracle stories in the New Testament are borrowed from religions such as Mithraism extant in the Roman Empire at the time. These stories follow the archetypal patterns set up for "heroes," "sacrificial kings," and "sons of the sun" in Egyptian, Sumerian, Babylonian, and ancient European cultures. One would think that the consolidation of these myths in a dominant new package would be useful, but the Christian story had one devastating flaw that still haunts us today. That flaw has led not only to the loss of many stories but also to the loss of whole cultures.

Christians said that Jesus was *the only* Son of God. This twist to a familiar story negated all other myths and stories for all other people. It required all people who wanted salvation or redemption to believe in only the Christian story. This tragic flaw opened the door for the murder of millions of people and the wholesale destruction of countless cultures—in the name of the Christian story. Most Christians today are appalled by what has been done in their name and have moved far from this narrow, ethnocentric view of their religion, but unfortunately, the growing wave of fundamentalist Christians has not seen the need for change.

Stories that could not be incorporated into those approved by the church in Christian Europe were branded either "pagan" or heresy, and those who told or valued the stories were persecuted. The Inquisition and the witch burnings from the twelfth through the sixteenth centuries in Europe are chilling examples of the suppression of stories and the beliefs that they represented. If we sometimes feel cut off from our roots, unaware of the true nature of our tribal origins, whether they be in Asia, Africa, Europe or the Americas, it may be this suppression of early stories and myths that is at the core of the problem.

All of our ancestors, no matter where we are from, were members of tribes or clans. If you scratch our surface, you will quickly discover, underneath the thin veneer of "civilization," a tribal person. In the history of the evolution of the human species, the present rational, industrialized, urban, cosmopolitan, and often monotheistic culture that we now inhabit is a brief episode. Our longer and psychologically more powerful inheritance is of living in close, intimate, extended family groupings. These groups bonded cooperatively with other groups in tribes or other social units that shared their oral traditions, histories, stories, and myths, often around the fire at night. Because of this history, which is lost to many of us, we still respond deeply to stories, poetry, and other oral traditions. We feel most alienated and alone when our stories are lost or cannot relate to the lives we are living.

Fortunately, the human storytelling urge is unstoppable. People like Jakob and Wilhelm Grimm collected European fairy tales, and one can now find collections of stories and fairy tales from every part of the world in our neighborhood bookstores. With movies and television we are constantly retelling old tales, embellishing the best of the timeless stories, and perhaps even creating a new mythology (at least the outward symbols) for the times. It would not be an exaggeration to say that we now have more access to a full range of myths, sagas, fairy tales, and stories than ever before. This is due to the omnipresence of television and movies as well as the written word and traditional storytelling. These media reflect motifs from around the world, in addition to our own national or cultural myths. Trying to stay parochial is getting harder and harder.

Marie-Louise von Franz writes in her classic *Interpretation of Fairy Tales:* "In myths or legends, or any other more elaborate mythological material, we get at the basic patterns of the human psyche through an overlay of cultural material. But in fairy tales there is much less specific conscious material and therefore they mirror the basic patterns of the psyche more clearly"(von Franz, 1982:1). If we heed the implications of this distinction we may find a clue to salvaging the heart of our mythological inheritance while leaving behind some of the cultural baggage. We can look at myths and stories as bringers of common messages but under different circumstances. We may be able to find in fairy tales the distilled versions of larger cultural myths and recreate their deeper meaning without having to buy into the ancient worldview that they carry. As they rise to the level of fairy tale, stories have often been purged, through their repetitive telling, of the religion, politics, morality, and economics of the time. They speak directly to the unfolding of consciousness through the human self.

Myths are linked to a people. When we think of the myths surrounding the Trojan War, we think of the Greeks; when we think of White Buffalo Calf Woman we think of the Lakota Sioux. These myths may make less sense for other cultures, as each speaks to the unique history and nature of a single culture. Still, the myths contain archetypal motifs that speak to the development of the human self, a self that is situated in a time and place.

Along with the psychological-spiritual components, myths often carry historical information and in some cases involve actual historical people. The stories in the Old Testament reflect the embellished and ethnocentric stories of the Hebrew people but certainly contain some useful historical information for those capable of disentangling it. While many have doubted the historical authenticity of the Trojan War, there is now a developing body of knowledge to suggest it did indeed occur. We need to recognize the cultural usefulness of history that has become mythologized, but we also need to be able to tell the difference between historic material and content whose purpose is the promotion of the growth of consciousness.

Edward Edinger, discussing Jung's "new myth," is very much in step with the idea of the development of a postmodern Western consciousness-based mythology when he says:

The new myth postulates that the created universe and its most exquisite flower, man, make up a vast enterprise for the creation of consciousness, that each individual is a unique experiment in that process; and that the sum total of consciousness created by each individual in his lifetime is deposited as a permanent addition in the collective treasury of the archetypal psyche (Edinger, 1984:23).

While myths are paradigmatic and give meaning and direction to the existence of large groups of people during a particular historical epic, stories contain the wisdom of our ancestors concerning living one's life. Stories give insight into the trials and tribulations of growing into maturity, the tasks required at various key points in one's life, initiations that need to understood and endured, the meaning of our feelings, the bad things that happen to good people, the good things that happen to bad people, and the individual pathless path to awakening. In short, stories instruct us about the meaning of life events and the qualities and attitudes required to live a good life.

Creating New Stories

We don't need to look far to discover new stories that can touch the depths and instruct our new generations. There are stories being written constantly that convey the wisdom of the psyche. Many of these stories, which are available to each new generation, are almost (but not quite) as free of cultural bias as a fairy tale, because they are emerging out of a multicultural, postmodern, and intellectually free society. They do, however, often carry the biases of modernity, rationalism, and individualism. Many of the writers of the stories and directors of the films made from them have searched outside of the cultural boxes for fresh ways to package these timeless teaching stories.

Film is an exceptionally powerful way to impress important stories upon people. There is nothing entirely new about this. Our ancestors from Greece to Elizabethan England have used stage plays to share the cultural stories. This type of medium allows individuals to give themselves over to the story, lose themselves in it, and find lost pieces of

12

their psyches in the characters of the play. Film, especially with the incredible special effects now available, can capture and immerse the mind in a manner unparalleled in our history.

My wife Jan and I sometimes teach a course that we call "Our Stories, Our Lives." It is all about seeing and understanding symbolism in stories. The students read stories and fairy tales, watch films, and write autobiographies using myth and symbol, rather than straight prose. The last time we taught the course, the power of some of these stories was impressed upon me again. This is an intensive three-week course, taught in three-hour blocks each day. On the third day, after seeing some of Joseph Campbell's *Power of Myth* videos, talking a lot about the sequence of the "hero's journey," discussing the meaning behind a couple of stories I told, and watching *The Dark Crystal* (Jim Henson's beautiful little myth) the students were about ready to revolt. "Who cares about all this stuff anyway!" was a pretty common sentiment. "Why not just get a good job and have a nice life?" was one student's comment, and who can argue with that?

The next day I showed the movie *The Matrix*. They changed from a rebellious street gang to a group of innocents with seeking hearts. We talked about why Neo (the lead character) would give up his normal life in search of something more. They shared moments from their own lives when they had glimpsed something greater, using Robert Johnson's term "grail castle experience" (Johnson, 1974:49). We talked about the names in the story: "Neo," meaning new, and Trinity (the anima/soul figure in the movie), referring to Knower, Known, and Knowing, or Love, Lover and Beloved, the full trinity of life. Could this mean that when the two of them unite we have a new life, a new world, new consciousness? The students really got into it. It was the turning point in the class. This is the power that myth continues to exert. Each generation needs stories to which they can relate, and when they find them, they will respond to them. There are many other films out there that are carrying important stories; I will share a couple of my favorite scenes.

I am always captivated by a scene late in the film *Return of the Jedi*. Han Solo, and Princess Leia, symbolically represents for me the questing

13

heart and the soul respectively, are fighting below on the forest planet, and Luke, representing the individual spirit or higher will, is confronting the emperor and his father, above, on the Death Star. This "as above, so below" sequence powerfully portrays the qualities of courage and daring (below) and mastery (above) that are needed to overcome one's own hidden barriers to growth.

Recently Jan and I went to see *The Fellowship of the Ring,* the 2001 version of Tolkien's story about hobbits, a ring of power, and a dark time. A scene that struck me as beautiful was that when Boromir, who had been the protector of Gondor, but never its king, was dying, and Aragorn, the rightful king, was comforting him. Many in the theater were sniffling or sobbing, but my eyes were mostly dry, although they had not always been dry during that movie. I was moved not by loss, but by the mythic image of the lower self that had been carrying the burden in the absence of the king, now turning over the task to the one destined to accomplish it, the king, or higher self. It was an awe-inspiring and powerful image.

There are many other little myths out there that I love and that have affected my life greatly. I especially like *Joe Versus the Volcano, Ladyhawke, The Emerald Forest,* and *Excalibur.* Sometimes these stories have come along just at the time when I needed something that they had to teach, or when I was down and needed a shot of the "hero's journey" or "alchemical marriage" to boost my resolve or give me courage. We don't always need to seek out spiritual guides or wise mentors; sometimes the stories around us can teach us all we need to know, once we have learned to speak the language of myth.

Myths We Can Do Without

I am often very concerned about two types of stories that I feel have outlived their usefulness and may be more a hindrance to growth than a help. These two motifs are the "tragic love story" and the "sacrificial king story." Both story types are incredibly interwoven into Western culture. They reflect a development of consciousness and a paradigm that has become outgrown. I think the damage that they can cause far outweighs their possible benefit. There are other ways to promote the growth to which the stories point.

Tragic Love

From Shakespeare's *Romeo and Juliet*, to the movie *City of Angels*, tragic love stories promote the idea that "true love" cannot last in this world of the flesh. Maybe it is thought that love as profound as this can only be hinted at on earth and must be waited for until we go to another world beyond this one. It might be that "true love" is seen as a metaphor for our relationship with God, and therefore can never be consummated between mortals. Possibly, from a psychological perspective, "true love" is an externalization of the *conjunctio oppositorium* within (the marriage of the inner feminine and masculine) and needs to be owned rather than projected. Whatever the reasons for the continuation of the tragic love motif, I believe it is a grave mistake.

Love is one of the greatest, most sublime, most transforming, and most useful of human emotions—why should it be doomed to failures? Yes, we certainly have difficulty in maintaining our loving relationships, but this could be partially a result of faulty mythology, not its cause. Following the lead of the Sufis, the medieval troubadours sang of a love that could not be fulfilled in life but rather became an ideal for which to live.

The romantic love of the troubadours had a civilizing effect on a brutish European culture, but it has changed greatly since that time. Today, at least in the West, love is the foundation for marriage and long-term commitment. Today, love is one of the few counterforces to a faceless, soulless machine-like existence. Love is an affirmation of commitment and a rejection of transience. Love rescues us from the isolation of individuality and challenges us to be "in relationship." Love requires us to go beyond our adolescent preoccupation with ourselves and consider at least one other person. Love is also a crucible that refines our personalities and opens our hearts.

Love serves us in all of these ways, and instead of supporting the powerful functions of love, our culture continues to propagate the story of tragic love. Could it be that love is too radical an activity to be easily accepted by monolithic states and religions? Love might require us to work fewer hours, to dedicate ourselves to our beloved and our families rather than the workplace. If we loved we might not be as willing to dismiss this life as inferior to spiritual realities. Love might keep us home during times of war, rather than leaving our loved ones to fight for the state. Love is a very radical political activity. Love not only transforms individuals but is also capable of transforming the world. Love is dangerous to the status quo. I am not hinting at a conspiracy here, only saying that old ways die hard, especially when they have a way of preserving things as they are.

What if we began telling more stories where "true love" was triumphant? Would that have a "snowball effect" and create more support for people seeking guidance in their own process of loving? Would the psychological effect of learning to love more completely have an impact on the inner process of uniting the masculine and feminine sides of the individual? Would more outer and inner harmony between lovers, between anima (the inner feminine) and animus (the inner masculine) begin to heal the cultural divide between men and women? I believe it is time for us to try.

The Sacrificial King

In a *darshan* (an in-depth spiritual interview) some years ago, a spiritual guide told me that I was "too impressed with sacrifice." I know that this is true. I know that I resonate very deeply with the archetypes of the sacrificial king and sacred warrior. If you would bore to the center of my being and divest me of all other qualities and identity, you would find the sacred king archetype. After much soul-searching, I believe we need to develop a new view of this ancient construct.

The sacrificial king is more difficult to discuss than tragic love. It is far more ancient, and it has a more crucial spiritual component. The idea that the chief, king, pharaoh, or emperor somehow embodies the spirit of the people and that his (and it is a "he") life is a reflection of this relationship, carries a power and inner truth that cannot be ignored.

If the ancient insight that "woman is life, and man is its protector" can be taken as indicative of a certain understanding of inner reality, then the "king" of our psyche, the ego, must be periodically sacrificed in order for soul to grow into the fullness of its life. The ego must go through a death and rebirth when it is too small to support the next step of the feminine side of our life, what we sometimes call the soul.

There are outer manifestations of this process, when the ego of the culture, often reflected in the leader or leadership, has too limited a perspective to lead the culture into its next great stage, and must be changed. The reality behind the stories of sacrificial kings, from Mithras to Jesus to Arthur, is profound and necessary and needs to have its place in our cultural stories. My concern is with the extent to which we have replaced "living" with "sacrifice." I think it is better to live for my country than to die for it. I think it is better to live for my family than to die for it. The sacrifice of lower desire for the benefit of the community or the growth of the individual has become, in the hands of nation-states and religions, a horrible weapon. The affirmation of life, which is what the inner meaning of sacrifice is all about, needs to be placed back in the forefront of the myth of sacrifice. Martyrdom for state or religion can no longer be seen as affirming of life, but instead as a bringer of death at the behest of a bureaucracy. There will most likely still be times when individuals must sacrifice their lives for higher ideals, but I would like to suggest we also need a mythology and stories that provide us with multiple pathways to live for our ideals and propose sacrifice only when the more life-affirming paths prove ineffective.

Life is by no means always rosy—as a matter of fact it seldom is—but we almost ensure failure to make life better when we continually impress upon the psyche that the only way to make life better is through death. Sometimes, especially when it is metaphor, death brings about a rebirth, but all too often death is simply death. It may be that the most radical idea that I will continually return to in this book is that of the affirmation of life. Life lives and death dies. If the hidden treasure that is the divine is to be found anywhere, it is in the sweet, vibrating, ever-present, yet ephemeral moment we call life. While sacrifice is sometimes the act of a great heart, it is sometimes more important to learn how to live for your purpose rather than die for it.

Myths and stories shape our world, sometimes for the better and sometimes to our detriment. Humans can be said to evolve through their cultures, and we are a species that is at a turning point in its evolution. Much of the world has moved beyond the stories that have given their cultures meaning and stands poised to take a leap into an unknown future. It will be crucially important which myths and stories we choose to take with us.

TWO

The One

HUMANS HAVE ALWAYS invented God
or gods to fit the times, conditions, and levels of consciousness prevailing in a region of the world. We need some kind of conceptualization
of cause and purpose in order to explain to ourselves why life is the
way it is and especially why we die. I am not sure that we would have
invented higher powers and religious forms were it not for death. But
the fact is, we do die and therefore some sort of understanding of ultimate causation and ultimate direction has become a part of virtually all
cultures. There are many other questions besides "Why do we die?"
that are sought in religion and ultimately are laid at the feet of a god-
figure. Mostly these are questions that human beings feel inadequate to
answer, especially if the issues in question relate to situations that seem
unfair or senseless. Questions like "Why do some people suffer more
than others?" and "Why do children sometimes die?" strain our ability
to make sense of our world. We want there to be some higher reason
or purpose behind the conditions under which we lead our lives. Gods
may be invented to answer these questions, partially because they cannot be held accountable.

Other questions, whose answers seem clouded in the mists of past
or future, such as "Is there a purpose for my life?" "Will my life make
sense in the end?" or "Is there another life after this one?" are given to

a god to answer, since we feel so inadequate to answer such questions. The unanswerable questions begin to have answers when we provide a god to whom we attribute omniscience. The qualities of the cultural "God Ideal" will determine the types of answers that aspirants receive.

The God Ideal

The God Ideal, as I will call the God that we create, is a term used by the Indian Sufi, Hazrat Inayat Khan. It serves the important function of providing a transcendent ideal toward which people can strive. (The God Ideal differs from the ineffable, the conception of that energy which is "beyond the beyond.") When one works with the concept of the God Ideal, God becomes the highest reality conceivable. An important point to remember is that we are discussing human concepts, not ultimate reality.

In this way of thinking, the concept of God is the elevator that transports us from one level of consciousness to a higher level. (Pir Vilayat Inayat Khan has used the wonderful British word "lift" in referring to this model.) Those caught in entirely materialistic preoccupations can use a fairly concrete conception of God to draw them out of their self-absorption and into seeking beyond the personal. Someone with a concrete consciousness can, by encountering a more abstract concept of God, develop latent capabilities of higher-order thinking, which in turn can lead to deeper and more complex understandings of ultimate reality. In this way, the God Ideal becomes an evolutionary push for individuals and cultures, toward higher consciousness and deeper understanding.

A third area in which the God Ideal is of utmost importance and yet sometimes invisible is in the formation of cultures. If one thinks that the God of a culture is "the Truth" and not a cultural construct, then the role that this ideal plays is invisible to those within the cultural group. Certain conditions like male dominance are seen as right and natural because they flow from a "father god" perspective. They become truths rather than choices. In this way the foundations of all cultures seem inextricably tied to the cosmological view of the people at the early stages of their cultural formation. The God Ideal of a small group of people can eventually spread and be forced upon millions of people. It is only in modern individualistic cultures that more than a handful of "enlightened" people can break out of this rigid cultural perspective. Profound contemplation of ultimate reality was previously only available through paths of renunciation or deep mystical study. Now, as more people disentangle themselves from singular cultural perspectives, there is an opportunity for either more confusion and alienation or more depth and understanding. It all depends upon what support can be given to individuals seeking to expand their perspectives.

From the preceding discussion it becomes clear that our conception of divinity is central to our individual and cultural viewpoints. The existence of God, gods, or "no god" cannot be easily dismissed as irrelevant. Certainly, the wholesale slide toward fundamentalism in the world today is a good example of people's need for a God Ideal to guide their lives. If the wise among us cannot capture people's imagination, then the dogmatic will.

The central questions of religion and myth become "Is there a God (or gods) of some sort that is ultimately responsible for our lives and who could answer questions if we were able to get his/her attention?" and "What might be the nature of such a God (or gods)?" These have certainly been the primary questions that men and women have asked throughout the ages. A unique way of approaching these questions, one that has not been discussed much in the past, is to see the God Ideal as a ladder that helps transform human consciousness.

This God does not require pronouns like "he," "she," or "it," nor will most people need to think in childlike anthropomorphized ways in order to conceive of this God. I am quite certain that many thinking individuals have viewed the divine at least partially this way for centuries; this perspective probably would not be considered foreign in any esoteric school of our day. I believe it is now time for these insights to be shared with the general public. We no longer can afford to keep the vast majority of humanity in the dark regarding the nature of reality. Human consciousness has evolved too far (though sometimes it is hard to see) to believe in the stories of childhood.

Such belief systems magnify the dangerous power of people who wield the power of life or death over their fellow humans or the planet itself.

A God Ideal to Contemplate

The understanding that we create God (rather than the other way around) is not a strange idea to those who have trod inner paths. Human beings create a concept of God and then install this God in some sort of otherworld reality, also of their own making. The truth is that *reality* is beyond concepts, and therefore any true ultimate creative energy is by definition beyond concepts. With minds that are bound by time and space, we simply cannot know that which is beyond time and space. We cannot experience within three or even four dimensions that which is beyond dimensions. We cannot attribute "beinghood" to that which is both all being and beyond being.

Some conceptions of divinity seem to be more useful to the evolution of consciousness than others. For instance, holistic viewpoints that stress the interrelatedness of all things are much more useful than highly dualistic perspectives. Holistic perspectives can promote physical, psychological, and cultural integration, whereas dualistic viewpoints divide the vast oneness of life into artificial categories. Discernment is necessary, but our choices are related to the needs of our organisms in time and place—not to a causal dualism inherent in nature.

A related but more specific issue is that narrow conceptions of divinity that limit God to a perspective favoring a certain race, ethnic group, or gender can be toxic in a global village. Not all God Ideals are equal. We have come to a point when we must recognize the need to nurture the evolution of human consciousness without poisoning our future with narrow, racist, misogynistic perspectives. God Ideals that promote harmony while challenging us to grow are the need of the future.

Since ultimate *reality* is unknowable—or it may be too simple for our complicated minds, I would like to discuss briefly what has become my God Ideal. I expect that by the time I finish this book I will have moved beyond these words and found another viewpoint that will propel me to another, more profound, vision of reality, but for the moment I am enjoying contemplating the horizons emerging from this perspective. God Ideals are not meant to last; they are meant to assist the development of consciousness. So please do not read this description as "true," but rather see it instead as the most recent page that I have turned in the book of my life.

All creation has arisen out of the primordial nothingness. The vast, primordial, fertile void, which is not yet any thing, lies at the heart of all. From this emptiness an Urge has emanated, sometimes thought of as the urge "to be." One can conceive God to be this vast fertile void or as the urge to be, which I will from this point on call "Life," or the "One Life."

I believe that a trinity flows from the fertile void, each aspect of the trinity taking existence from the impulse before it. *Life, consciousness,* and *momentum* constitute this God Ideal. This triune nature of reality is the stuff out of which all else emerges. It should not be confused with the current scientific understandings of these words; they are just shadows of the magnificent effulgence we are attempting to grasp. Words are cultural forms and can never describe the felt experience, and the felt experience is not large enough (since it uses the limited human body and mind) to contain the reality.

Along with many others, I used to think that everything was spirit. Matter is just solidified spirit, and all things are just spirit in various forms or stages of manifestation. But then what is spirit? Spirit is life. Spirit is life in its ever-creative, ever-emerging impulse to be. Life is the urge to be, it is not conscious, it simply becomes. It is the power and all being, and it is impersonal. It does not know; rather it is constantly becoming, and there is no end to life. It will continue to be forever. Life does not think, "I will create"; it is Creator, Created, and the Creative Process.

Enfolded within the oneness of life is the duality of awareness. When this ever-emerging life begins to become aware, consciousness begins, and when this awareness becomes aware of being aware, human consciousness begins. Consciousness, like life, pervades all things but appears to reach its most advanced (so far) stage in humans. Human beings not only know, but they "know that they know." Human beings think about thoughts, think about feelings, and have feelings about their thoughts and feelings about their feelings. We are very complex creatures, and sometimes very strange creatures. But we are creating creatures, who take the all-pervading life and create physical, mental, and emotional forms and then inhabit them. We often forget that we created them and wonder where they come from. We are incredible creatures and as far as we know, the best vehicle for carrying consciousness that life has so far created.

The emergence of consciousness from the unknowing flow of life is generally what religious forms point to in their creation myths. Prophets and reformers come onto the scene and represent the emerging consciousness of the times, attempting to convey to the general populace something of the nature of the consciousness that is developing in that time and place. This is done within the constraints of not only the prophet's level of consciousness but, more importantly, the level of consciousness of the people listening to the message. Whether we call these exemplars of the cutting edge of consciousness "prophets," "avatars," "wise ones," or some other culturally appropriate appellation does not matter; the effect is the same. They are human beings who, through spiritual practice, develop the ability to reflect back to the majority of their culture some new understanding of the meaning and purpose of life. As consciousness is constantly changing, often expanding and sometimes contracting in scope, there is an ongoing need for a fresh outlook that reflects the state of consciousness in a given culture. Religions take the lives and ideas of the messengers and attempt to freeze them in time in an effort to make the teachings fit all times and all places. Any good, self-respecting prophet would tell us to move on toward the next level of understanding!

As we have seen so far, out of the oneness of all-creative life a duality emerges, that of knowing and known, or consciousness. I think that if we wish to name these two aspects of the One, we could call the first *spirit* and the second *soul*. They are not exactly one, as in the Christian Trinity, because life is the one, all-pervading reality, and consciousness flows out of life. Consciousness is a byproduct of immaterial life meeting and interacting with the material part of life, like the interaction of sea and shore creating the breaking waves of consciousness. It is only perceived as a duality until consciousness emerges; before that event it is still all one. This is the mythical "fall" from oneness into multiplicity. It is from this point on that the tree of knowledge (consciousness) does all the work. All of human culture—material, social, psychological, scientific, and religious—flows from the birth of consciousness out of the One Life.

Whenever we talk about the mind and mind worlds, spiritual hierarchies, spiritual realms, and all sorts of other spiritual, religious and psychological concepts, we know we are actually exploring things that human consciousness has created. Life is the transcendent reality that is beyond human understanding, and all else is the work of consciousness. Consciousness orders and organizes the One Life as it perceives it and makes it comprehensible to our current capabilities of understanding. Life pours forth its effulgence, and consciousness organizes it (actually only some of it, since a huge amount remains undetected, hence unknowable, by human perception).

The third aspect of triune divinity is *momentum*. Since we know that so-called spirit and matter are really the One Life in different aspects (just as matter can exist as gaseous, liquid, and solid), we can easily understand that certain principles of science may be applicable to nonmaterial existence. We know that objects set in motion will continue until some other force slows, stops, or diverts them. We also know that objects at rest require force to get them to move. We understand gravity, centrifugal force, and centripetal force. I believe that what is called karma in the East is simply the activity of these natural laws upon consciousness. We need to be careful not to blindly buy into a cultural understanding of karma that is more appropriate for those of the Hindu religion, as the Theosophists did at the end of the nineteenth century. I will purposely stay away from using the word "karma," since there is much misunderstanding of that term.

When we set our consciousness in motion along a certain track, it will likely continue along that track until something strong enough changes its course. We are quite aware of this in large and small ways in our everyday life. Attitudes, habits, pastimes, goals, perspectives, and interests all have a quality of momentum that will carry us along their path unless something happens to change our direction. We know that often it takes a tragedy or major life event to change our direction. This quite obvious reality works on all levels of human existence. It can help us understand the good and the evil that people do. It can show us that winning has a momentum and losing has a momentum, as do sickness and health. It can remind us that every decision we make, no matter how small, is part of the direction of momentum being generated by us in our lives. If we could only understand and be conscious of the consequences of every action in our life, we could become the masters of our own momentum.

If consciousness lasts after bodies die (and I believe it does), then for good or ill we carry the direction of our momentum into the conditions that follow physical life. Here is the hidden truth behind the teachings of religions regarding reincarnation, heavens, hells, karma, and even resurrection. Consciousness continues, only the physical body has died, and therefore the direction, intensity, and quality of consciousness are carried into the afterlife. If it is true that a body dies but the consciousness that has been associated with that body does not, then it would make sense that the consciousness of the individual would carry on along the same path that momentum has been taking it in life.

Although there are limitations to this analogy, the dreaming state would be the best way to describe the afterlife. The mind creates the world in which the dreamer lives. Sometimes the world is pleasant and sometimes frightening. Without the limitations of the physical body, consciousness uses the malleable images of the mind world to create what it imagines. It is not at all difficult to see how the usual emotions, thought processes, and expectations of a person could then create a world that is just an extension of the momentum of his or her previous physical life. It is not surprising that people get what they expect after death. Their consciousness creates what it expects or fears out of the same mental material that is used to create dreams when the body is asleep.

Much of spirituality revolves around this insight. The choices and directions we make in our conscious, physical life establish the momentum for the future, both before and after death. What fills our minds and attracts our attention now will do so in the future, until an effort of will changes our direction. Momentum will carry us where we have set our sights unless we create a change. Change is not easy, and is most likely done best amidst the grossness of the physical plane where physical conditions can propel us to change in ways that are less available in astral, mind, and spiritual realms.

Many expect that once they die it will be much easier to change, because either God or angels will do it for them or there will be less distraction from the senses, but unfortunately that is not likely to be the case. The momentum pushing us toward whatever we value now will continue to push us in like directions for many lifetimes, as well as between lifetimes, until we exert our will and change our direction.

The act of "spiritual surrender" comes from the will as well. We often feel spiritual surrender when our ego, or lower will, has been battered and broken and finally our higher will shines through, though it feels quite impersonal. It is important to understand that my use of the word "will" does not involve personal assertion or ego. In fact, the will of which I speak is only occasionally something of which we are fully conscious. Often our will seems to descend like grace from some unknown place to rescue us from the folly of our life as we have been living it.

As you can see from this discussion of my personal God Ideal, I view life as a flow, or series of emanations, like concentric circles, from a central unknowable and ineffable source. That source, or the fertile void of being and nonbeing, is to my estimation the only thing that merits the term God. Yet it is not something that requires prayer, obedience, worship, or any other personal act. It simply *is*. Life, which I see as the first emanation and first duality since it separates into being and nonbeing, is the source of all that we know and experience, but it is not the ultimate *reality*.

Consciousness brings us into the realm of knowing and soul. It is usually the highest level toward which religion and spirituality can point. It seems to me that both the Buddha and the Christ were aligned with consciousness. They may be said to represent its essence.

Learning how to live a good and meaningful life brings us into the realm that I call momentum. Spirituality, morality, civility, love, and learning to live a good life are traces of the wisdom of our ancestors. Our ancestors have tried to outline for us the ways that worked best for them to avoid being captured by lower emotions and desires. They made an attempt to teach us how to channel our energies in directions that are good for our communities and, in most cases, also ourselves.

We have outlined above the worlds that spirituality may explore. It is becoming clear that much of what is called spirituality today deals primarily with what I call momentum, although some attempts have been made to explore consciousness. Let's look at some of the other aspects of divinity and briefly mention some attempts to touch these realms.

I have always been impressed by the ability of Buddhists to describe the "One Mind" or the "God Realms." Perhaps it is because they have avoided the trap of monotheism that they are able to think about things that are more impersonal. *The Tibetan Book of the Great Liberation,* attributed to Padma Sambhava, the bringer of Buddhism to Tibet and what is now Nepal and Bhutan, very powerfully clarifies the difference between Ultimate Reality and human concepts. The Evans-Wentz translation of this work shows a spiritual teacher intent upon cutting through the religious concepts of the day in order to provide a glimpse of something beyond. For instance:

> There being no duality, pluralism is untrue.
> Until duality is transcended and at-one-ment realized
> Enlightenment cannot be attained.
> The whole Sangsara and Nirvana, as an inseparable unity,
> Are one's mind (Evans-Wentz 1968:206-207).

And:

> The one Mind, omniscient, vacuous, immaculate, eternally,
> the Unobscured Voidness,
> void of quality as the sky, self-originated
> Wisdom, shining clearly, imperishable, is Itself the Thatness.
> The whole visible Universe also symbolizes the One Mind.

By knowing the All-Consciousness in one's mind, one knows it to be as void of quality as the sky (Evans-Wentz, 1968:230-231).

When I first discovered this work, my spiritual mentor, who was not a Buddhist but a Sufi, suggested to me that I should read it out loud to myself at least one hundred times as a spiritual practice. The actual work by Padma Sambhava is quite short and very worth reading many times over. Its teachings, which say that ultimate reality is beyond our mental concepts and yet can be found by looking within, are at least as relevant today as in Padma Sambhava's time.

I have often been impressed by the ability of what we might call *natural spirituality* to point to a holistic, interconnected reality that combines the transcendent and immanent in daily life. Natural spirituality includes the various types of shamanic, nature-honoring worldviews and practices of indigenous people around the world. I have had the opportunity to know and spend time with several Native American elders and have also encountered natural spirituality during travels in Asia.

One example of a holistic perspective involves the use of the six directions: east, south, west, north, above, and below. When invoking the "grandfathers and grandmothers" of the six directions, we are putting ourselves in harmony with the physical and spiritual forces represented by each direction. We are also connecting with the ancestors and the complete circle of life, both immanent and transcendent. This almost universal magic circle places one in the center of the universe and in touch with everything-always. It is the coalescing of all in the singularity of self. What a powerful act! It is far from primitive. Natural spirituality flows out of an organic nonduality that uses the images of everyday life to point to the transcendent. We have lost touch with this process in the dominant culture. It could be that in our rush to eradicate paganism, we lost what was best in ourselves and what tied us most closely to the divine.

I have found that certain aspects of Sufism are designed to take us beyond the lower levels of reality. They help us to discover the heights and depths of consciousness as well as the nonduality of the One. The Western version of Sufism that I have studied is quite clear in this regard. One of the primary spiritual practices of Sufism is the repetition of *dhikr* ("zikr"). When the Sufi says the Arabic words *La illaha illa 'la,* he or she is literally saying, "There is no god but God." The Sufi, however, evolves the meaning over time. The meaning of dhikr may begin for the Sufi as, "Nothing exists except God." Over time the dhikr will take on multiple meanings such as: seeing God as all, seeing self and God as One, becoming lost in the oneness of being, seeing the clarity of unity, and many more states of consciousness. It appears that dhikr leads one to the same realization of nonduality that was spoken of by Padma Sambhava.

Common realizations spoken of by Sufis, especially in states of ecstasy, are, "I am the eyes through which God sees," or, "I am the actions of God," or, "I am the truth." During these episodes of higher consciousness, the distinctions between knower and known, subject and object, become erased, and only the oneness remains. This is the ultimate spiritual purpose of Sufi practice, to transcend duality.

When the realization of Oneness is reached, there is no need to invent new God Ideals. Oneness fills the heart with the knowledge of unity and the mind relaxes its mania to create dualistic concepts. In this state we finally feel the peace which passes all understanding.

THREE

The Mystery

OUR WORLD AND our lives are full of
mystery. There is much that we cannot fathom, and when we allow
ourselves to fully experience the world around us, life becomes even
more mysterious. Scientific and religious explanations for the mysteries
of life are attempts to explain events that, given the paradigm of the
moment, are unexplainable. The problem of mystery lies not in the
mystery itself but in the paradigm that tries to explain it away. The vast
potentiality of life will not go away in spite of the best attempts at
human conceptualization. The small boxes in which we attempt to con-
fine reality are simply inadequate to hold life's effulgence. It is this vast
potentiality for life to manifest its wonders in myriads of ways that is at
the heart of all that we see as mystery, occult, hidden, and miraculous.

In this chapter, I will describe mysteries that we sometimes contemplate—in spite of the fact that they do not fit well into our common
views of life. My choice of mysteries is based upon personal experience and interest, and is certainly not exhaustive. We will organize
these mysteries into categories of synchronicity, earth mysteries, mind
mysteries, and mysteries on the path. Each of these mysteries holds
wisdom that, if explored, could significantly improve the quality of life
on this planet. Our discussion will be illustrative of some of the more
common puzzles of life. We humans will never be able to completely

31

comprehend the rich and diverse world in which we live, much less the inner worlds that we unknowingly touch every moment. We can, however, explore the mysteries of our lives with an open mind. The pleasure of this exploration is enormous.

Synchronicity

Carl Jung coined the term "synchronicity" to deal with the phenomenon of "meaningful coincidence." He was not comfortable with some of what he saw to be superstitious beliefs that existed regarding these phenomena, nor was he comfortable with scientific thinking that could not get past "cause-and-effect" explanations. He believed there must be commonplace explanations for synchronistic events, just as physics can account for discontinuities (Jung, 1973:102). Synchronicity has become popular for describing events that mysteriously connect in a seemingly meaningful way, although the popular meaning has become less precise than the "acausal connecting principle" that Jung had intended. I will be using the more popular understanding of the word, since that is now more commonly understood.

I have come to believe that life is our deepest teacher, and I pay special attention to events that seem to occur together in a meaningful way. The more attention I pay to such "meaningful coincidences," the more often they seem to occur. This is one of the primary ways that life teaches. There are many, often harsher, ways to learn from life, but synchronicity is one of the more amazing and mysterious variations. I do not know why or how synchronicity works—I just know that it does. Synchronicity has been very important in my life as a way of receiving guidance from the depths. The possibility of meaningful coincidence awakens one to each moment. Through being open to life's teachings, we create the possibility of making life and the world around us our primary mentor. I recall a point in my life when I was confronted with an ethical dilemma in my professional life. I was working in a mental health center as the Chief Psychiatric Social Worker and I felt that a new manager was acting unethically and wanted me to do so as well. I tried using all my skill to change the situation, but he was very inflexible. I seemed to have only two choices: either do as I was told, or be fired. I enjoyed my job very much, but I also knew deep down inside that I was stagnating. I therefore chose a third option. I resigned. I used this opportunity to go into private practice as a psychotherapist. I have never regretted that choice, primarily because it provided me the freedom and the time to pursue my spiritual path. Looking back at the situation I know that life presented me with an opportunity in the form of a crisis. It was a teaching in impermanence, being true to myself, and fearlessness. The dilemma and the choice that I made were also keys to the development of my spiritual path. In retrospect, the timing and direction of this choice were very synchronistic and yet at the time it felt like I was taking a leap into the abyss. Had I not taken the step that I took at that time, I probably would not have written this book.

Synchronicity is mysterious, and it can manifest in any form at any time and in any place. Natural settings, however, seem to provide exceptional possibilities for synchronicity to occur. Let me share a few examples of synchronicity between thought and the natural world that I have found meaningful. About ten years ago my wife and I were on a thirty-day spiritual retreat in a coconut grove overlooking the Indian Ocean in Bali, Indonesia. About midway through the retreat, I was wondering about the real purpose of my being there. All of a sudden I came across the little green snakes that inhabit the island. They were crawling up trees, scooting along the ground, and I even saw one on the beach. I had not seen one snake before that day. I usually don't like snakes much, but these little fellows intrigued me. The phrase "the nagas" also began going through my mind incessantly. My question was being answered for me by the world around me. To me (and that is what is important) the "nagas" (which is snake symbolism found in Hindu mythology) were bringers of wisdom, representing both the rising of the kundalini and the presence of the "old ways." I then understood that one of the purposes of the retreat was to touch the wisdom represented by the nagas.

A few years later Jan and I were attending a leaders' retreat for the Sufi Order in the Sierras of Northern California. I found myself questioning whether I should continue my association with the Sufi Order. I felt constricted and spiritually stifled, and was wondering if there wasn't

a new step that I needed to take. The issues involved the continuing efficacy of spiritual teachers, the lack of meaningful roles other than student
and teacher within the order (it seemed to me that students must remain
children, that teachers often get lost in teaching), and whether illumination is possible when living a life in the world. On the first day of the
retreat, we left the retreat camp and went off into the mountains on our
own. At one point Jan and I were sitting on a rock at the edge of Salmon
Lake discussing these issues when I blurted out, "We have to find our
own home, and it isn't here [meaning the Sufi Order] anymore." At that
very moment a large bald eagle flew very low over our heads and we
saw that it was being chased away from the lake by an osprey that we
had seen circling the lake earlier. We knew then what we needed to do.
We continued the retreat, but did so on our own. We saw very clearly
that we needed to find our eagle selves and our true domain.

This story makes more sense when put into the context of a spiritual journey with identifiable stages. Most serious seekers experience
these stages in some form. One of the more challenging stages occurs
when the seeker has reached the point of needing to strike out on his
or her own in order to make the teachings real in life. In the classical
Sufi tradition, teachers often told their students when it was time for
them to leave. In more loosely organized contemporary spiritual
schools, it may sometimes be difficult for the teacher to discern the
exact moment when the student needs to leave, so the student may
have to figure this out on his or her own. The student may not always
be conscious of the deeper reasons for the need to leave and may leave
in frustration, just as young adults who need to become more inde-
pendent may often leave their parents' homes in frustration over perceived restrictions or minor differences.

Now, over eight years after these events unfolded in the high Sierras retreat, I continue to be happy about striking out on our own. I
have nothing but gratitude for the Sufi Order. What we were going
through was a stage of spiritual development that is necessary, but
painful. If one looks at spiritual teachers and their schools as ferrymen
and boats that carry us across a river that we could not otherwise
cross, then the leaving of the boat and the ferryman should be a time

34

of joy and thanksgiving. One feels joy over having reached at least the first stage of one's goal and thanksgiving toward the teachers who have brought one there.

Once we took the steps to leave, a whole new world opened to us. This has taken us far past the experiences of earlier days, and also shown us how important what we learned in the Sufi Order was. Without the foundation of that initial training, we would have been lost and overwhelmed by the nature of the realizations and experiences that ensued.

Returning to the discussion of meaningful coincidences, we can see that two things are involved: a paired set of experiences and a meaningful interpretation of their synchronicity. It is easy to explain the ability of two college professors and sometimes psychotherapists to interpret events in a psychologically meaningful way. What might be thought to be more mysterious is to account for the nature and timing of the paired events. I could imagine that if one sat on that rock long enough, a person could witness an osprey chasing an eagle, but I doubt that the timing of my words with the event could be described as mere coincidence without meaning.

If this sort of event happened only rarely in a lifetime, it might not seem too mysterious. If it only happened on spiritual retreat, it might be explained by religious persons as divine intervention by a personal and involved God. But the fact is that events like the ones described happen all the time, day after day, year after year. One need only be tuned in and watching for them, and they will be there. They are not unusual, but they are mysterious. They are mysterious because they do not fit into the scientific or religious paradigms prevalent in our society.

Traditional societies have explanations for synchronistic events, but most of these explanations have been labeled superstition or worse by both the dominant monotheistic religions and the scientific establishment. I agree with Carl Jung, who was convinced that early humankind understood these things far better than we. From my perspective, the word "superstition" is often simply a label of condemnation placed upon religious beliefs that are not our own.

The examples of synchronistic events that I have shared were experienced in nature. It is certainly helpful to be in a natural setting, but synchronicity can happen anywhere and at any time. People can say or do things that trigger some sort of pairing with our thoughts, actions, or experiences. Horns can honk, phones can ring, and computers can crash. I remember sitting with Jan in a classy restaurant on the River Walk in San Antonio, Texas. I had an especially clear realization concerning the nature of our relationship, and immediately a ceiling tile broke loose and fell right next to me. Jan and I had fun with that one!

Earth Mysteries

Earth mysteries have long tantalized our imaginations. Many have associated all sorts of powers, miraculous happenings, spirits, hidden peoples, ancient rites, and special places with what we call "Earth mysteries." Often this is accurate, but we have sometimes been naïve or overly credulous in our approach. Others, primarily sky-centered patriarchal religions, have attributed only evil, degradation, and grossness to the Earth. This sort of ingratitude toward our life-giving home may be difficult to understand, but it has been the unfortunate state of affairs for several thousand years.

Anyone who begins to work with Earth-oriented practices or spends much time with traditional native peoples anywhere in the world will rapidly learn that the Earth and our natural surroundings are much more alive than most of us could ever imagine. Jan and I enjoy hiking in the mountains. We have often been struck by the difference in the atmosphere of places that have had little human disruption contrasted with places overrun by tourists. Some places, like Sedona, Arizona, are so powerful that the energy remains in spite of the overabundance of people, but other places are unable to sustain their aliveness when too many humans overwhelm the natural spirit of the place.

I can remember my first real encounter with this phenomenon when hiking on Grand Teton Mountain. As we climbed higher, and the other hikers began to peter out, the presence of this incredible mountain began to emerge. Its ancient, watchful grandeur became apparent. Late in our hike, about when we needed to turn around and head back to the trailhead, a mist appeared ahead of us for a brief moment, and we were flooded with feeling for the mountain's being. That being shares the pain of the Earth, which is suffering under the yoke of too many uncaring, unconscious people, but it also has an ancient dignity and grandeur that took our breath away. Today I am still grateful for the willingness of that mighty mountain to allow us to witness with it.

Even though nature needs no explanation, it may be useful to discuss this phenomenon. As we noted earlier, we can see that consciousness slowly emerges from the all-pervading life, a byproduct of life's creation and inhabiting of form. Consciousness, of one sort or another, is endemic to everything that has form, whether seen in the physical world or unseen on the inner planes of reality.

Jelaludin Rumi and other Sufis have addressed this with statements that, paraphrased, usually go something like: "I slept as a rock, began to stir as I entered plant form, became aware in my animal state, and achieved self-awareness as a human being" (Arasteh, 1972:118–120). The "I" in this statement is consciousness. That consciousness is, in its broadest form, God, and in its narrowest form, it is the individual psyche. But this statement is only meant as a doorway into the vastness of the realm of consciousness. All life in any form, seen or unseen, possesses consciousness.

Consciousness is the natural byproduct of life taking form. All life possesses consciousness—rocks, trees, mountains, animals, storms, stars, planets, suns, and moons all possess consciousness in greater or lesser degrees. Consciousness can relate to consciousness. If we tune in to our own consciousness, we can become aware of all that is conscious around us.

The many aspects of consciousness seem to be more easily apparent in some places than in others. Bali is one of those places where life sometimes seems almost transparent, and the consciousness in all things shines through. When Jan and I were on our thirty-day spiritual retreat in Bali, we also spent almost an additional month exploring several other locations, especially the area around Ubud.

In Bali, the people constantly acknowledge the world of spirit. Beautiful offerings of fruit and flowers are everywhere you look, by temples and shrines, at crossroads and bridges, and in front of homes. The women make these offerings not to a single deity but rather to both the "good" and "bad" spirits. The world of Balinese people is populated by many forms of consciousness, not only those that can be seen. Balinese people see themselves as being arbitrators between energies that are helpful and those that are unhelpful. They use the symbolism of a checkered cloth to represent the harmonious integration of positive and negative energies. In Bali people believe that it would be futile to try to get rid of evil as we in the West wish to do, but instead they try to integrate negativity in such a way as to balance or neutralize it.

There is great wisdom in this approach. Given our limited understanding of the depths of reality and the long-range consequences of our actions, we are often unsure of what might be truly helpful or unhelpful. When one spends some time in Bali, the atmosphere and rhythm of life bring one into a magical space where it becomes easier to experience the unseen worlds of consciousness, what the Balinese call "the spirit world." The slight haze created by wood fires combined with the sounds of roosters crowing, dogs barking, doves cooing, and the omnipresent sound of gamelon music creates an atmosphere that feels as ancient as time. Consciousness is taken beyond the personal into the ancient, impersonal oneness with creation. We found that returning to the comparatively "dead world" of Western life was a real shock to our systems, but the memory of what we touched in Bali is still alive and available.

The natural world can teach us much about the nature of reality, as in the case of our meeting with Grand Teton Mountain, encounters with the stars in the night sky, or an immersion in the ambiance of an ancient grove of trees. At those times we may experience something so deep that we are unable to articulate its beauty and wisdom. At other times we may only perceive a simple message or a warning.

Sometimes the natural world needs something from us. I have often watched Jan walking in the yard or past a houseplant and have seen her yanked, as if by an invisible hook, toward a particular plant. She then usually gets some water or fertilizer or something else needed by the plant and ministers to its need. Afterwards, when I ask her about it, she usually tells me that the plant was thirsty or needed something. She has an amazing "green thumb," and it is because she is tuned into the needs of the plants in her environment. Somehow her consciousness is open to the consciousness of plants. As I become more sensitive to the natural world, I seem to be experiencing a similar affinity with the plant world. Last summer, I grabbed a large pruning shears and was about to cut a volunteer black locust tree that was impinging upon another tree that I had planted. I experienced a very strong "No!" and backed away from the tree. It seemed that the black locust had a strong spirit and wanted to grow. I decided, instead, to move the other newly planted tree.

Mysteries of the Mind

We come now to the mysteries of the mind. Sometimes we label phenomena as mysteries simply because we lack understanding of consciousness. The mind, which is our individual container for consciousness, may be viewed as a more permeable, yet distinct, body with which we identify. Being more permeable and intangible, it is not as separate as we think from other loci of consciousness. Many of the so-called mysteries of telepathy, mind reading, and precognition are easily understood if we get past our faulty conceptions of the mind as being enclosed within our physical bodies.

Minds function in a "mind world" that is just as real as our bodies, but one that also has properties that are less imprisoned in the here and now. I remember a spiritual guide suggesting to a group that we get to know our neighbors better, since we share much more with them than we know. That's a scary thought, but a very important one. Mystics understand that we have several bodies, as opposed to only one. When we share physical space with others, our subtle bodies are actively in relationship, whether we know it or not.

Just as fascinating as the "psychic" implications of the concept of a mind world is what has been called "creative imagination." Creative imagination is nearly as ancient as human existence and involves the practice of working with imaginal realms. Imaginal realms are inner worlds created and explored through personal imagination, and yet anchored in a reality not totally personal or contained within the individual mind. Using the mind and its ability to imagine, in order to create, navigate, or explore imaginal realms is at the heart of shamanic practice in countless cultures. It is also central to creativity, poetry, and religion. People in the current Western materialistic culture often misunderstand the religious stories of previous ages because we are unfamiliar with the imaginal realms; it seldom occurs to us that we are one of the first cultures not to take these realms seriously. To our ancestors, events that took place through intention in worlds of our imagination (not fantasy) were just as real as events taking place in the physical world. The imaginal events had just as much impact on the individual and the community.

It is vital to note the importance of individual intention in negotiating the imaginal world. The shaman or adept is one who has trained the will and is capable of using the will as intention in the imaginal worlds just as in the physical world. There is a significant difference between idle fantasy and the working of a trained will in the world of imagination. If one were to understand the workings of the imagination, much that seems bizarre in certain religious stories can make perfect sense. Stories of gods or angels impregnating virgins in order to produce special offspring may be seen as a culturally approved way for a hero to enter physical existence, but they may be much more. Such stories may also point to a temple rite in which a male, in a deep imaginal state of attunement with a cultural icon, has intercourse with a woman, who is also in a deep state of altered consciousness. She is meditating upon a theme, and she has been chosen because of her exceptional characteristics to be the mother of a spiritual hero.

I have been working with shamanic practices for several years and have found them to be invaluable in filling in some of the holes in my understanding of reality. While the Sufi practices I've done for decades are, I believe, exceptionally good at refining consciousness and teaching about "higher" reality, most of them do little to address issues related to Earth mysteries and the energies surrounding us. Shamanism fills this gap. Although I have had several friends who have been elders or healers in the Native American community, I have not sought to take instruction from them. I made this decision because I had no desire to take on cultural beliefs along with shamanic techniques. I have done that in the past with Sufism, almost got lost, and didn't want to go through that process all over again. Michael Harner's "core shamanism" has been useful in providing access to the techniques and guidelines of shamanism without the necessity of accumulating more cultural baggage.

I found immediately, upon my first try, that *journeying,* a basic technique of working in imaginal realms, was second nature for me. Since I have been using this technique as one of my basic spiritual practices, much of what I had difficulty in understanding previously has become clear. The rather amazing thing about working with what has variously been referred to as creative imagination, active imagination, secondary imagination, guided imagery, and in some cases, meditation, is that there is an inner consistency and dynamic that interacts with my will, but is not totally dependent upon it. I have a relationship with these inner worlds and their inhabitants, and I can be an important part of their existence, but there is a reality that is not totally dependent upon me that will go on with or without me. I believe that this is a part of the "shared mind world" of the human race, and even though it may seem to be created by the individual shaman, it is also shared in common by all of us.

I'd like to share an experience that I had at a medicine wheel in Wyoming. About four years ago, Jan and I were driving to Montana to do some day-hiking in the Beartooth Range. We wanted to visit the powerful medicine wheel that lies on the western slopes of the Big Horn Mountains of Wyoming. We had been driving for a while through meadows brimming with blue lupine and purple asters and stopped and walked among them, feeling the vastness of this blue and purple field. An hour or so later we arrived at the turnoff that leads to the medicine wheel, an ancient circle of stones used for ceremonial purposes for hundreds of years by the Native American nations in this area.

About two-thirds of the way up the mountain, we found a parking area, ranger office, and barricade that had not been there ten years earlier, when we had last been there. We parked and as we approached the barricade, a young woman in a ranger's uniform approached us and offered information about the site. We told her that the last time

41

we had been there, we had driven nearly to the summit, and there had been no one around. She explained that about eight years previously, the park service had decided to try to protect the medicine wheel and to make it more accessible for both tourism and Native American ceremonies.

It felt good to be walking up a mountain road again. We always seem to walk faster in the mountains, and we're always happy. Remembering what a Navajo friend had told us about approaching Native American lands, we stopped about half way and took a handful of dry, rocky, mountain soil and asked the spirits of the place for permission to be there. Then we replaced the soil and continued our ascent. I immediately noticed that my shamanic power animal was running beside us (in my now heightened imagination), thoroughly enjoying himself.

When we reached the medicine wheel, there was a young, male ranger to describe the history and purpose of the medicine wheel and answer any questions people might have. We said we had been there before and didn't need much introduction and proceeded to enter the path that encircles the wheel. We began to circumambulate the wheel in a clockwise direction. My first reaction was a vivid memory of circumambulating Bodnath Stupa in Kathmandu, Nepal, about five years earlier. Even though that five years had taken my belief system far from the place it had been, it felt good to be walking around a sacred site again. I walked behind Jan, believing at that time that the visit was primarily for her, since she had some burning questions about purpose and direction for which she was seeking guidance.

We stopped at the eastern point and invoked the spirits of the east. Jan recited Black Elk's prayer from Harney Peak, which she had committed to memory many years ago. It was a still and pregnant moment, and I again noticed my power animal, very intensely present. As we turned to walk to the South, I had a powerful impression of "trailing clouds of glory," to use Emerson's terminology. I was experiencing being the point of a long line (more like an inverted pyramid) of beings. I had seen some of them before; they are what some people refer to as the "spiritual hierarchy." I first met them in a dream in 1982, and they have since become a normal fixture in my meditations. To me they had come to represent the more evolved consciousness of our world.

It seemed as though I was the tip of a gigantic group of shining beings reaching to touch the world at this sacred spot. I had never experienced them this strongly before, nor was I all that used to a visionary experience this intense. I asked them, mentally, "Why are you here?" Their answer was both breathtaking and poignant. They wished to apologize and seek help from the spirits of the Earth. Their pain was profound. They were very aware of how the patriarchal, otherworldly religious and spiritual traditions of the past 4,000 years have inadvertently sown the seeds of spiritual and physical destruction upon the Earth and its inhabitants. This unintended consequence of good intentions, along with the foolishness of those who exploited their teachings for power and wealth, has left our natural world, including us, at the brink of annihilation.

The apology for this state of affairs and the desire to work together with the forces of the Earth were so heartfelt that my tears were flowing like a spring from the depths of humanity's heart. I felt like I was a witness to a meeting of profound import between the Earth and sky energies seeking reconciliation. My tears would not stop, and I felt my heart would burst before it could tolerate the pain and ecstasy of the moment. We sputtered out (at least I was only able to eke out some faint and garbled words) an invocation to the spirits of the south, and Jan said Black Elk's prayer again, also eyeing me closely, wondering what was going on. Then we circled to the west. It is amazing how something that internally feels monumental and eternal can fade away into normal life. By the time we were standing facing west the experience had ended, leaving behind only a whiff of the rapture that had been. It has been my experience that all experiences of this order waft away leaving me asking, "Was that real?" The sense of deep peace that lingered answered the question.

Two more invocations of the spirits of the directions, three more recitations of Black Elk's prayer, and one more circumambulation (leaving offerings at each direction), and we were again walking on the mountain road, this time down toward our car. Jan had received the guidance she was seeking, and I had received much more than I had expected. For me, the most important personal (and I don't believe this experience was entirely personal) effect of this experience was that I was beginning to develop a new respect for the spiritual beings attached to patriarchal religious traditions. I had all but written them off as irrelevant and dangerous to our times, but I began to see that they were concerned with what is happening on this planet. The possibility to feel unity in the inner world had begun to unfold.

Even if the religions of the day were continuing to do things that I found to be troubling, at least I knew that a move toward bringing heaven and Earth together had begun. I could feel at one with the founders of those religious traditions, knowing in my heart that they, too, saw the problem. They seemed to understand the problems of our times, rather than being distant, aloof, father-like beings seeking to be worshiped. This "spiritual hierarchy" was intimately involved in seeking solutions to the problem of the giant chasm between heaven and Earth that is at the heart of today's malaise. Leaving this place, I felt that a connection had been made that would have a life and momentum of its own. The beings, which have made a step toward forging an alliance and possibly a union, will continue to play out the implications of their desire to help humanity and the planet.

You may have noticed that I have given no indication of a response from the telluric or Earth powers. We could certainly understand if the Earth would be a bit reticent to accept an alliance with sky powers whose misguided representatives have spent more than four thousand years attempting to suppress and destroy people and traditions that honor the Earth and its powers. It would be reasonable to think that the Earth might be better off without this cancerous growth of humanity, and therefore it might just let us destroy ourselves. But I got no sense of that. I felt that it went without saying that the spiritual hierarchy was welcomed, like the prodigal son, back into the family of life.

Although this discussion of my visionary experience in the imaginal realms stresses its external implications, I am also aware of the intrapsychic implications of the experience. My psyche was undoubtedly dealing with the healing of my own inner splits among body, mind, and spirit, as well as father issues that I bring from childhood. These psychological aspects of the experience are also valid. It is often, if not always, true that dreams, visions, stories, and myths have several layers of truth. It is a mistake to devalue one level in order to emphasize another.

For my own spiritual growth, this experience was a watershed that marked a shift where I could let go of the "not this, not this" *via negativa* that I had been traveling for several years after leaving the Sufi Order. I had experienced the unity but could not reconcile it with life in the world. Now I felt the impetus to discover more of "what is" instead of "what is not." This experience in the mysteries of the mind had a transforming effect.

Mysteries of the Path

We now move to the mysteries of the spiritual path. These paths can be related to either Earth mysteries or sky mysteries, or in some rare cases both, but they are primarily time-tested methods of inner growth. For me, the most mysterious and amazing aspect of the spiritual path is that it works! Initiation, which forms a bond with a lineage of wise ones and the practices that one learns and uses, accomplish the purposes for which they are designed. In a world where spiritual and religious thought are seen to be fuzzy, feel-good illusions, it is absolutely amazing to discover that the path works. I will be devoting several later chapters to issues like teachers and spiritual transmission, sound, and breath, so we will postpone a major discussion of these topics until then. For now, we will simply acknowledge the power of these aspects of the path.

When we mobilize our will sufficiently to enter a spiritual path, we make a commitment at the deepest level of the psyche. In spite of the fact that we may not consciously know what we are doing at the time, that commitment has profound consequences. By making the commitment, we set ourselves upon a path that has a momentum of its own, of which we are only vaguely, incompletely aware. From that point forward a process of change, including what Hazrat Inayat Khan called "mental purification," ensues.

If we are lucky and do our work, the path will transform us into someone we can only dimly imagine. The depths of the inner work are typically almost unconscious. I can hardly count the number of times I have been advised or came to the realization that my conception of my own spiritual progress is more likely to be wrong than right. Times when I think I have finally "got it" I am usually farther from it and times when I think I am lost I am actually making more progress than I can imagine. We often have no clue as to what our internal processes are up to and what deep churnings and purgings are going on. Taking that step and entering a spiritual path is a thing of wonder and mystery.

I marveled that after my initiation into the Sufi Order, my life began to change dramatically. I was often not sure what was happening or where it was all leading, but my psyche seemed quickened. There was both a new intensity and a peace in my life. Beyond that, my essential hypertension, an inherited form of high blood pressure that I had had since my early twenties, disappeared almost entirely (and remained that way for seven or eight years, at which time it began to slowly re-emerge). I have no doubt that will and intention, coupled with the transmission of a spiritual school (energizing spiritual energy, explained in chapter 8), work at deep levels of the human psyche to quicken and transform personality and the consciousness from which it flows.

A continuing relationship with a spiritual teacher is usually formed at the moment a person enters a path. That relationship becomes a teacher-student dyad. The student and teacher become linked in a very profound manner and, at least for a while, much of the transformative work occurs within that pairing. There is a mutuality in the dyad that is capable of deepening the teacher in order to meet the learning needs of the student, just as the student is drawn deeper by the association with the teacher. There is much that can go wrong with this relationship as it manifests in our times, but the relationship is at the heart of learning how to refine and develop consciousness. Not only do we learn the ABCs of pathworking from our teacher, but the relationship also provides a heart-bond that is a constant source of illumination. Although we must discover how to take the potential for exploitation out of the teacher-student relationship, it is for a while the most important and transforming agent in the student's life. There is magic in this relationship that is truly mysterious. Many Sufis believe that no oral teaching is necessary if the hearts of the student and teacher are sufficiently tuned to the relationship. The teacher is a very real stepping-stone to the infinite.

Sound is the other mystery of the path that is truly amazing. We will discuss this mystery more deeply in chapter 13. My purpose here is to acknowledge the truly magical effect that the use of sound can have on an individual. There are many stories that can be told of sages, particularly in India, extolling the virtue of repeating "the Name." *Mantra* or *Jap yoga* in the Hindu tradition, and *wasifa* and *dhikr* in the Sufi tradition, are thought to be the essence of spiritual practice. Meditation is important, but repeating the name(s) of God is what gets the inner work done. We will discuss the possible reasons why this is true at a later time, but the truth lies in the experience.

Sound practices are essential to virtually all spiritual education, and only seem absent in those traditions where individual spiritual work has been eradicated in favor of seeking salvation (which makes little sense to me) through faith and the knowledge of others. Yet if we seek sufficiently deep we can find the use of sound as a spiritual practice even within these traditions. For instance, in Christianity we can find monastic chanting and liturgical song as methods of creating a sacred atmosphere throughout most of its history. The main difference between these Christian practices and others is the lack of the use of individual sound practices designed for specific individual spiritual advancement. Still, the early Christian desert fathers used repetitions of the "prayer of the heart" as an important method for purifying the heart and connecting with the Divine.

The Sufi path, the path with which I am most familiar, uses sound as a primary practice, second only to the teacher-pupil relationship. One set of practices with sound is called wasifa, involving the repetition of words used to describe God in the Qur'an. These are called the *99 Names of God* or the *99 Beautiful Names.* The wasifa represent latent qualities that exist in each person and can be strengthened through concentration and repetition. The teacher suggests specific wasifa to be repeated by the student each day in order to accomplish the desired personality transformation. I have used wasifa in my spiritual practice and have found them to be an effective means of change. They work slowly over time, but they work to bring out or strengthen qualities in a remarkable way. At times along the way, when I have had to struggle with doubt and lack of faith in the process, I only needed to look at the remarkable changes that seemed directly related to doing wasifa to quell my fears.

Dhikr (pronounced "ziker") is the repetition of the phrase, "There is no God but God," *La illaha illa la,* which may better be understood as "Nothing exists except the One." The multiple use of the "ahh" sound has a profound effect upon the consciousness, but the phrase is more than that. It is a sweeping away of the everpresent duality and the substituting of the knowledge of Oneness that does the incredible work of the dhikr. People who engage in repetition of dhikr can be swept into the world of nonduality *(zat)* and can experience moments of sublime peace and wholeness. People who do dhikr over a lifetime can free themselves from the constrictions of dualistic thinking and attain spiritual freedom.

These mysteries, from synchronicity and shamanic journeys to heart connections and sound practices, are all part of my experience. Although there exist other types of mysteries, I wish to share only those that I have experienced directly and repeatedly. Therefore, this discussion of mysteries should be seen as only the tip of a very large iceberg. Much that cannot be explained by our current religious and scientific paradigms occurs on a regular basis and is experienced by many people around us; we have just learned not to talk about "such things."

Throughout my life there have been many relatives, friends, clients, and students who share so-called paranormal experiences they have had, but did not feel they could discuss with most people. When a very large portion of the population has such experiences, and therefore must deny very real and profound experiences in order to fit in, it seems it is time for our cultural paradigms to change.

FOUR

The Moral Life

TO LIVE TOGETHER in groups, people
require some set of expectations to guide interactions at various levels
of the group. Whether people are gathered in a community, or interacting with family and loved ones, sets of rules and expectations evolve
to guide behavior. Societies generally place great importance on being
able to count on all of their members to act in accordance with a single set of expectations for behavior. Traditionally, morality has most
often been linked to religious beliefs. When this is the case, informal
controls toward conforming are especially strong, since they are often
linked to one's sense of self-worth as well as expectations for reward or
punishment in the afterlife. The fear that terrorizes the hearts of the
defenders of the religious status quo is that, when the religious myth is
called into question, moral decay will prevail.

It is true that morality is built into all mythologies, but only in the
broadest sense. Morality is built into religions, but this is because religion is based upon culture. Morality is cultural and reflects the time-
tested wisdom of a group of people regarding how best to live
together, prosper as a people, and accomplish the accepted purposes of
the culture. These informal rules for guiding behavior become institu-
tionalized in the structures of a society, such as family form and socialization of youth, economic relationships, political structure, and, of

49

course, religious practice. Morality is interwoven into all areas of life and cannot easily be disentangled from all the other social institutions. When the morality of a culture and its mythological/religious basis start to drift apart and lose their hold on a significant portion of the population (as has happened today) all aspects of society are affected.

Life at the turn of the twenty-first century in the postindustrial West may sometimes feel like a normless void where we must invent our own morality. This is not an easy thing to do. The need to stop and think, rather than just being guided by whatever everybody else is doing, is always difficult. Even those who still hold to the morality of the past are open to the ravages of normlessness, because they must interact daily with those who do not hold their same values. The disintegration of the central myth, along with a pluralistic society with many competing religions and mythologies, has brought about the need to find the nonreligious basis for morality. The cultural reasons to live a moral life are just as relevant today as ever. The specifics may change, but the need to live in harmony with others and with the natural world is probably more important and more difficult today than ever before.

The Social Contract and Consciousness

Let us look at a basis for moral behavior in keeping with this new perspective, then we can compare this approach with what it replaces. A morality based upon the premise that the evolution of consciousness toward an authentic spirituality is the highest good might, at first blush, sound abstract, but if one investigates the implications, it may not be that abstract at all. The "morality of consciousness" would by its very nature have to include much of the best of what we have called "morality" for millennia. We may add to the morality of consciousness a "morality of social contract." These two moralities become the two hands of moral action—social contract and consciousness.

All of us must live within the context of groupings, ranging from our culture and society, down to neighborhoods and families. The oil that lubricates interactions in all these circumstances is, at the informal level, manners, norms, and the expectations placed upon us because of the roles we fill. At the formal level, we are bound by laws and contracts. Being held accountable, by informal and formal social control, to live in harmony within our communities, is what is meant by the term "social contract." While religions have taken credit for this type of morality over the millennia by placing words in the mouths of their prophets or avatars extolling certain virtues, it is clear that the morality of contract is more an evolution of "best practices" for living in community. There is often great wisdom in the shared morality of a people with regard to living in that particular time and place. Sometimes, however, time and place change and the morality of contract needs to change as well. We will return to the morality of contract shortly, but first let's examine the concept of the "morality of consciousness."

The Morality of Consciousness

What is it that hinders the expansion and evolution of consciousness? Things that constrict the human spirit. I propose that a morality of consciousness encourages expansion of consciousness and discourages those interactions that force others to constrict their consciousness. What do I mean by "expanding and constricting consciousness"? This is far too big a question to answer completely now, so let's look at a few examples. Expansion of consciousness may involve "walking a mile in another person's shoes," while constricting of consciousness might involve recoiling from another's experiences out of fear or hate.

Expansion of consciousness often requires time and space for reflection and contemplation; constriction is what we do when we hurry or fill our lives with habits and addictions. Expansion involves allowing ourselves to be sensitive to the feelings of those (people, animals, plants, and even minerals) around us, while constricting involves ignoring, neglecting, or negating the feelings and impressions we receive from our environment. Expansion of consciousness involves opening ourselves to wider, deeper and more subtle aspects of life.

Oppression, poverty, violence, hostility, and unwanted intrusion into the life and possessions of another cause human beings to constrict and retreat from awareness and life. These are all ways in which people can interfere with the development of the others' consciousness. (There are certainly ways in which we hold ourselves back in our development, but that is not the topic at hand.) Let's look briefly at each of these and attempt to discern their effect on consciousness.

Oppression

Oppression, or the lack of freedom, confines the body, mind, and emotions of individuals within rigid parameters. When people are not allowed freedom of movement, their world shrinks, and their life experiences are less full than the lives of those who have freedom. When people are deprived of the opportunity to seek knowledge beyond a rigidly prescribed boundary, consciousness is squeezed even more, and the human capacity for expansion, creativity, and awe is severely wounded. The refusal to allow emotional expression (within reasonable boundaries) keeps the individual from becoming a whole person.

Cultures, governments, religions, scientific/academic disciplines, families, and bullies of all kinds attempt to oppress others by imposing their will and perspectives on their victims. When this is allowed to happen, the consciousness of the individual being oppressed must contract into a self-protective mode and either identifies with the aggressor, or seeks another means to stay out of harm's way. Outside of reasonable law and social convention, the imposing of constrictions that are too tight on any other human being, or group of human beings, may be called oppression. If the creation of consciousness and the evolution of consciousness is the way in which the One Life becomes known to itself, and if this is the ultimate purpose of human existence, then oppression is at the top of the list of immoralities. Any act that oppresses another human being becomes by its very nature an immoral act.

Poverty

Poverty is a cruel breaker of souls. Poverty consigns a unique expression of the One Life to an existence that drains and destroys consciousness instead of nurturing it. Poverty is a despicable evil that would not be necessary if human beings had the will and the heart to eradicate it. Any act that perpetuates poverty is an immoral act. Yet we live in a world where the gap between the rich and the poor gets larger with every day.

In 1997, in the richest country in the world, the United States, 35.6 million people (13.3 percent) lived below the poverty line (Segal and Stromwall, 2000:521). Starvation and famine ravage parts of Africa and Asia. In China, India, and many other countries in Asia, Africa, and Latin America, a large segment of the population live on less than two dollars per day (Dandaneau, 2001:29). It is not that the world cannot produce sufficient resources to address these ills; it is rather that we are unwilling to develop economic systems and technologies that would serve the purposes of the world rather than the privileged few. Visionaries such as R. Buckminster Fuller have called for changes that would enable us to eradicate poverty and have given us suggestions on how to do it, but we have always refused to entertain the possibility that it could be done.

As a social worker, I have had opportunities to work with low-income people. In the United States, being poor is different from being poor in Mexico or India, but the felt experience is still of poverty. While I have known some courageous low-income people who have been able to cultivate a loving and wise level of consciousness, it has more often been my experience to see the devastation of poverty in people's hopelessness, despair, and sometimes, in psychological problems. People sometimes overcome poverty, but it is more often the case that poverty overwhelms the poor. Our systems of social stratification have created huge class disparities of income, wealth, and power, and movement from one class to another is restricted by a host of social mechanisms, including racism, sexism, and the loss of jobs in our big cities.

Violence

Wanton violence is violence without a constructive purpose. It is most likely wanton violence that we would all agree needs curbing. When one is on the receiving end of violence of any sort, provoked or unprovoked, justified or unjustified, the tendency is to contract physically, mentally, and emotionally. It is true that there are adrenaline junkies who, after participating in battle or some other violent activity, crave the "high" that can be experienced at times of violence, but these are very few. Most of us are severely traumatized by violence.

My stepfather fought in two wars, the Second World War and the Korean War, and was tortured in a Japanese prisoner-of-war camp. In spite of being a career soldier—and he was quite good at being a soldier—he spent over the last fifty years of his life waking almost every night with horrendous war and POW dreams. He also displayed most of the other symptoms of post-traumatic stress disorder. For whole generations of men, the violence of war is the defining experience of their lives, and they spend the majority of their lives emotionally constricted and wounded. Death is not the only sacrifice in war; living with the wounds to the soul caused by the experience of war is almost as tragic.

Despite its horrors, I still wish not to completely condemn all violence. Unfortunately, there still are times when nations as well as people may be called upon to defend themselves. I am not in favor of giving free rein to forces of oppression, poverty, and others that wish to limit and constrict humanity. In civilized societies, we employ armies and police forces and give them permission to engage in violence for our sake. The only problem with this solution is that all too often these forces become too powerful and despotic, and we find that we need protection from those we have authorized to protect us.

As we begin to construct a morality that is in the service of human consciousness, violence is certainly an enemy of the creation of consciousness. Violence is also often the means for the promotion and continuation of oppression and poverty. Violent acts, without an overriding and compelling need in order to protect oneself, loved ones, or community, are immoral acts.

Hostility

While hostility may seem similar to violence, let us broaden it to include attitudes and viewpoints that seek to do emotional and mental harm to people, and also harm to the natural world. Plundering natural resources, polluting air and water, destroying cultures, civilizations, and species, are not dissimilar from harassing women, bullying a playmate, or ruining a competitor. All of these behaviors involve a disregard for the well-being of others and a narcissistic sense of privilege, which makes the hostility acceptable to oneself. When people are harassed, bullied, and demeaned, they may close down, put up protective walls, strike out at others, give up, or in some cases strive to overcome. These responses are detrimental in many ways; they require repair or damage control rather than creation and expansion of consciousness. Certainly in lives dominated by the need to protect oneself from the bullying of others, there is little time for growth.

When nature is harassed, bullied, or demeaned, there is also a loss. Sometimes it is easy to see, as with the loss of the ozone layer or lack of safe water to drink, but other times it is a more subtle loss that not everyone can see. We have disregarded the importance of Life and Consciousness for so long that we are often incapable of seeing the true nature of the intricate web of Consciousness and Life and how it is all wound together in Oneness. The price we pay for our ignorance is becoming more apparent every day. The natural world is becoming more like a dead world, and is less responsive to the inner needs of humanity. To use traditional terminology, we are killing God every day, and we don't seem to care or even notice. Hostile acts toward people and nature, whatever form they take, are immoral acts.

Unwanted Intrusion

Just as violence and hostility cause contraction into emotions like fear and anger, invading or appropriating another's person, home, or property causes contraction into fear or anger, and usually leads to some sort of retaliation. We again find a situation where, due to the actions of others an individual or group, people must engage in self-protective or retaliatory behavior that draws them away from self-awareness and into contraction or "externalization." Externalization refers to the common human tendency to see issues of consciousness "out there" rather than explore them in oneself as a means of creating more consciousness. Always seeing the evil "out there" rather than looking at one's own dark side is easier to do when there are things being done to you by others. The more oppression, poverty, violence, hostility, and thievery that an individual has to tolerate, the easier it is for him or her to externalize all the "bad guys" and avoid self-knowledge and the discovery of the shadow within.

Consciousness is served in a civil and reasonably ordered society, where there is a minimum of oppression and a maximum of opportunity. When people deepen their consciousness to the point where they become authentic human beings, their sense of morality transcends cultural norms and dictates that the person act in accordance with a higher morality. This first order of morality, which I believe to be beyond culture, is a step toward what I describe as "the morality of consciousness."

Morality of Contract

Now we may return to the morality of contract, which is the morality that derives from culture and is therefore culturally relative. Cultural moralities are important in that they allow for an understanding of the social contract by all of the people with whom one lives, works, and plays. At any time and in any place there is a need to know the rules that must be followed if one is to be an accepted member of the community. These rules range from manners to taboos. In a *gesellshaft,* or formal society, like most Western industrialized nations, many important rules are enforced by law.

It is not realistic to talk about the myriad of behaviors regulated by informal or formal controls within a given culture or society, but we might take one area that seems of moral concern to just about every society and view it from a cultural rather than a religious perspective. By taking this perspective we can evaluate the implications of changes over time, and we can look at moral choices as situated in time and place rather than as eternal truths. This type of moral regulation becomes the "morality of social contract." It is fundamentally different from the "morality of consciousness."

The Regulation of Sexuality

Because sexuality is something that all cultures have seen the need to regulate through moral codes, it can provide us insight into the reasons behind an evolution of morality. The Western sexual morality that is dying, along with the myths that supported it, emerged largely out of the experiences of the Hebrew people in the last centuries of the pre-Christian era and those of the early Christians in the first three centuries of the Christian era. What we know about families during this time suggests that marriage was more like a contract between families and a means for maintaining economic stability than the love relationship it is today. We also know that a high value was placed upon knowing beyond a reasonable doubt the paternity of a child, especially if it was a boy. Property and inheritance rights followed the male line, and fathers wanted to know that the male children were their own. This ensured the continuation of the father's bloodline and also made the allocation of inherited wealth less problematic.

To ensure the proper allocation of inherited wealth, women's sexuality needed to be controlled so that men could be certain of their offspring. Two other practical issues were at work in the morality that developed during this time. First, both the Jewish people and the early Christians wanted and needed to grow. The Jewish people were building their nation after being decimated by war and the Babylonian captivity, and the early Christians sought safety and power in numbers. Much attention was paid to the "proper" and orderly creation and socialization of new members into their societies. Children were desired, and they needed to be protected and taught by strong families dedicated to the beliefs of the larger community. It would not have been helpful to have a lot of confusion about parentage affecting the stability and dependability of the family.

The corollary to the above concerns is obvious, but not often discussed. Birth control was not dependable. Heterosexual sexuality very often led to pregnancy, and this fact of life colored all other considerations. The freedom to experiment with sex that came about with the advent of the birth control pill was simply nonexistent. There may have been other hidden sexual norms among the priestly and wealthy classes, but among the general populace these were the sexual conditions.

Compare the conditions just described to the current state of sexuality, marriage, and family. Sociologists describe today's marriages as "companionate," in other words based on love and companionship rather than economic or other social considerations. Today people choose their own life partners. Women need not be as financially dependent upon their husbands as in the past and are able to choose a husband who is emotionally and mentally (as well as physically) capable of being a partner and friend. Inheritance does not simply go to biological sons, but to any or all children or relatives, according to the couple's wishes. The extended family, in which people have their noses in everyone else's business, has been replaced by the highly mobile nuclear family and, in many cases, the "binuclear" family created upon the divorce of a couple.

Dating and the sexuality of young never-married members of our society are also quite different from two thousand years ago. Today's mobile, unchaperoned youth, who vaguely understand that their relationships will not be like those of their grandparents, undergo dating rituals as in any other culture. Generally, they are not looking for a spouse that will please their parents or add to the family's wealth, but rather someone with whom they feel they can be friends and have a good life.

Sexuality is a part of that good life. As important to our discussion of sexual morality as any of the above factors is the change in birth control. Couples, whether married or unmarried, can now engage in sexual intercourse and be 99.9 percent certain that pregnancy will not occur. This creates very different conditions for the regulating of sexuality. Today's dating is training for today's marriage, not yesterday's.

To understand the evolving sexual morality, one more factor must be understood. We do not need more people. We live in a world of six billion human beings. Every day we experience the growing population density when we step outdoors. Anyone over forty can remember when there were a lot fewer people to contend with in stores, on the freeway, and in any other public place we find ourselves. Even in the United States, where we have more room than most places in the world, we are getting mighty testy because of the constant press of people in our lives. It will not be long before we will begin to have major water problems throughout the world, including the U.S., and we are already plagued by pollution and waste management problems that may be unsolvable. We do not live in a time in which we should be encouraging people to "be fruitful and multiply." In this context, who among us would say that the only purpose of sex should be procreation?

Sex has changed and so must the morality that regulates it. Sex continues to serve the function of perpetuating the species, but it is no longer seen as an evil that must be put up with only for that purpose. It now is being seen by a growing number of individuals as a means of expressing love and deepening intimacy. It is part of the companionship of life partners. Sexual expression can serve to unlock the sometimes mutually exclusive prisons of male and female, bridging the gender gap. Sex can expand our limited consciousness through its push toward empathy with the partner as well as the experience of ecstasy, which may serve to provide a glimpse of eternity. In other words, sex is very important in our lives, and its regulation should be out of reverence for its transformative beauty, rather than fear and dread.

This is a very different morality regarding sex than that of the ancient Hebrews or early Christians, but it is a morality that matches the deepening relationships and evolving level of consciousness of the times. What we see around us is the conflict between this emerging moral perspective and the dying proscriptions of the outlived morality of older times. The evolution of these two perspectives became very evident in the Middle Ages, when the myths and stories related to romantic love and personal choice emerged in the twelfth and thirteenth centuries. The important thing to realize is that tying sex to love and individual freedom of choice is a major shift in consciousness and has paved the way for the far more individuated consciousness that humans possess today. This change in sexual morality is interwoven with evolutionary strides in consciousness.

In spite of this tie to consciousness, we can also still see sexual codes and their variations from culture-to-culture as both reflecting and influencing the cultural milieu in which they dwell. Sexual morality reflects the specific needs and beliefs of a culture with regard to the regulation of family and sexual expression. Heterogeneous societies, such as those in the United States and Western Europe, allow for a wider variety of moral choices because of their diversity, whereas homogeneous cultures, because of their limited diversity, allow for much less freedom in moral choice. One can see this very clearly not only in areas of dating, premarital sex, marital and extramarital sex, and divorce, but also in birth control, abortion, and homosexuality. These hot-button issues rise to prominence in the West primarily because of the lack of unanimity of opinion and room for choice and individual freedom provided by a diverse society. A diverse society such as ours must learn how to use emerging moral standards to inform public debate and policy, rather than remain bound to unworkable moralities of the past that are tied to dying religious dogma.

The Immorality of Morality

The morality of the past was not always very moral. This means that yesterday's morality was not very moral, using the measure of today's standards. This is especially obvious when looking at the behaviors of larger groups of people and of nations. Let's spend some time looking at examples of Christian morality and its historical manifestations. If we realize that the morality we thought was working in the past was at least partially responsible for great suffering and destruction, we might be freed to explore a more compassionate, human-centered, freedom-enhancing morality. We may begin to realize that it is only our concepts that are holding us back from being awakened to the cry of humanity resounding around the globe for a more compassionate life-affirming morality.

While one might choose to study the Roman Church from the time of Constantine and the Council of Nicaea through the many crusades, inquisitions, conquests, annihilations of indigenous peoples, that would

THE MORAL LIFE

be a book in itself. It is also beyond the scope of this book to discuss the contemporary crisis triggered by the revelation of the sexual exploitation of children by priests. We will look at a few examples of the immoral actions of Christian countries and rulers to make the point that we would not be giving much up if we chose to shift toward a "morality of consciousness and social contract."

There are four primary moral problems that have plagued Christianity from its inception. These problems have affected the other monotheistic religions to some extent as well. The first issue is the highly ethnocentric perspective that Christianity is the only "true" religion. Secondly, there is a dualistic, otherworldly leaning that treats the physical world on this glorious, garden planet as unworthy of our love and respect. Third, linked to the second, we find a rejection of the feminine in all its manifestations. Last, a literalism that fuels the other three is all too often present, especially in forms that seem designed to convince the masses of the righteousness of whatever church or state is doing.

The belief that one's own religion is the only right religion, and must be thrust upon everyone else, may be the most destructive impulse ever visited upon humanity. The life and teachings of Jesus can be viewed as a teaching story filled with symbolic importance and potential to liberate the soul, or it can be used as a prison designed to deprive non-Christians of opportunities to learn from their own cultural experiences, to follow their own hearts. This is not because the teachings of Jesus are not profound and useful, but rather because in the European power politics of the last seventeen hundred years, church and state have been inseparable partners in oppression and imperialism.

We will explore a few examples that point to the enormity of the problem. I focus on Christianity because it is the religion of my childhood and lies at the heart of American culture. We could examine similar moral ambiguities from other monotheistic religions, but I believe that it is better to challenge the community to which one belongs than others.

- Early Christian zealots destroyed the irreplaceable history of human culture contained at the library of Alexandria, Egypt.

61

- Constantine's power politics at the Council of Nicaea in A.D. 325 sealed the fate of Christianity as a closed system by eliminating differences of opinion as to the nature of Christ and other crucial issues. The key issue is the idea that Jesus was the "only" Son of God. This implicitly makes all other religions inferior, since Jesus is by definition the "only one."

- The Albigensian Crusade exterminated over two million Cathers in the south of France. The Cathers were far more dualistic than the Roman Church, and saw things of the world as evil; they also rejected the divinity of Jesus and believed in reincarnation. They were developing a large following in southern France and were becoming a threat to the Roman Church, partially because they lived austere lives that reflected their deeply held beliefs.

- The conquest of the Americas by Spain, Portugal, and later England and France was another factor. The Church worked hand-in-glove with these imperialistic states, especially Spain, sanctioning their brutal destruction of whole civilizations in order to bring "true faith" to the heathens. For example, both Pope Alexander VI and Julius II were instrumental in giving permission to own and divide up the New World for Spain and Portugal. How incredible that they thought it was theirs to give! Alexander the VI proclaimed in a papal bull that all lands discovered west of a line one hundred leagues beyond the Azores belonged to Spain. Julius II granted Ferdinand of Spain the "right of royal patronage" in the Americas (Crow, 1992:67–68). Besides the wholesale slaughter and greed involved in this church-backed endeavor, the mind boggles at its self-righteous pomposity. For example, the young priest accompanying Balboa, upon seeing the Pacific Ocean, rushed into the waves with his crucifix shouting, "I take possession of this ocean in the name of Jesus Christ" (Crow, 1992:69).

- The Inquisition, which lasted from its inception during the Albigensian Crusade in the early thirteenth century until the witch hunts of the seventeenth and early eighteenth centuries, used torture and church-sponsored execution to control ideas with which it did not agree. The various inquisitions successfully prolonged the age of darkness and ignorance in Europe, while just to the south and east the Muslim world was awash in intellectual and spiritual awakening.

- Our final example is the "Christian Right" in today's American political scene. With a zeal that may rival the Inquisitors, these self-righteous denizens of the "true faith" have already dismantled much of the economic and social safety net for needy Americans and are working on destroying the American form of democracy itself. Their means include demonizing not only the poor and culturally different, but also those who would wish to preserve the human rights of all people. All of this is being done in the name of Christian morality and the "old-time religion."

The dualistic perspective that the physical world is to be despised and that only the spiritual is to be valued is tied to a misunderstanding of the holistic nature of reality. There is no "up there" and "down here"; there is only "here." Unfortunately, this misunderstanding has become synonymous with most Christian beliefs. This was particularly true of the Roman Church and did not change much with the Reformation. Other monotheistic religions had gone out of their way to distance themselves from this sort of literalistic, "God is up there and we are down here" perspective. Karen Armstrong notes, "Jews, Muslims, and Orthodox Christians had all insisted in their different ways that our human idea of God did not correspond to the ineffable reality of which it was a mere symbol" (Armstrong, 1973:352).

The idea that humans are better than the rest of creation and must subdue, conquer, or even be stewards of the rest of creation is also part of the problem. Reuben Snake, a wise, astute, and humble elder of the Winnebago Nation in northeastern Nebraska, and a family friend, used to make the very important point that humans are the least of the Creator's creatures. We are not strong like the bear, nor swift like the deer, nor ferocious like the lion. We cannot fly like the birds, we are not protected by fur, and we must go through a lot of trouble to build

63

a place to live. All and all, we are a rather sorry lot and have much to learn from our brothers and sisters who run on four legs, fly in the sky, swim in lakes, streams, and oceans or crawl on their bellies and shed their skin.

It is this humble desire to learn from the natural world that is missing today. Reuben also believed that the native peoples of the world, especially the Native Americans, could help the rest of us learn how to live on this planet, if only we would reach out and seek their advice. He used to lament that there were so many of us (white people) and so few of them (Native Americans), so it was a huge task. He had done the math and would tell us with a big grin that each native person would have to adopt several hundred (about four hundred, I think) European Americans in order to accomplish this great work!

The point is that this dualistic, antiphysical bias that has troubled Christianity from the beginning is first of all wrong-headed, and secondly, it is largely responsible for the ecological problems of today and the ecological disaster that awaits us. It is also behind the oppression of women and non-Christian cultural minorities, as well as the repression of healthy sexuality and life energy.

The denial of the feminine in all of its manifestations, as women, nature, native peoples, love, the body and sexuality, is certainly the curse left us by the warlike patriarchal tribes that brought us monotheism. Judaism, Christianity, and Islam have had to wage incessant warfare, both physical and spiritual, in their attempts to combat the tendency of human beings to seek the feminine side of divinity. After the Hebrews left Egypt, bringing their tribal-war God with them, they first had to engage in genocide against the matrifocal cultures of Canaan. Then they spent centuries having to suppress continually the same matrifocal, or feminine-centered, tendencies within their own population. When one looks at the lives of Jesus and Mohammed, one sees many women at the very center of their circles of followers and families, yet once the followers of the followers started creating dogma, women were relegated to secondary status. This is very odd if looked at from a spiritual perspective, but from a political perspective it is perfectly understandable. The problem is that no religion can claim to convey truth if it does not recognize the unity of feminine and masculine.

The fear of the feminine and prejudice against the matrifocal societies that were displaced or destroyed by patriarchal expansion has been generalized to all things that are associated with the feminine. Mother Earth, because of her association with woman, becomes something to be dominated and despoiled. People with a stronger feminine influence in their mythology are labeled pagans, witches, or devil-worshipers. If you want to know some of the sacred places for precolonial Native Americans, just look for place names like "Devil's Tower," Devil's Lake," or "Witch's Hollow." This is what Christians thought of the religions of native people. This dualism turns potentially harmonious groups into warring, self-hating factions that can never understand, empathize, and accommodate each other. This is the sad, sad state of affairs of the modern world of religion and of men and women.

Finally, we must talk of literalism. We have seen that literal interpretations of religion provide fuel for an ethnocentric, misogynistic, world-hating morality. While at any given time and for any given person, this morality might be quite different from that which I am portraying, it is when literalistic interpretations are strong within a culture that religious morality becomes an antimorality. Most monotheistic religions have tried valiantly to avoid this literalistic trap. Those who are wise understand that literalism is the way of children and that when people become adults they need to be shown the symbolic nature of the words or images. However, too often it is tempting to invoke literalism to support political power or cultural domination. It is at these times that immorality rules the day.

It is simply not possible to put the ultimate reality into a box. Symbolic images and metaphors are used to try to relay as close an approximation to ultimate truth as human consciousness is capable of comprehending at a given time. Hardy, warlike, patriarchal people use metaphors that reflect their experience, and sedentary, peace-loving, agricultural societies use metaphors that reflect their experience. Which one is right? Both groups are right, and neither is right. Cultural groups use metaphors for that which human beings cannot describe or even comprehend. It is when primary knowledge of the nature of reality is lost that we warp our gods and religions to fit our small viewpoints; then we visit upon ourselves the kinds of immorality that we have witnessed in the last two thousand years.

Children in the dominant culture in the United States usually believe in Santa Claus. They may even believe that he is watching them all the time and they will be rewarded or punished accordingly at Christmastime. Sometime, usually before the age of six or seven, children realize that Santa Claus doesn't really exist and that it has been their parents who have given them gifts all along. It is time for them to realize this fact, because it is also time for their intellects to develop capabilities beyond childhood fantasies. Usually no one regrets their having believed in Santa Claus, just as no one regrets their growing out of the belief. It is just part of growing up and understanding the way in which the world works. Children also need to develop a more mature reason for being "good." If it is not because Santa is watching, then why should they be good?

When children begin to become a little less reliant on external authority, they enter a long process of moral development and gradually become more self-regulating and inner-directed. Young children make appropriate moral choices out of fear of punishment or desire for reward. Mature adults make appropriate moral choices based upon concern for others, welfare of self, allegiance to community, and principle. The day of religions that force moral behavior though literalistic fear of punishment and hope for reward is fast coming to an end, as human consciousness moves from its childhood into its adolescence. The female Sufi mystic, Rabia, spoke to God with words something like this: "If I come to you through fear of Hell, then cast me into Hell. If I come to you though hope for Heaven, then you should also cast me into Hell. If I come to you simply out of love for your divine presence, then take me to your bosom for eternity" (Inayat, 1978:21). Now *there* is a woman who understands.

PART TWO

Understanding the Core of Spirituality

THERE ARE CENTRAL processes relevant to all forms of spirituality, regardless of the cultures in which they are embedded. Understanding these processes is crucial. Some of the most important areas are opening the heart, mastery, creating personality, spiritual teaching and transmission, and spiritual freedom. If we are to disentangle spirituality from its varied cultural inflections, we must make sure that we do not "throw out the baby with the bathwater." The central processes I will discuss in the following chapters are beyond culture because they are necessary for the expansion of consciousness under all cultural circumstances. Of all of these issues, the first two chapters are paramount.

FIVE

Opening the Heart

WHAT IS MEANT by "heart" in spiritual traditions? Is heart only the muscle that pumps blood throughout the body? Do we mean by heart the fourth chakra (to use the common terminology derived from the Yogic-Hindu tradition) in the human energy system of the subtle bodies? Is heart synonymous with courage, as when a person is said to have a lot of heart? Is heart just another way of describing emotions? Actually, the meaning of heart to the mystic is all of these things and yet more. The awakened heart is the ultimate in human achievement, as it is the bringing together of heaven and earth in the form of human existence. The awakening of the human heart is the ultimate purpose of human life, as the "hidden treasure" becomes manifest in the mirror of the heart. In other words, consciousness transcends its captivity in the usual narrowness of human life when it comes to fruition in the vastness of the awakened heart.

The Feeling Nature

One way to integrate the various definitions of the heart is to refer to it as the feeling nature. This may include courage, love, and sensitivity, as well as "higher" emotions like exultation, bliss, and ecstatic love. The emotional nature is also related to the heart center in the subtle body.

Some emotions are related to lower centers. For instance, power (unless used for the benefit of others) is usually related to the solar plexus center. The heart is the seat of feelings that involve caring, healing, joining, and all other feelings that seek wholeness rather than separation. All feelings, even the most rageful or base, can be transformed by the awakening heart into useful aspects of the psyche. Transformed anger and rage can become the strength and magnetism. Transformed depression can become depth of feeling. Most human beings have access to only a small range of emotion. Opening the heart to a larger range of feeling is one aspect of what we are talking about. Becoming sensitive to the feelings and experiences of others is also involved in the opening of the heart. Refining the typical feelings one experiences is another part of the journey. While this process involves the subtle center referred to as the heart chakra, the evidence of an opening heart is seen in one's activities and relationships in everyday life. It does not require a psychic reading to determine the degree to which one's heart is open, only observation of the way one treats one's fellow human beings.

Developing the feeling nature is crucial for spiritual development. If we seek wisdom without an open heart, what we often get is cynicism or dry intellectual pomposity. If we seek power without an open heart, we become cruel, domineering, or callous to the needs of others. If we seek psychic abilities without an open heart, we are often overwhelmed by them or can cause damage to others. All things that can be gained by spiritual development must be mediated by an awakened heart, or they may become horrors rather than blessings. The lessons of history are legion in this arena.

On the other side of this coin lie overemotionality and being victimized by our own emotions. Some people seem to have little ability to filter or control what seems to be a vast reservoir of emotion just below the surface that intrudes upon their ability to cope with their lives. Other people have difficulty in separating self from other sufficiently not to be flooded by the emotions of another. It is important to keep in mind that a wounded heart (which often lacks boundaries) is not necessarily an open heart. Ego strength and adequate boundaries are essential in order to develop spiritually. People whose feeling nature presents problems in everyday coping need instruction in the development of heart, just as surely as those who have a difficult time feeling; the instruction needs to be designed to deal with their specific needs.

All too often I have seen a "one-size-fits-all" perspective applied to the development of heart qualities, to the detriment of overly sensitive people. Spiritual paths in patriarchal societies have been designed to break down men's egos. Women and very sensitive men were often not taken into consideration, as spiritual schools were developed in the context of patriarchal religions. Today, when at least an equal number of spiritual aspirants are female, we may be confronting limitations in spiritual teachings that arise from male-oriented spiritual schools.

The Process

The most important question in spiritual development often becomes "How do we open our hearts?" Put another way, how do human beings transcend the narrow, self-encapsulated, low-key existence that is considered normal by cultural standards? How do individuals heighten their sensitivity, receptiveness, compassion, empathy, passion, psychological courage, and myriads of other aspects of the feeling nature, while remaining capable of functioning within their own culture? How do we become fully conscious of our feelings while maintaining the capacity to function in a sometimes harsh cultural environment? These have been the difficult questions that have plagued spiritual seekers since the dawn of time. The important thing to realize is that progress has been made in this area by those courageous souls who have trod the inner paths before us. There are techniques that have stood the test of time and continue to work to this day.

The heart does not open in a few days or weeks or months. It is a gradual process that generally requires years of dedicated work. Spiritual teachings typically employ more than one method when working on the heart. There are several stages that usually must be passed through. Let us begin by looking at the stages of opening the heart. We must realize that this kind of sequential description is only a convenience, and that individuals will have their own idiosyncratic ways of doing the inner work. We can, however, learn much by looking at a typical sequence. There is a natural sequential growth that could conceivably bring open hearts to many as they proceed into old age. Unfortunately, this natural process is often subverted by cultural circumstances, beliefs, and dictates that inhibit the development of the psyche.

There are very few spiritual seekers today who do not enter the process with deep wounds to the heart. To hang out with spiritual people is to hang out with wounded people. People come with "father-wounding" and "mother-wounding"; some people come with "too much world," and others come with "not enough world." People come with karmic wounds (unfinished fallout from the momentum of previous lives) that seek to repeat themselves over and over again. Many come with an existential alienation toward a world that makes no sense to them. Some people have been used and abused by those around them and bear the scars, while others bear the guilt of having been users and abusers. I remember asking a well-known spiritual guide why so little esotericism was taught in his spiritual group. He told me that very few people are ready for it. I suggested that most of us had a lot of healing to do first; he looked a bit startled by my statement at first, and then he just smiled.

A Safe Place to Heal

The first thing that is needed by all of these seekers is to be *seen*. Whether we are talking about a spiritual guide or other members of a group of like-minded individuals, someone must see the person for the unique and beautiful spark of consciousness that he or she is and somehow reflect that beauty back upon the individual. This is why it is so difficult to grow spiritually without a teacher or a group; there are points at which another being is an absolute necessity. If that other being is wise and able to see and has an open heart, it is much easier for this encounter to play itself out in the most useful way. If the other is either unaware of what is happening or uses it to gain control over the individual (as in unscrupulous cults), the process is usually stifled.

A healthy atmosphere is often created naturally within loving relationships and is what we hope sets families apart from the rest of society (although this idealized image of the family is not usually borne out in real-life families). It is quite common that people in small spiritual groups see their groups as more like a family than most experienced in their families of origin. A trust and sense of belonging is built that counteracts much of the alienation and wounding that people bring with them. From this trust and sense of belonging can emerge either the perfect place for psychological and spiritual growth or a repressive cult of domination and alienation. The direction will depend upon the wisdom, skill, and motivation of the leaders.

Once an individual feels seen and accepted by a spiritual mentor, spiritual group, a lover, or a therapist, a safety zone is created. Within this zone of safety, whether it be the relationship or some sort of group setting, a numinous atmosphere exists. If this atmosphere is honored, the heart of even the most wounded person can be gently opened over time. The creation of such a zone of safety is partially the reason for the emphasis upon the teacher-pupil relationship and the fellowship of seekers (e.g., the *sangha* in Buddhism) in most religions and schools of inner study. This is also the area of most potential for abuse, when spiritual mentors fail to live up to the trust that is placed in them.

A common difficulty found in spiritual schools that train both males and females is the sexualizing of spiritual relationships. Especially when a male mentor uses the relationship with a female student for sexual purposes, we can see opportunity for deep damage to the bond of safety. It is so easy for admiration of someone who represents our spiritual aspirations to be misinterpreted as sexual attraction. Spiritual teachers and students need to be taught to know the difference as soon in the process as possible. One can readily see that wounding within this zone of safety can be the worst of betrayals.

Taking Charge of the Process

With a safe place to grow, the heart can be guided through a series of experiences designed to strengthen and expand it. These experiences

73

are generally of two sorts. First, spiritual practices can be used as an exercise program for the heart. Meditations on themes that expand or deepen the loving nature can be incorporated into daily spiritual practice. Breathing techniques that visualize the breath working with the heart can also be used. (See chapter 12 on breath.) Possibly the most effective meditation technique, sound, can be used to work with the vibratory aspect of the heart chakra. (See chapter 13 on sound.) All of these techniques will have a profound effect on the heart over time, if made a part of daily spiritual practice.

The second and most important factor in the strengthening of the heart is the conscious expansion of love, compassion, and empathy in everyday life through the use of will. The meditative practices are essential to prepare the heart and the will, but the real work never happens simply by magic. Spiritual practices and techniques are not enough. We must, as human beings, exert our will in order to change.

Since will is very much connected with the heart qualities, we need to discuss what is meant by "will." We often hear that we should align our personal will with the Divine Will, and much fuss is made about the difference. I don't necessarily see it that way. Yes, individuals can certainly make their own lives and the lives of others miserable when they force things to happen. This is folly, not true will. I reserve the word "will" for that which is the heart's desire; this is the divine intention. The heart's desire is the will of the Soul and is not usually an entirely conscious phenomenon. The will of the Soul is triggered when the heart's desire becomes conscious intention. We may not know what we are doing, but when we set out to achieve a desire from the depths of our hearts, something profound happens.

I have often tried to use what I thought was my will in order to get something I wanted, like a better job, more money, or more recognition. My experience has been that most of the time I failed when I tried to use my will to accomplish this sort of mundane thing. I have been fortunate in my life, as I have all that I need (although like most people, that is not all that I want), but things like good jobs and money and relationships have come to me basically through a natural progression of cause and effect, rather than through the conscious use of will.

What I understand now about my will is that it follows the dictates of my Soul and is at work in granting me my heart's desire, which is spiritual understanding. Setting my will upon anything smaller never works for me, and now that I understand what is going on, I am glad for that.

I feel confident in saying that if we engage our will in the pursuit of opening our hearts, we will always be doing the work of our Soul. We noted earlier that the heart opens through use of the will and is not done in some magical way. Sometimes after we have done a huge amount of inner work and experience the wonderful results, it feels like something magical has happened. The actual process is quite comprehensible, however. We start the process by intending to expand and deepen our heart. Intention is will in disguise. Real will does not feel willful, and it is better described as intention. "Willfulness" engages too much ego and too little Soul.

If we consider the engaging of the will as the first step in the process of opening the heart, the next step is to engage regularly in meditative practices to stimulate and soften the heart. Simultaneously, life will bring us a multitude of opportunities for working with the breadth and depth of our hearts. For the spiritual seeker, every event in life becomes a lesson in heart.

Every time we look at the faces of our spouses or friends, we have an opportunity to see them in all of their splendor and depth, rather than as just our projections upon them. Every time we drive our cars, we have the opportunity to see the drivers around us as being equally entitled to the road. Every time we see someone in need we have the opportunity to feel their need and our own response. In the past those who found it difficult to love those around them could profess to love God and by doing so get off the hook, but more than loving a distant God is asked of us today. We are asked to love each other, and by doing so we are indeed loving God, who is Life itself and the Consciousness that flows from it.

Opening the heart has been described as being similar to peeling an onion or the opening of the petals of a rose. In other words, it is not a single act. The heart gradually opens, layer after layer or petal by petal,

75

over time. Sometimes it feels so profound that we feel that this must be the end, as it could not get any more profound, but it is not the end, and, it does get even more profound. After engaging the will through intention, doing spiritual practices, and making everyday life our teacher, the heart just starts opening. Sometimes we are startled by the seemingly magical experience of our hearts opening when we feel we have done nothing out of the ordinary to provoke the change, but when that happens, we are experiencing the cumulative impact of many years of work.

We often have experiences that signal that our hearts are opening. People may remark that our faces seem softer or more open. We may begin to feel the pain of the world, and for a time we may feel overwhelmed by it. Sometimes our newfound sensitivity is difficult to get used to and we may have difficulty keeping company with the same people or doing the same activities as before. As our hearts open we may by necessity have to change our lifestyles or circles of friends in order to protect our emerging hearts.

I recall my first spiritual retreat. It was a three-day retreat, during which I was in total silence and seclusion in a small hut in upstate New York. I began sobbing (for no apparent outward reason) on the evening of the first full day and did not stop until the afternoon of the third day. Afterwards my retreat guide told me that I was experiencing the "broken heart of God." I did not doubt that conclusion for a minute, since it had certainly felt that way.

For me, the "broken heart of God" entails our participation in the tragic, beautiful, absurd mystery of existence. All of us carry our own tragedies and triumphs within us, and as we touch the depths of our hearts, we may encounter our unacknowledged personal pain. Facing our personal pain may tap into the collective human tragedy, which is vast. That this seemingly endless flow of sorrow has a name is helpful, because by naming it we can learn to separate the personal from the collective sorrow. The next step in the process is to work to heal our personal pain. To focus on the collective pain before healing ourselves is to engage in a "spiritual bypass," an avoidance of the hard work of dealing with our own baggage. Eventually we become capable of connecting with the deep fountain of compassion that pours healing out upon the collective broken hearts and helps to lift them up beyond the abyss of pain.

Meeting the Fullness of Life

As the heart opens, we begin to feel more. We do not just feel more emotion. As a matter of fact, sometimes as the heart grows bigger it is able to encompass more emotion, and this has a reverse effect; we feel less overwhelmed by our personal emotions. It might be more accurate to say that we become more aware or more conscious. Without the barriers to awareness that are set up when we block feeling, much more of life becomes available to us. The opening of the heart may be described as opening to life in its fullness. An awakened heart is the key to all of the mysteries and the depths of existence. People are likely to experience this awakening in different ways, according to their own temperaments.

Spiritual awakening unfolds uniquely for each individual. The first signs of an opening heart are varied. Some people begin to develop wisdom and seem to understand life in new and remarkable ways. Others may not seem any wiser, but they grow powerful and magnetic. Some people develop a healing touch or glance, while others may develop psychic abilities. While the uniqueness of individual temperament explains some of these differences, there are other factors, like karmic momentum, that also play a role in the direction of the changes that are the result of the opening of the heart. It is quite likely that as the heart becomes more alive and open, many new abilities will evolve, but it is typical that one or two will remain prominent.

The development of wisdom, seership, healing abilities, and power is related to the heart's ability, when freed from its restrictions, to know and touch all that is around it. The human heart, which is the seat of the Soul, serves as a link between the situated self, which is located in a cultural context, and timeless reality. Once we have freed the heart from its prison, it serves as a door between us and all that appears to be other than ourselves. We become linked to the universal mind and can

77

know things that we would not normally know. If this sounds too far out, don't fret, because it is a slow process, and people don't just wake up one day and know all things. Just as the heart opens over time, it also learns how to become aware over time. I have often had the experience that I felt I was on a "need-to-know basis" with the universe. It is only when a situation arises that requires me to know something, that this intuitive "knowing" emerges from the background. There is nothing bizarre or psychic about it. It is simply a faculty of the heart.

Some may be wondering where the mind is in all of this discussion of the heart. The Sufis have long contended that the mind is the surface of the heart. I find no reason to disagree with them. The mind seems able to know only that to which the heart is open. When the heart is open only to material and surface appearances, then that is what the mind knows. When the heart opens to new worlds, the mind gets busy trying to know all it can about those worlds.

Most of us have had the experience of not being interested in something and basically ignoring it until, through some experience or inner drive, we become awakened to the subject. Then we devour all we can on the subject and wonder why we didn't have this interest before. It is like the opening of a rose; as each petal unfolds, the rose becomes more beautiful and fragrant. As the heart opens to new possibilities and eventually to hidden realms, we humans become more beautiful and wise. The awakened heart is never bored; it is always waking up to something new and exciting. When you spend some time with people with open hearts, you will discover that they are always excited by what is around the next corner, physically, intellectually, emotionally, and spiritually.

My Grandmother Ida was my first spiritual teacher, and even after meeting many spiritually realized beings, I've found that she still ranks up there as one of the most saintly human beings I have ever encountered. About two years before Grandma died (at the age of ninety-one), I asked her to dictate her life story into a tape recorder that my cousin had bought her. She thought that was a great idea, since she had had quite an interesting life. She had been the first woman barber in the state of Wisconsin, an early exponent of women's rights (especially contraceptive rights), and a healer of some renown in the Midwest.

Grandma would never take money for her services as a healer, even though phone calls and visits from people in need often kept her busy. She had met just about every guru or spiritual teacher that came to Milwaukee or Chicago between 1920 and 1950. Her main spiritual practice in her seventies and eighties was serving as the greeter in a Lutheran church and cutting hair for aged residents in a Lutheran nursing home. These were her means for bestowing her wellspring of blessings upon the people who came her way.

I listened to Grandma's tapes a few times. They usually started out with a story from her youth. One of my favorite stories is about Grandma's helping a psychotic neighbor by following what her spirit guides told her to do. (Grandma's spirit guides were with her throughout her life.) Upon learning about my grandmother's actions, her father, a Lutheran minister, told her that she was evil. My grandmother, who was only nine years old at the time, stopped her hellfire-and-brimstone father in his tracks by asking, "Can evil do good?" He did not interfere with her work after that. After recording such stories, Grandma would apparently enter into an ecstatic state, and all I would hear on the tape was her exclamation, "It's just so beautiful, it's so wonderful." That was indeed how her life was, beautiful and wonderful, not because she did not have problems like the rest of us, but because her open heart was focused upon the sublime. That is the nature of life for the saintly among us; they are often just too happy, giving, and loving to be miserable.

Psychological Opening

Optimally, all of us would work on our hearts on the psychological level before beginning our spiritual journeys. The opening of the heart is related to psychological development as well as to spiritual growth. Work on the psychological level represents an intermediary stage of the development of heart qualities and the emotional life that is available to everyone, although this work is not easy. The heart begins to open when we begin to take responsibility for all of our feelings and thoughts. A very big part of this process is what the Jungians have stressed, dealing with the "shadow." From a Jungian perspective the shadow contains the unacknowledged, and often unwanted, aspects of our psyche. They are often seen as our negative or dark side, but can in truth be any quality or tendency of which we are not conscious. Another equally important area of heart work is freeing oneself up from chronic emotional restrictions.

Many of us bring from our childhoods injunctions regarding what it is acceptable to feel and what it is not acceptable to feel. There are certainly gender restrictions that are based upon societal norms regarding men and women, but there are also family taboos and restricted modeling of feeling. For whatever reason, most of us begin our adult lives with a less-than-full access to a range of emotions. We often find one set of emotions, such as anger and rage, acceptable, but find ourselves unable to feel or even conceive of feeling opposite emotions, like vulnerability, openness, or love. The constellation I have just described is a typically male pattern, but I have met women with the same pattern. We could describe many such patterns, such as another in which a person is able to feel weak, fearful, or dependent emotions but finds it difficult to feel competent and powerful, but I think the point is well understood in our society.

What the issue boils down to is that human beings generally have access to a much smaller portion of their emotional and psychological inheritance than is useful. This kind of restricted emotional existence is neither good for individuals nor society. What is needed here is also opening the heart, but at what might be termed the psychological level rather than the spiritual. It is, however, equally important, and while it is not necessarily a prerequisite to spiritual opening, it hopefully precedes or accompanies the spiritual opening.

If one develops power or other spiritual abilities without this psychological wholeness, there can be dire consequences. The annals of the guru hunts of the 1960s and 1970s are full of stories of somewhat spiritually mature but psychologically immature spiritual teachers. I have personally known some very beautiful and wise spiritual teachers, but there were some who could not live up to their billing. It is important for all of us to recognize that a certain amount of spiritual maturity may coexist with psychological immaturity. This incongruity may confuse or even deceive some seekers who lack a sophisticated understanding of human psychological functioning.

As we have noted, the heart is awakened, or opened, both psychologically and spiritually. Psychological awakening involves healing of early wounding and freeing up a full range of emotional responsiveness. Spiritual awakening involves freeing the heart to reach out beyond its boundaries to experience and encompass more of the world around it, both manifest and unmanifest. This is a process, and it unfolds over time. Sometimes the psychological and the spiritual unfolding go hand in hand, and sometimes one develops before the other. It is usually not a problem when the psychological precedes the spiritual, but when this process is reversed, there are a myriad of problems that can arise.

There are many examples in the late twentieth century of individuals who developed a degree of spiritual power and magnetism, but because they were either unbalanced or immature psychologically, they caused suffering to those around them. One need only think of leaders of cult leaders such as Jimmy Jones or David Koresch to see examples of spiritual magnetism run amok, unchecked by a wounded psyche. Other spiritual leaders have developed great knowledge and power, but lacked the psychological maturity and self-discipline to keep the heart open and personal desires checked amid the temptations of the West. Bhagwan Rajneesh was the poster child for this sort of unbalanced development.

Overview of the Heart-Opening Process

Let's now retrace the process of opening the heart. First, all of us begin our spiritual process with wounds to our heart. It seems that life in this world is always going to have some wounding effect on the human heart, so we can just assume those wounds are there. What is required to awaken the heart, even with the wounds, is a safe psychological environment. This safe environment is often provided by an individual or group of individuals who are capable of *seeing* the beauty of our souls in spite of our woundedness. If this safe environment remains stable and

81

trustworthy, we can engage in spiritual practices that soften and help to heal our wounds. We can also consciously work on expanding the scope of our hearts. Expansion of our feeling nature leads us to a deeper empathy with the world around us, both seen and unseen. From this "at-one-ment" gradually emerges the spiritual realization we have been seeking.

Hazrat Inayat Khan often used the word "sympathy" to describe the quality needed to take certain important steps toward realization. I once had difficulty understanding that word, because I saw it in light of its more modern usage. Now I understand that what Inayat Khan called "sympathy" we now describe as "empathy." It is empathy with all of life and all of nature that is what the wise ones have from the earliest times called spiritual realization.

The more we progress spiritually, the more we become aware of the condition of everyone and everything around us. It is more difficult than ever before to ignore the joy and suffering of our fellow humans. We are also far more aware of the natural world around us and the myriad of seen and unseen beings that populate our surroundings. Tears of joy and of sorrow can flow, sometimes at very inopportune times, much more readily than ever. These tears are mostly responses to the fullness of life that surrounds us. The vibrant, teeming life around us is a constant reminder of the oneness of all life. It is through the empathy of the open heart joining with all of life that the oneness is experienced.

SIX

Mastery

THE INDIAN SUFI, Hazrat Inayat Khan, has said, "The purpose of life is to attain to mastery" (1982,4:119). Sadly, we have heard far too little about this essential human quality in the spiritual explosion that has gone on since the 1970s. The '60s and '70s were a time of questioning authority, doing your own thing, and trying to break old worn out structures. It was not a time for self-discipline or renunciation. We had forgotten the wisdom behind the practices associated with mastery, and that led to a questioning of its purpose. Those qualities that make up the complex called mastery had become identified with "shoulds," "oughts," and "musts," not conscious choice and growth. We have a great need today to reclaim the wisdom of mastery.

The word "mastery" is used to describe a complex of qualities that revolve around the practice of self-discipline. It is greater than self-discipline, because it also relates to being as fully aware of one's own motivations, blind spots, psychological issues, and biases as possible. Mastery is also the ability to accomplish one's desires in life. It is not repression of feelings and impulses, but rather the ability to feel fully and yet be in control of one's behaviors. Awareness of and control over the expression of all of one's actions, impulses, thoughts, feelings, and eventually even one's atmosphere, are the signs of mastery.

83

One of the metaphors used in the Bible to communicate that Jesus had attained the fullness of mastery is his walking upon the waters of the Sea of Galilee. It is a very apt metaphor, because water in the form of lakes, seas, and oceans often represents the unconscious human processes. Animal instincts, including self-preservation, dominance, and unsocialized sexuality, along with repressed anger, rage, sorrow, hatred, greed, and many other emotions, are a part of the unconscious processes. We can add to these the collective mind world of the human species.

Normally people may be seen as swimming in the sea of our collective mind world, able to keep their heads above the waters and get around, but still very much subject to its conditions. People in psychotic states, such as schizophrenia or those experiencing delirium due to illness, seem to be drowning in these waters, unable to have control over the processes. Mystics, psychics, shamans, and seers submerge in these waters but are able to emerge again with visions of the inner world. But the one who has attained mastery is in control of the waters of the unconscious and walks upon them as if they were dry land. This person is "master of both worlds," fully aware of the content of the unconscious shadow, but able to choose the direction, content, and feeling of his or her actions.

Mastery is a continual process of becoming, rather than something that is easily attained and incorporated. It is something that the wise have always struggled to attain, but very few have claimed to possess. The progressive development of mastery is of the utmost importance on the spiritual path, because as we pursue insight, power and awareness, we often fail to understand how truly shattering these experiences can be. Without sufficient mastery the seeker can be destroyed by the impact of that which he or she has been seeking.

Mastery is a power over oneself that is created by three things: an awakened heart, self-discipline, and self-confidence (Inayat Khan, unpublished Sangithas). Largeness of heart in the form of compassion, sympathy, empathy, and love is at the core of mastery. It is not mastery to withhold action, speech, or feeling out of narrowness of heart; that may instead point to a pathology like paranoia or obsessive-compulsive personality. Mastery starts with a large and loving heart that sees all and forgives all. To that magnanimous heart the masterful person adds self-discipline and self-confidence.

There was a point in my life when I was feeling narrow of heart and miserly and knew that it was essential that I open my heart to accommodate a new situation and new people, but I was having difficulty figuring out how to do it. My wife Jan and I were beginning a new marriage and putting together a blended family. Our children were better at handling the situation than we could have possibly hoped, and my wife was the great love of my life, yet I found myself feeling petty and irritable.

One evening while meditating I saw, in my mind's eye, a giant, ruddy-faced, smiling man in a Boy Scout uniform. Up to this point, this is the way my spiritual life had often seemed. While others reported seeing archangels or the opening of the heavens, I only saw a big blond guy wearing shorts and merit badges! (Sometimes the heavens had opened up, but that had been the exception.) While grizzly bears or wolves had delivered messages to some, I got this message from a giant Boy Scout—and I had always had some doubts about the Boy Scouts. Such is the nature of concepts!

This giant Boy Scout was so joyous, open and magnanimous that the answer to my dilemma became obvious: the heart is opened through joy, empathy, and love, not through "should" and "ought." The answer was, "Be it and you will become it!" To this day my wife and I often discuss the "big Boy Scout" whenever we feel the need to broaden or deepen our hearts. I have grown to appreciate the quirky nature of my unconscious processes and today might be much more likely to doubt the validity of my meditations if they came in a too patently "spiritual" form.

We can break mastery down into mastery of body, mastery of mind, mastery of emotion, and mastery of self. If the purpose of life is to become more conscious, then living an unconscious life, moved about willy-nilly by outside or inside forces over which one feels no control, is the opposite of a life well lived. Mastery requires human beings to exert more control over their own lives. People have often tried to control their lives by ignoring the chaos within and trying to control the outside world. This externalization has simply led to oppression, violence, and destruction in families and communities, without addressing the true problem.

Examples of cultures, religions, and nations demonizing others rather than dealing with their own problems or attempting to control or destroy others rather than developing an orderly and compassionate center comprise the bulk of our historical experience. When we seek to control others rather than ourselves, we may create smaller examples of oppression or violence, but it is equally objectionable. Domestic violence, discrimination, and hate crimes are just a few examples of mistaking the task at hand and trying to control some aspect of the environment rather that dealing with the inner issues.

If, on the other hand, people choose to deal with the chaos within and learn about themselves and how to control or channel their feelings, thoughts, and impulses, they not only become masters of themselves but also learn to master their environments. Many wise teachers of the past have exhorted us to avoid picking the mote from our neighbor's eye until we have removed the log from our own.

Mastery of the Body

We can see in religious traditions around the world practices to promote physical mastery. From giving up certain things for Lent and fasting during the daylight hours during Ramadan to the physical austerities of Hindu yogis and rishis, one thing is clear. Spiritual traditions recognize the necessity to awaken and affirm the actor within the actions. The consciousness that adheres to and animates the body needs to choose its actions and experiences, rather than falling into habitual and addictive patterns. From a spiritual perspective, we could say that all patterns not freely chosen by the conscious will can become addictions. Eating, sleeping, watching television, craving chocolate, having sex (not making love, which involves the will of the heart, and may be the closest that most human beings get to spiritual realization), and a myriad of other behaviors in which the body engages without thinking or choosing can be seen as addictions.

Of course it is necessary for all of us to eat, sleep, and have some sort of sexual outlet, but beyond the basics required to stay alive and remain healthy, eating, sleeping and sex, along with myriads of other behaviors, can become habitual and detract from rather than enhance life. Learning to take charge of these habits is what is behind many religious practices involving renunciation. When a Christian abstains from eating meat one day a week during Lent, she is beginning to take control of the body and its needs, rather than being controlled by it. When a yogi succeeds in controlling his heartbeat through breathing practices, he is asserting his will over bodily functions. In both instances the person is asserting the will in the service of the highest ideal, which guards against inflation of the ego. This is what mastery of the body is all about. It requires waking up the will, so that it, rather than unconscious habit, is in charge of the self.

For the most part, Western traditions have lost sight of the reasons behind austerities, and they are either seen as superfluous to religion or as being done to please God. They are neither; they are a form of exercise for the soul, and they are actually very important to anyone wishing to develop mastery and grow their heart. Making a conscious choice by saying, "I, not my habits or desires, am in charge of my body," is the first step toward mastery. This discipline is entered into in service of the ideal, which protects the aspirant from the insufferability and hubris that can accompany asceticism in service of the ego. A certain degree of mastery of the body is required before one can attain mastery in other areas.

How does one develop physical mastery? Mastery develops like a muscle; the more you use it, the stronger it gets. It is important not to overwhelm ourselves early in the process, so one needs to begin with small things. You could say to yourself, "This week I'm not going to drink coffee," or, "This week I'm not going to eat chocolate." The trick is to set goals that are realistic, and then not to get lazy. Once you have had success at giving things up for a short time, you can begin to make larger commitments or lifestyle changes. You might decide to get up a half-hour earlier each day and meditate or to do yoga over the noon hour each day. The task is to continue to take more and more control of your life and always be chipping away at your habitual patterns.

Several years back I belonged to group that met about once a month, and one of our practices was to give something up each time for the coming month. I thought I should give up watching television, since it was something I really didn't want to give up. I committed to giving up TV for the month, and a few days later the Gulf War broke out. While people all around me were watching smart bombs slip down chimneys, I got my news from the newspaper and felt quite left out of the action. It was one of my most powerful experiences. I built a great deal of will power with that exercise, enough that people around me began to comment on how I was changing. Had I simply been out of the country and missed the war, it would not have had the same effect. It is the conscious use of will to inhibit habit that transforms sleepwalking humans into wide-awake powerful beings.

Mastery of the Mind

When exploring the topic of the mastery of the mind, we will speak of two things. The first is the mastering of impulses or urges, and the second is the mastering of thoughts. It is very clear that power is lost whenever a person gives in to impulse; power is gained whenever impulses are controlled. What kind of power are we talking about? We are talking about will power, one of the building blocks of mastery, and we are also talking about the ability to accomplish the things one wishes to achieve in life. Through this process we learn that mastery of self is also mastery of life.

Impulses are often automatic reactions to environmental stimuli, whether positive or negative, and the tendency is to act blindly upon impulse in response to the environment. The mastery of impulses not only builds strength of character in the form of will power, but it also puts the individual, not the environment, in charge of her actions. We are placing our consciousness at the forefront in our lives, making it the prime principle acting in the theater of life. Consciousness should not be confused with our egos, or the everyday sense of self, but rather should be seen to be the basis of the Self, which we will discuss later in this chapter.

The method of mastering impulses is the most simple and straight forward; it may also produce some of the most powerful early results. We simply become aware of the impulse and then inhibit it. If we have the impulse to engage in a reflexive action in response to some stimuli and we inhibit it, we build character, power, and mastery. When we are driving on the freeway and someone passes us and then slows down and we have the impulse to utter a profanity at them but consciously choose not to, we have practiced mastery of impulse. This sort of thing has nothing to do with morality and everything to do with building character and power.

Mastery over our thoughts brings us into a realm of control that is much more difficult than control of body and impulse. We need to have done some practicing and building of will power and concentration before we will have much success with controlling our thoughts. Meditation and spiritual practices that serve to focus the mind on certain set thoughts or images are the primary ways to build this ability. The primary purpose behind meditation is to develop concentration and the ability to hold certain images and thoughts in the mind. Likewise, meditation can teach us how to avoid holding thoughts or images in our minds.

Anyone who has attempted meditation has found that at first the mind is quite unruly. When one sits down to meditate, the tendency is for both the body and mind to get fidgety. The body rebels at being made to be still, and the mind rebels at our attempt to control it. With practice the meditator slowly brings the body, and even more slowly, the mind, into harmony with the intent to meditate. This is not something that can be rushed and may take a lifetime to perfect, but the resultant peace and will power are extremely satisfying, even early in the process.

Once we have some practice with controlling the mind through meditation, we can move to the more advanced practice of mastery, where we watch and control our thoughts throughout the day. Most of us experience having thoughts that we are glad no one else is aware we have. Our minds are often full of nonsense, at best, and sometimes, anger, meanness, self-depreciation, doubt, and myriads of other not very useful thoughts. These thoughts not only interfere with our daily activities and diminish our self worth and confidence, but they also affect our general atmosphere, thereby affecting those around us. One of the reasons it is so liberating to be around a person who has mastery over the mind is that the person's atmosphere is clear and peaceful. The atmosphere is clear and peaceful because the mind is clear and peaceful. The mind is clear and peaceful, not by magic, but through the mastering of thoughts.

The mastering of thought is a two-fold process. The first step is to develop the tendency to watch our own thoughts from a somewhat detached perspective. Notice which thoughts are in harmony with your self-image and ideals and which thoughts are not. Notice which thoughts come unbidden or unwanted and which have an obsessive quality to them. Getting a clear picture of our mental clutter, sometimes called roof brain chatter, is a sobering experience. Paying attention to what clutters our daily semi-conscious mental activity sets the stage for introducing the element of choice into this chaos.

The second step is that of choosing not to think certain thoughts that enter our minds. How do we accomplish this heroic feat? Not by confronting the thought directly—that just strengthens it. Instead, we insert another thought to replace it. The use of ongoing mantra (called *wasifa* by the Sufis) is one method that has been used in spiritual traditions for millennia. In the use of mantra, the thought is replaced by the mental repetition of a word or phrase, eventually crowding the thought out of the mind. Since the mantra is a positive or helpful phrase, one is replacing an unhelpful thought with a helpful one. The mantra need not be from another tradition or in another language in order to do its magic, but it helps if it has a numinous quality to it. I have always found the phrase "Toward the One" to be helpful, because it is connected to the Western Sufi tradition from which I received my training, and because it is also my heart's desire. Recently some spiritual groups have developed whole lists of phrases, affirmations that may be used for this purpose, if one does not have a tradition from which to garner a mantra of some sort.

Another way to eliminate unwanted thoughts is simply to watch them until they change into something else. This takes both discipline and quiet time, both of which are rare commodities in today's world. If a person adopts a meditation technique such as Zen Buddhist zazen and is disciplined enough to sit regularly, this simple technique of watching the mind may be superior to all others. It is useful because it does not involve the superimposing of a concept over other thoughts in the mind; therefore it promotes mental clarity. It is important to understand that trying to change one's thoughts by just getting upset with them is the least useful way to attempt to master the mind.

The process of mastering the mind is one of the most gratifying things to which a human being can devote effort. The very real benefits involve feelings of peace, clarity of thought, power to accomplish tasks, and a magnetic atmosphere. It is a lifelong process, but even small strides produce gratifying results. A certain amount of accomplishment in mastering of the mind is also a prerequisite for spiritual realization. In addition, without mental mastery, any psychic abilities that develop may become more of a curse than a blessing, because psychically sensitive persons may feel unable to control their psychic impressions and feel at the mercy of the inner environment.

Mastery of Emotions

Development of mastery in the realm of emotions can be a very difficult process. Somehow, emotions seem more identified with the inner self than thoughts are. Emotions are also often less understood. It is common in our culture for some people to dismiss emotions as irrelevant to getting things done. Other people feel overwhelmed or over-identified with their emotions. Because our culture values consciousness at the expense of unconscious processes, we have a history of being suspicious of emotions, which seem to emerge from the subconscious depths and interfere with our conscious plans and ideas. Emotions have been relegated to identification with the feminine, watery, dimly understood depths of human experience, and, like most things feminine, have been ignored or condemned. The triumph of masculine, feeling-rejecting scientific paradigms seems almost complete, now that we can control our emotions through the use of psychotropic medication.

Jungian analysts talk of the moodiness that overtakes men who have little access to their emotions. Women in general complain about unfeeling men. Men, who have been forced to stuff their feelings in order to fit in, wonder why they feel empty inside. Personality disorders, which are lifelong patterns of pathological behavior and inner experience, are overtaking anxiety disorders as the most prevalent form of psychological problem. (The important thing to understand about personality disorders is that they usually involve patterns of behavior designed to compensate for a loss of the capacity to feel.)

These trends are related to our cultural rejection of the world of emotions. Much of the malaise of modern times in Western societies can be traced to a cultural phobia regarding the role of legitimate emotions in understanding the human condition. We have a history of trying to diminish or negate the emotional nature of humankind through scientific and religious neglect or condemnation. Yet because of our loss of access to our emotional depths, Madison Avenue can use a type of overemotionality to sell everything from automobiles to soap.

How do we propose to master emotions when we wish to deny them or find ourselves overwhelmed by them? We who live in the Western world have few cultural resources to help us understand them. We may not be able to easily learn from Eastern religions and mystical traditions because of the very real differences in how the world is experienced. A life of seclusion or renunciation that is often prescribed in the East in order to deal with emotional and physical overcoming is much less practical in the West. As I once heard Pir Vilayat Khan say, "There is not much room in the Western world for dervishes."

In traditions where the seeker renounces the world, it is necessary to stay away from stimuli that would draw one back. We need only look at the private lives of many an Indian guru who came to the West in the '60s or '70s to see that their mastery over physical and emotional entanglements did not last very long. The reality is that they, too, had been misled by the patriarchal phobia regarding sexuality and emotionality. It is likely that living a normal life with spouse and family is, while difficult, far preferable to the life of a renunciate for the majority of spiritually oriented people in the West. It is also likely that one can reach the same level of realization, although it may manifest differently when living a life in relationship to family and community.

Living our lives in the context of relationships with our spouses, children, parents, friends, employers and employees, and community is the greatest of spiritual tasks. Maybe early religious leaders and reformers did not believe human beings were ready to take on such a formidable task, but times are changing, and if true spirituality will be found anywhere the twenty-first century, it will be found in the hearts of those people embedded in meaningful human relationships. The time has come to overthrow our fear of the emotional context of life and seek meaning there.

Before emotions can be mastered, they must first be felt. They must then be understood and placed in the living context of our lives. I think that the saying "You don't know what you don't know until you know it" is important for this discussion. We only know our feelings to the level that we can feel them. Many of us have slowly and methodically cut ourselves off from the power and depth of our feelings over our lifetimes. We believe that we feel, but there is a potential qualitative difference that we can't be aware of unless we deepen our feelings.

Nearly twenty years ago, in the midst of forming the most important relationship of my life, I experienced what can only be described as a primal scream. I was behind the wheel of my car at the time, and as this blood-curdling noise began to rumble forth from my depths, I grabbed the steering wheel and pulled over to the side of the road. The scream broke the painful mood of the moment, and Jan and I just looked at each other. Neither of us had heard such a sound before. Painful as it was, the result was something that has continued to evolve to this day.

That scream opened up the depths of my feeling. From that moment, my feelings became qualitatively different, stronger, more clearly defined, and more alive. For me the world of feelings (and I had always been considered a feeling person) began to grow and intensify on that day, and the development continues today. The primal scream was obviously only one overt experience amidst thousands, as Jan and I consciously embarked upon our road as spiritual partners.

93

The first step, then, in mastering the emotional world is awareness and acceptance of emotions, both pleasant and difficult, as an integral part of our daily lives. The next step is to learn to control our reactions to our emotions without repressing the emotions themselves. For this the spiritual practice of detachment is crucial. By detachment, I am not referring to a cold, unfeeling condition or a spacey, otherworldly condition. It is more like having a sense of humor about oneself and about life. We need to develop the ability to look dispassionately at ourselves and at what we are experiencing, and while we still feel the pain or joy of the moment, we understand that "this, too, shall pass." Knowing and understanding our emotional nature, we make a choice whether or not we wish to become identified with the roller-coaster ride between elation and depression and back again. This sort of detachment makes us large enough to contain the opposites within, as we view (sometimes with a chuckle) our unique life experience.

Mastery of emotions is not an easy task. Total mastery may be unattainable for most of us. We can, however, make some strides toward the goal. These strides, small though they may be, will have significant impact on the quality of our lives. Developing a loving, kind, compassionate sense of detachment in the midst of the turmoil and uncertainty of everyday life in families and the workplace usually leads to a kind of magnanimity, rather than the aloofness that most people fear. It is this magnanimity that is seen in those spiritual giants that we occasionally encounter when seeking after spiritual role models.

I once did a thirty-day spiritual retreat in a coconut grove overlooking the Indian Ocean in Bali, Indonesia. Jan and I made the retreat together. We ate vegetarian food and maintained silence (except for brief interactions with each other and our retreat guide) for a full thirty days. We also spent many hours doing spiritual practices. We were under the direction of a trusted spiritual guide with whom we would check in once a day. We began to notice that as the retreat progressed we were given (and seemed to need) far fewer spiritual practices.

Our daily life began to be more centered and masterful. The quality of time changed. The natural world became more alive and gave us the teachings we needed. Conscious, fully lived moments became our primary experience. We were a little confused at the time, because everything seemed so normal and unspiritual. This realness was sometimes so simple that we hardly noticed it. We wondered (as do many seekers when experiencing states that confront our spiritual concepts) whether this experience was real or whether we had somehow lost our spiritual focus. After several days we asked our retreat guide about what we were experiencing. He simply replied that we were doing an "advanced retreat." It took quite a few years to process what that meant. I know now that there were many lessons in that retreat, and that a central lesson involved mastering our typical emotional responses in order to create a sacred space.

Mastery of Self

The self-aware wholeness that is at the center of our actions, impulses, thoughts and feelings may be called the Self. This deepest and most complete aspect of who we are has also been called "the Soul." We will refer to the higher Self as Soul from this point in our discussion. Most people, being primarily identified with their actions, thoughts, or feelings, are unaware of the individual Soul. The Soul is incarnated into conscious life when we become aware of it; until that point we may be more accurate to view humans in the mechanistic scientific paradigm. However, once the Soul is made the center of our conscious world, we will never be able to view existence from a mechanistic perspective again. It is this birth of the Soul that is alluded to by those that talk about the "second birth" or being "born again." It is unfortunate that so few people who use the phrase understand the truth behind the words.

As with all forms of mastery, the first step toward mastery of self is awareness of Soul. Once this step is taken, it becomes obvious that it is the Soul that becomes the master. From my perspective, mastery of self is identification with the Soul. When my thoughts, feelings, and actions come from my Soul, and when my impulses are the impulses of my Soul, it is then that I have attained mastery of the self. At this point the sayings of the early Sufis such as "I am the Divine Glance" or *Ana'l Haqq* (I am the Truth) are understandable. The individual has shifted his identification from the ego to the Soul. The seeker is also the Sought. The lover is also the Beloved.

Along with an awakened, compassionate heart, mastery is the clearest sign of a spiritually realized person. The Sufis use the term *wali* to indicate the quality of mastery, and as with all Arabic words, there are many levels of meaning. I have always resonated with the level of meaning where *wali* means "friend of God." When one has attained a certain degree of mastery, it is the will of the "Divine Friend" that is acted upon in the world, not the will of the individual. We should be careful not to see mastery as something that one "gets" before moving on to bigger and better things. Mastery is the beginning of spiritual progress and the end, the alpha and the omega.

While traveling in the Kathmandu Valley in Nepal, we visited Kopan Monastery, a Buddhist monastery fairly close to Bodnath Stupa. Our son Nathan, who had spent a month at the monastery, told us that the monks there had said that the primary mantra of Gautama Sidhartha, the Buddha, was *"tayata om muni muni mahamuni so ha."* When we realize that the Sanskrit word *muni* also means "mastery," we understand that even a person as spiritually realized as the Buddha felt the need to work continually on the quality of mastery.

SEVEN

Creating Personality

THE PHRASE "THE art of personality" was used by Hazrat Inayat Khan to describe the building of character and the development of an increasingly refined personality. The phrase succinctly defines much of the purpose of spiritual pursuit as well as life in general. If we recognize that the One Life becomes self-aware in the physical world through the vehicle of the human being, it becomes understandable that the quality of that consciousness and vehicle matters. Our personalities are the total of our accumulated character, interests, abilities, and qualities, as they manifest in our lives.

The care we take to insure that our personalities are a purposefully created work of art, as opposed to an unconscious mass of impulses, determines our success or failure in the fulfilling the purpose of our lives. The artful creation of personality is not just the individual ego's desire to look good. How we create our personality affects the quality of life on all planes of existence and may be considered the "great work" of our lives.

We have previously discussed opening of the heart and mastery, two important aspects of personality development. These two core qualities are prerequisites for further personality development; they also represent the culmination of continued work with personality. Heart qualities and mastery are woven into the fabric of personality and are related to all other aspects of spiritual growth.

When impasses in personality development are reached, it is often because more mastery or heart is needed. When impasses are reached in the development of mastery or heart, some other quality needs to be developed in order to progress. All aspects of personality are works in progress and are dependent upon each other for continued growth. The vast potentialities for human psychic evolution are far too many and varied to be fully covered in this book, so we will limit our discussion to two relatively broad areas: wisdom and altruism.

There are so many divergent opinions about the nature of wisdom. We will begin by observing what lies beyond the scope of wisdom. Wisdom is not knowledge, although wisdom can encompass knowledge. Wisdom is not critical thinking, although critical thinking can be a step toward wisdom. Wisdom is not faith, although wisdom can understand the place of faith in human psychological and spiritual evolution. Wisdom is not, as many have said, the mixture of knowledge, experience, and time. This is one way that wisdom can come, but it is highly dependent upon the kind of knowledge and the quality of one's interpretation of experience. We all grow old, but a significantly smaller number of us become wise. In the next section we will explore three concepts related to the development of wisdom: discernment, perspective, and understanding.

Discernment

Discernment relates to the ability to see and the ability to judge. The individual who possesses discernment is able to discriminate one thing from another. In a physical sense discernment is the ability to discriminate clearly figure from ground. Psychologically speaking, it is the ability to clearly discriminate wise from foolish, useful from nonuseful, or benign from harmful. In the realm of spirituality, discernment allows us to discriminate spiritual freedom from spiritual captivity and truth from falsity.

Discernment serves two monumentally important tasks. It helps us in the "unlearning" process, which is essential to wisdom. In order to discover more accurate and sensible understandings of life and the world around us we must first unlearn what we currently believe to be the truth. Without discernment to unlearn the knowledge that no longer serves us, we can never learn something new. Knowledge builds upon prior knowledge, and if the earlier knowledge will only accommodate a certain type of material, that is all that we can learn. If we want to be able to learn something new, we will have to eliminate knowledge that limits our scope.

For instance, if we "know" that Columbus was the first European to come to the Americas, we will avoid, dismiss, and be blind to all indications of earlier Nordic exploration. We will dismiss the possibility that there was copper mining in 7000 B.C.E. in the Great Lakes by sea peoples from the Mediterranean (Bailey, 1994). If we see Columbus as "the discoverer of the Americas," we will likely ignore the amazing variety of First Nations cultures that existed in this hemisphere long before Columbus's voyage. Discernment helps us decide what needs to be eliminated, what knowledge needs to stay, and what new knowledge is worthy of our efforts.

"No" always seems to come before "yes." As toddlers we learn to say "no" before most other language is developed. Young people, especially in today's difficult youth culture, need to learn to say "no" to many of the temptations facing them in order to avoid pitfalls that could ruin their futures. All adult human beings need to learn to say "no" to others who would use them and hurt them. The Sufis have understood this truth for millennia as they have repeated, "There is no god, but God." The first part of this declaration is a negation, which is followed by an affirmation.

"No" is an important word. "No" is at the heart of discernment. We always need to learn to say "no" when we find ourselves being trapped in too small a box to contain our developing selves. Toddlers say "no" to their parents in order to escape the early symbiotic relationship and become an individual. In their teen years these same individuals must repeat the "no" to assert their emerging adulthood. Adults learn to say "no" as they take responsibility for themselves and others and to avoid exploitative people and situations. "No" sets boundaries and refuses violation. One aspect of discernment may be seen as the equivalent of "no" in the cognitive realm.

Discernment is at the heart of adult postformal thought and critical thinking. Discernment is about analysis and choice. Freedom to inquire and gather information, to analyze that information, to make choices based upon our analysis and then to evaluate the results of our choices is what is required for informed adult learning and cognitive development. The degree to which we take advantage of this freedom to think is what makes all the difference between the seeker after truth and the rest of the population.

The seeker of truth is willing to discern the underlying assumptions in a wide spectrum of knowledge. The seeker will challenge and eventually unlearn those assumptions when they prove too small to contain growing awareness. Discernment is a sword of truth, which cuts through the fog of cultural illusion to reveal new worlds of possibility.

The second monumentally important task of discernment is that of making choices about what to say "yes" to in our lives. Each "no" needs to be followed by a "yes." The toddler says "no" to his or her previous existence as a totally dependent little child and "yes" to the emerging self. The teenager says "no" to continued living in the shadow of parental rule and "yes" to adult responsibility and freedom. The adult says "no" to a stultifying relationship or condition and "yes" to new freedom of opportunity. The mystic says "no" to oppressive, childish, or materialistic gods and "yes" to the One Being and the doors that this decision opens. There must be a "yes" that follows the "no" in order for our lives to keep moving. Making good choices in what we affirm in our lives takes just as much discernment as deciding what we reject.

Critical thinking is as crucial in saying "yes" as it is in saying "no." Freedom to think outside of the boxes in which we are placed by paradigms that are too small is one of the greatest gifts of life. Unfortunately, this freedom comes to far too few people. But discernment is needed when we have freedom, because not all choices are equally good for us, our families, our communities, and our species. The problem with choice is that when we step outside of the cultural boxes there are fewer guidelines, and we can get ourselves in a real mess.

The ability to anticipate the consequences of our actions, to discern the moral implications, and to choose wisely is required of all who have the courage—or audacity—to move beyond the commonplace. Developing even a small measure of wisdom takes us beyond the commonplace, and life often requires the wise to deal with difficult issues whose resolutions may involve thinking far beyond the realm of cultural clichés. The wise must often obey two sets of guidelines, the cultural norms and rules as well as the rules of a liberated conscience. This is the proverbial razor's edge.

Perspective

Perspective is the second quality of wisdom that we will explore. Perspective in this context involves a wideness of view, which includes the ability to see from differing points of view. Perspective can be gained in several ways, but it usually involves a degree of detachment. A typical spiritual perspective is sometimes said to be "getting high." Many practices taught in spiritual schools make the individual feel as if he or she is in a high place, detached from earthly cares and concerns. From this high place it is possible to see a whole picture of life without emotional involvement or the expectation of action. From this perspective we can often see multiple causation, the interconnectedness of life, and a vaster array of options for our own lives.

Another form that perspective takes is empathy, which is the opening of the heart to others sufficiently to experience what life is like for them. This, too, is widening our perspective. We detach from our self-absorption enough to enter into the perspective of another. Empathy is a natural developmental milestone for children. It is supposed to happen sometime when the child is approaching the age of six or seven. This is a time when children begin to formulate conceptions of right and wrong, based upon how events would affect others.

How sad it is that empathy is such an undervalued capacity! Empathy needs to be an ever-deepening and broadening quality throughout life, as it infuses all of our relationships and interactions. Empathy might be seen as the great facilitator of relationships. Unfortunately, some of us never get past our childhood egocentrism. Even more of us avoid any deepening or expanding as we get older, a time that seems perfectly suited for such growth.

Empathy could not only make our world a much better place but also could be a major catalyst for refining our consciousness. Empathy is the secret of spiritual attainment. The wise broaden their experience and perspective by loosening their personal boundaries sufficiently to understand the depths of others; in doing so they approach the depths of the divine, the One Life.

A passage from the works of Hazrat Inayat Khan illumines the quality of empathy. Inayat Khan uses the word sympathy in a way that I believe is synonymous with contemporary use of the word "empathy." The word "empathy" has only come into popular usage since Carl Rogers wrote about it in the 1950s. (When Inayat Khan was talking about sympathy in the first three decades of the twentieth century, he did not have the more descriptive word, *empathy,* available to him.) Just prior to the following passage, Inayat Khan discussed methods of spiritual development achieved by "getting high," and then he said:

> And it is only one power, the power of one's sympathy, that assimilates all poisonous influences . . . The world seeks for complexity . . . But if I tell you simple things like this, that it is the deepening of your sympathy, the awakening of that sympathetic spirit in you which is every power and magnetism, and the expansion of which means spiritual unfoldment, then there will be few to understand. For human beings do not want simple teaching, they want complexity . . .
>
> And then there is another stage of expansion, and that is trying to look at everything from another's point of view also, trying to think also as the other person thinks . . . In this way one extends one's knowledge to a degree that no reading can give. Then one begins to receive from all sources; one will attract knowledge from every plane as soon as the mind becomes so pliable that it does not only stick to its own point of view. This process is called unlearning . . .
>
> If you go further then you unite with everything. In this consciousness distance is no longer distance; if you can extend your consciousness so that your consciousness touches the consciousness of another, then not only the thoughts of that

person but his whole spirit is reflected in your spirit. Space does not matter; your consciousness can touch every part of the world and every person, at whatever distance he may be. And if you go still further, then you can only realize that you are connected with all beings. That there is nothing and no one who is divided or separate from you, and that you are not only connected by chains with those you love, but with all those you have known and do not know—connected by a consciousness which binds you faster than any chains. Naturally one then begins to see the law working in nature; one begins to see that the whole universe is a mechanism working towards a certain purpose. Therefore the right one and the wrong one, the good and the bad, are all bringing about one desired result, by wrong power and by right power, a result meant to be, which is the purpose of life.

Then naturally one holds oneself back from that dogmatic spirit: "you are wrong" and "you are right," and one comes to the spirit of the sage: saying nothing, knowing all, doing all, and suffering all things. This makes one the friend of all and the servant of all. And with all the realizations of mystical truth and spiritual attainment, what one realizes is one thing, the only thing worth while, and that is to be of some little use to one's fellow man" (1982:123–126).

I might suggest that the reader go back and read through this quotation one more time. We could search a lifetime and not come up with a better brief description of spiritual realization than this. Who among us would have guessed that it is through empathy, the opening of our hearts to our fellow human beings, that our much-sought-after realization can come. This is truly personality in exalted form.

We can see from the above examples that the development of perspective requires the capacity for detachment from the personal vantage point. Whether one chooses to use height or vastness or the intimacy of empathy as one's concentration, one must overcome the personal perspective. This does not mean that we don't have a personal perspective, only that we are not entirely confined by it. We can, when circumstances call for it, detach from the total identification with ourselves and experience life from a different perspective. It is this different perspective that provides us with the opportunity to see what cannot be seen from our more restricted vantage point. This vast perspective may, if carried to its furthest extent, result in realization of the profoundest sort.

Understanding

The third aspect of wisdom that we will discuss is understanding. Understanding involves more than just knowing information; it involves the full processing of that information and comprehending all the implications and depths of the information. Robert Heinlein, in his science-fiction classic, *Stranger in a Strange Land,* coined the word "grok" to indicate this sort of knowing. We don't have a word in English that quite carries the implications that I wish to express with the word "understanding." To use more metaphorical language we could say that understanding is knowing with mind, heart, and spirit.

Understanding is a quality of knowing in which the mind has a full grasp of all the intricacies and subtleties of the subject of knowing; the heart feels the depths and rightness of the subject of knowing, and the spirit is exalted in the consciousness of knowing. To say "I understand" is to feel at one with that which is known. Understanding is the unity of knowing, and it is the purview of the wise. The wise are not surprised by unintended consequences of actions, for they expect them. The wise know that nothing is entirely right or wrong, good or bad, smart or stupid. Everything is a unity. We demonstrate understanding when we recognize that everything is interconnected. Understanding transcends dualism.

We can see that wisdom is a multifaceted quality and that it does not just happen; it needs to be developed. The development of discernment, perspective, and understanding is an activity engaged in when we are purposefully working with the expansion and refinement of our consciousness. To be effective, working with consciousness must be done not only in meditation and retreat, but also in everyday life; this is what we refer to as the creation of personality. As we grow, we become increasingly cognizant of the implications of all of our behaviors and interactions, and we work to create a personality that is a thing of beauty.

The artful creation of personality becomes even more obvious when we look at the realm of human behavior generally referred to as altruism. As with the preceding discussion of wisdom, we will break altruism into three components. We will explore a trilogy composed of kindness, compassion and magnanimity. Let's begin with kindness.

Kindness

In 1982, I attended the first Kalachakra initiation led by the Dalai Lama outside of Tibet or India, in Madison, Wisconsin. Since that time the Dalai Lama has conducted several more of these initiations around the world. The Kalachakra initiation is the initiation of the bodhisattva in the Tibetan Buddhist tradition. It is a four-day ceremony involving about a dozen monks as well as the Dalai Lama. There were several hundred of us Westerners in attendance; it was a high and beautiful ceremony. In the midst of all the beauty and pageantry the Dalai Lama emphasized being kind to one another as the most important spiritual act we could undertake.

That is certainly great wisdom. It also points to the hidden truth that at the heart of all religious traditions is the same ancient wisdom, the wisdom of the heart. What an incredible world it would be if we could all follow that advice. Kindness seems such a little word, not very sophisticated at all, and yet acts of kindness are the truly sacred events in our world. The kind heart is the awakened heart.

Kindness naturally flows from the heart of one who considers others as well as self. We often see kindness in families, especially from parents toward their children, because there is still some cultural mandate for parents to put aside their own interests for the sake of their children. But kindness seems to be dying out in this culture of individualism. We are taught by everything around us, including some of the experts of human personality, psychologists, psychiatrists, and to a lesser degree, social workers and sociologists, that we must put ourselves and our needs before others. Our individual success and happiness is paramount, and although we can help others, we should help ourselves first.

It takes a strong and confident individual to recognize that while an egocentric perspective may be appropriate for early adolescence, adult maturity involves interconnectedness and reciprocity. We live in a culture that stresses adolescent virtues of independence and self-involvement as its highest value and sees adulthood as old-fashioned. We don't wish to return to an old-fashioned, oppressive, patriarchal morality, but the self-absorbed and narcissistic focus on self that seems to be today's morality is equally destructive.

It would be false to say that kindness is extinct in our culture because there are many kind people and acts of individual kindness continue to be found in daily interactions. Especially in times of crisis we will see the best of human qualities rise to the surface, such as happened after the terrorist attacks in New York City and Washington, D.C., on September 11, 2001. Where I live in the heartland of the United States people are especially kind to their neighbors, though they may be distrustful of strangers. My concern is that we are trending away from kindness. We have fewer expectations of encountering kindness and it is less often held up as the ideal.

One who consciously engages in acts of kindness as a spiritual practice is building a beautiful temple of personality. When we take the time to pay attention to what another might need or want, that is the first step. How often do we really pay attention to the needs of others? The next step is to take whatever time or energy is needed to accomplish the kind act. This becomes even more difficult in this time of multitasking, when we barely have time to do the essential tasks of life. Are not kind acts even more important in hectic times like these, when none of us ever gets enough of what we need?

Then the most important thing: no expectation of reward or thanks. When we are kind and expect kindness in return, that is a business arrangement, not a kind act. Kindness is done from an open heart with no expectations. We simply act in a kind manner and move on. When kindness is suggested as a spiritual practice, one proviso is often that you cannot let the recipient of the act know that it was you who did it or hang around in expectation of thanks. These need not be grandiose, readily observable, one-time kind acts; in reality, the kind personality is at work in all interactions.

I am not suggesting we all be saint-like and give, give, give, and never get back. There are times when we need to make demands, and there are also times when we need not to give to others for one reason or another. By developing the quality of kindness, we develop our own spiritual depths and create harmony in our environments.

Compassion

The second of the three aspects of altruism is compassion. Compassion means to "suffer with." This means that one must be able to be with someone rather than isolated or alienated. Being with someone requires making room in our world for the experience of another. We need the self-discipline to control the bleeding through of our own opinions, ideas, and perspectives into the experience of the other person. We also need subtlety and fine-tuning in order to perceive the experience of the other, rather than our projections upon them or our ideas about them. It is this refined and sensitive nature, accompanied by sufficient self-discipline to avoid projection or overidentification that are the signs of truly compassionate people.

In the previous chapter I recounted the story of visiting our son Nathan in Nepal, where he was spending a year abroad studying Tibetan language and culture. When he shared with us the mantra reputed to have been the mantra of the Buddha, we recognized immediately that it was a mantra stressing mastery. Contemplating the way that this mantra puts the compassion that is at the heart of the Buddha's teachings together with the practice of mastery was an enlightening experience.

One cannot be compassionate without the self-control necessary to deal with one's own emotions. Self-control is also critical in developing and protecting one's sensitivity in a world that does not value fineness and gentleness. It is obvious that mastery is a necessary prerequisite for compassion, if it is to be an ongoing and sustainable aspect of the personality. Most people can be compassionate on occasion, but far fewer can make compassion a central feature of their personality.

The second aspect of compassion involves "suffering." There are two basic meanings to the word "suffer." The first meaning has to do with endurance or the undergoing of something. The second is related to the experience of pain. Compassion is primarily related to the first meaning, endurance and being with another, since we cannot very well actually feel the pain of another. Since we have felt our own pain, we can imagine what it might feel like for another person, but we cannot feel it with them. Compassion is more directly related to "hanging in there" with another person while he or she undergoes an ordeal. To be there (emotionally and maybe physically) with others while they suffer, without judging them, with kindness and an attention to their needs, is the essence of compassion.

Compassion, like kindness, involves action as well as emotion. We may feel sympathy for the victims of famine while we sit in front of our television sets, but compassion does not enter the picture until our hearts are moved toward some sort of compassionate act toward those with whom we have been moved to "suffer." We cannot take on all the problems of the world and be actively compassionate toward all; it is just too big a world with far too much suffering. But those who have built compassion into their personalities *live* this quality on a daily basis.

Compassionate people use their skills, knowledge, and feelings with love and kindness to relieve as much suffering as possible in the lives of those around them. Compassion is like a good virus; it can be spread through contact and may impact far more people with its good will than we could ever imagine. It is true that in order to save the world, each of us must start with ourselves and our own little corner of the planet.

In some early tribal societies people believed that they (the tribe) were the only real people. All others were somehow less than human and therefore could be treated in a less-than-human manner. Some of us still operate in this manner, although now it is usually our nation or religion that we feel is the only good or true thing. This ethnocentric perspective is destroying us. Our stature as humans can be measured by the size of our hearts, and our hearts can be measured by how many people we love.

The love of which I speak takes many forms. It includes those we passionately love and to whom we make love, but it also includes children, parents, and other family members, friends, and acquaintances. From this personal and somewhat spiritually restricted position, our hearts may grow in wider and wider circles to encompass eventually not only all of humanity but all sentient beings.

The trick to this kind of growth is to avoid concepts that constrict the heart. Our concepts are often our most prized possessions. We have come by them through the school of hard knocks, and we passionately wish to defend them. They are our interpretation of the way life works and why our life has gone a certain way. They are often cultural beliefs that can be dangerous to challenge. They serve as interpreters of reality, and without them we can feel adrift in a sea of meaninglessness. Our concepts limit our world, but they help us to feel safe.

To broaden our compassion we need to broaden our concepts. Why live by stingy, constricting concepts, when there are vast and limitless perspectives available to us? Why make our hearts puny and mean, when they can expand and in doing so create vast joy for us as well as for others? If we remain captive of our too-small perspectives, we hold others around us in their grip—what an awful thing to do to someone we love. Opening our hearts through compassion for others creates joy and healing in the world around us.

Magnanimity

The ultimate in the development of personality in the realm of altruism is magnanimity. Magnanimous people have a largeness of heart that transforms and empowers those around them. Magnanimity is the divine power represented in the Arthurian legend by the sword Excalibur. This divine power is at the heart of the patriarchal myths of the past several millennia. Webster defines magnanimity as "greatness of

soul, rising above pettiness or meanness and being generous in overlooking injury or insult." These qualities of magnanimity are true signs
of spiritual evolution.

About twenty years ago I became acquainted with Otto, an eighty-
five-year-old man who lived in a nursing home. Otto had been an
architect and had worked on the first New York City subway system.
He could do logarithms in his head (actually he said he must be getting
a bit senile because he was having trouble with this ability of late) and
translated Greek and Sanskrit. He had studied mysticism with Rudolf
Steiner in Europe and had also been involved in Theosophy most of his
life. The person who introduced us knew that we had similar interests
(not the logarithms, I must add) and thought that we could benefit
from each other's company. Otto used a wheelchair and had very few
visitors. After our first visit, he began calling me "mahatma" whenever I
came. It was a good joke, since it was obvious that it was Otto that was
the great soul in disguise as an old man in a nursing home.

I watched with dismay and amazement as the nursing staff treated
Otto as if he were a child; he accepted their motherly doting with a
wink and a chuckle. Even in these circumstances, seemingly designed
to make one small, Otto's heart remained large, and his sense of humor
remained intact. Otto's heart was bigger than his circumstances, and his
mind comprehended the transient nature of youth and life itself. Otto
was magnanimous and was returning life in full measure for the life he
had lived.

There was only love, no resentment over having outlived his family
and friends. There was only generosity toward those who could see his
failing body but not his fullness of spirit. There was only gratitude for
the opportunity to share memories and wisdom with a younger man
who at least partially understood. I have had several experiences with
those who have grown old and wise like Otto, and it is always the
rarest of joys. The magnanimity of truly great souls transforms the lives
of those around them who have the eyes to see.

Magnanimity is a creative and generative force. In people where this
heart force is active, we generally find success of one form or another.
I have known some magnanimous people who work in the corporate

world, and they tend to be dynamic leaders who are often at the center of what is new and exciting. I have known families where the magnanimity of the parents flowed over into successful and dynamic children. I have known spiritually awakened magnanimous people whose presence helped liberate those around them from the weight of their struggles and propelled them toward their own realizations.

This magnanimous spirit is not dependent on any certain type of personality or belief system, but is rather a quality that seems to arise from an exuberantly open and loving heart. When we are in the company of such a heart, we are lifted out of our troubles and into our possibilities. Magnanimous people bring hope and inner freedom wherever they go. This is certainly the culmination of the creation of personality.

Like wisdom and altruism, many human qualities, when cultivated, may blossom into radiant components of our personality structures. We could examine characteristics such as nobility, self-sacrifice, perseverance, generosity, enthusiasm, a sense of justice, beauty, and many others. In their highest stages of development in the human personality, these qualities bring a sense of what is truly the potential of human consciousness. The personality represents a deep pool of potential waiting to be tapped by those who can truly appreciate the nature of an enlightened spirituality. As we mold our unique personalities from this pool of possibilities, we are doing work that benefits the whole; the future of humanity may depend upon it.

EIGHT

Paths, Transmissions, and Teachers

TODAY AS ALWAYS, some of us have become dissatisfied with exoteric religions. The exodus from established religions may be greater today, because of the weakness of our central myths and because of the strength of the scientific and mechanistic perspectives. Some, believing that the failings of religion reflect a lack of spiritual authenticity, reject the world of spirit altogether. Others of us recognize that the mythic stories of a culture are, in religion, packaged for the masses. We seek the inner meanings and teachings of spirituality that have not been given to mass audiences, but instead have been reserved for those with the desire and ability to penetrate the mysteries.

Cultures abound with alternative stories of spiritually heroic souls who have left the beaten track and found spiritual realization through an arduous inner journey. Today we have an entire genre of spiritual self-help books that share these stories and give advice to the aspirant. Some portion of our postmodern culture still recognizes the need to feed the evolution of consciousness. We intuit that consciousness requires a deeper search into life than is generally offered. Yet embarking upon a search for depth in our understanding of life can be very confusing.

Setting out upon the inner journey is confusing for several reasons. First we are confronted with the dilemma of whether we should seek a formal inner path or embark upon a very individual journey. This way of individuality was the way of the Grail Knights of the Western European tradition, as described by Joseph Campbell:

> They thought that it would be a disgrace to go forth as a group. Each entered the forest at a point that he himself had chosen, where it was darkest and there was no path. If there is a path it is someone else's path and you are not on the adventure (1999: vii).

There is certainly truth to the assertion that each of us must follow our own individual path, but one needs to also realize that very few of the Grail Knights attained the Grail. So while the pathless path is an option, we are not usually sufficiently prepared to succeed this way.

Another perspective suggests that there are tried-and-true inner paths that have successfully guided aspirants to realization for thousands of years; we should follow a "true and complete path," or we could end up in severe psychological and spiritual trouble. Hazrat Inayat Khan has likened treading the inner path without a teacher to trying to cross the ocean in a rowboat. It can be done, but it is not recommended. We find here a true dilemma: we leave exoteric organizations to seek realization for individual reasons, and then we must choose between remaining individually directed or submitting to group instruction through a spiritual school.

I do not believe that this needs to be an either/or question. It must instead be viewed as a process that involves both individual spiritual adventure and submission of the individual will to an educational process. As a matter of fact, much of this process has its parallel in the intellectual maturation process. Just as we must leave the security of home and high school, sources of order for our understanding of the world around us, as we spiritually mature we may need to leave the safety of the church, synagogue, mosque, or temple. If we are to continue learning, the next step after leaving home is not usually complete independence, but rather we engage in further education through college, travel, or some sort of mentoring process. The same holds true for spiritual growth. The next step is usually further education.

We must seek those who have traveled the path of expanding consciousness before us in order to learn the ABCs of spiritual growth. The ABCs I am referring to are methods for working with consciousness, however these will most likely be coupled with cultural beliefs and practices. We must remember from the outset that we are entering into a process similar to a college education. Our professors have much to teach us, but we will eventually be leaving them to make our own way in the world and will not spend the rest of our lives in their classroom. Similarly, we may need to seek to develop our own unique "pathless path" eventually, but often our first step is more education.

The next major issue is what sort of path to follow. Should we try to find an inner path that is related to the exoteric religion of our childhood? Are we so disappointed or wounded by the weaknesses of our childhood religion that we want to find truth as far from it as possible? Does an inner path associated with our religion offer us the depth that we need, without having to learn completely new cultural history and symbols? Those of us coming of age in the 1960s and '70s often chose Eastern paths such as Hinduism, Zen Buddhism, Tibetan Buddhism, or Sufism. Today it is more likely that dissatisfied aspirants in the United States will seek depth through exploration some sort of New Age "channeled" material or be drawn toward a fundamentalist group.

New Age groups centered around channeled teachings are spotty in their usefulness, and fundamentalism is a mistake for long-term growth, although it can sometimes be useful for the heart in the short run. In other words, the pickings are getting slim when it comes to finding good spiritual instruction, especially in the United States. There is a stronger esoteric tradition in Europe, where Western mysticism is much more alive. So how do seekers find a group of like-minded souls and a spiritual mentor today? Often this question is answered for us by synchronicity. We must realize that any path we choose will probably carry cultural baggage with it. This is just part of being on a path, and it is not at this entry stage that we can do anything about it.

Finding a Teacher

"When the student is ready, the teacher will appear." This phrase has been around for a long time, and it is still true. The difficulty is that early in the process we may not have the eyes to see when one of the many teachers we usually encounter enters our lives. The teacher might not announce himself or herself as such. "She" might not be the "he" you were expecting. "He" might not be the "she" you were expecting. The teacher might look like a normal person, not the image we have in our mind of the perfect spiritual teacher.

The typical experience of someone seeking an entrance to the inner path is of meeting many incidental teachers or short-term teachers who prepare the way by giving us little pieces of information and get us going in the right direction. Some of these individuals know that they are guiding you and others don't. The trick at this stage of life, or any stage for that matter, is to see everyone and everything as your teacher. Life, and all the people that enter our life, brings daily pieces of information that can be used to further our development if only we will recognize what is happening. Keeping a strong dose of reason operative at all times but accepting guidance from all that life sends us is the sign of one who is ready for the inner journey.

Through the workings of synchronicity we may eventually encounter options to join with like-minded seekers in a spiritual group of some sort. At that point we need to decide about making a commitment to pursue a particular path. We again have a decision to make. We may have met one person who swears by the guidance of a particular psychic and the classes she gives and also have a friend who believes that Tibetan Buddhism is quickest way to enlightenment. At about the time we are checking these two paths we receive a brochure in the mail announcing a workshop by a Zen *roshi*. The picture of the roshi somehow captivates us, and we feel drawn to the workshop. And so it goes.

A certain amount of spiritual window-shopping is not a bad thing. This sort of struggle to find one's "right path" is common, as thousands of us who have wrestled with this dilemma can attest. Generally, over time our hearts will draw us to a path and teacher that are right for us.

For some, with too much doubt, too much thinking, or too much fear, the struggle will be difficult indeed. For others with a bit more trust, clear heads, and an adventuresome spirit, the choice will be made and the path engaged.

I used to think there were only a few paths in the world that could lead the aspirant to enlightenment. I don't believe that anymore, although I am skeptical of much that passes for spiritual training today. Paths are a spiritual heritage and often feel to the beginner as if he or she has finally returned home after a long journey. A true path is usually not easy or simple, but it does feel somehow "right." The path that is right for us at a given time usually involves a "momentum" carried by our soul from before our birth, as well as a sense of having been drawn to it. A teacher or mentor usually stands at the entrance to the path, and we feel a strong attraction to the teacher.

We sometimes make the mistake of hero-worship, because we don't realize that the teacher is the *door* to the path—we mistake the door for the path itself. That is why we project such power over our soul upon him or her. The teacher, like a favorite professor in college, seems to embody the very knowledge we have been searching for. Unlike a college professor, a spiritual teacher may also hold the "keys to the kingdom" in the form of the spiritual transmission of the path. We will find, as we often do in college, that the teacher may not really be as wise or powerful as we think, but instead carries our projection of spirituality. We will discover over time that our own inner resources are even more important to us than our teacher's wisdom—and any authentic teacher will tell us that. We will also feel eternally indebted to the teacher who opened the portals of the path to us for the gift of the transmission that came with the teaching.

Spiritual Transmission

What is spiritual transmission? It is a mystery, an infusion of energy and a deep connection that can be felt and whose effects can be seen in the life of the spiritual seeker. Anyone who has ever taken initiation into a spiritual school will attest to the change that followed, but few can find the words to explain the experience. One example of the power of transmission that occurs with initiation occurred for me after a particularly powerful "past life" experience.

While traveling in the American West one summer with my wife, the environment rang some very old bells for me. I was experiencing deep sorrow, and the words of Jesus, "Why have you forsaken me?" were flooding my mind. I was in a very deep space that I had experienced before. It seemed that whenever I entered this very deep place, either through remembering part of a past life as I was this time, or getting deeply into my consciousness on retreat, I would begin sobbing and feel as if life was far too painful to endure. This was never a suicidal place, just a very deep, often impersonal experience of what some Sufis call the "broken heart of God." This time the pain seemed more powerful than ever before. Jan prompted me to seek my spiritual guide inwardly to ask for help. When I called Pir Vilayat to mind, the image of him giving me *bayat* (initiation) came to mind in such a powerful way that I knew that it was the answer to my wounds.

Since that moment I have never again experienced that degree of suffering when I have gotten to certain deep spiritual places. I was until that time blocked from going beyond the invisible barrier of the psychological pain. Once I had fully incorporated the depth of the transmission given in initiation, I was able to break though the barrier of suffering. A whole new world of spirit and emotion has opened to me since that experience.

What happened to make that difference? I believe it was the mystery of transmission. As the door to a spiritual lineage or heritage, the teacher through initiation can connect the aspirant to a stream of consciousness and energy that is beyond the personal. Sufis see this as a heart connection. The impact is deep and lasting. A true Sufi teacher will never abandon an initiate inwardly, even though there may be times when circumstances may limit the outward contact.

I remember doing some spiritual emergency work about twenty years ago. The person who came to me for help was a very psychic young woman, who was becoming unbalanced partially because of spiritual guidance that was opening her psychic abilities without sufficient work with her heart qualities. After talking with her for an hour I gave her some practices to do to help in the development of heart qualities. She came back a week later and told me of a vision she had had while in a state somewhere between sleep and waking. She had experienced a line of "little men in turbans" pouring a golden liquid into her heart. She watched this process, for what seemed to be hours. She awoke from this "dream" feeling stronger and more solid than she had felt in a long time. I find it interesting that I hadn't told her that I was a Sufi. I don't claim to know how this works, but there is a strong link with one's spiritual heritage that does much of the work in transforming consciousness.

Transmission may be the hidden reality behind what Christians call grace. I am quite sure that much of the growth I have experienced is not of my own volition but rather the grace of transmission. In my case it continues in spite of the fact that outwardly I no longer follow a specific teacher or path. I may have entered the pathless path, but I remain connected with the lineage anyway. I wonder if this is not the way in which a path is supposed to work. Through an initiatory process we experience a transmission and receive spiritual practices; later, after reaching a certain level, we may embark upon a more individual quest for realization.

Beauties and Abuses

We live in a time when it is important to acknowledge both the rewards and the dangers of entering a path and taking a teacher. At the time I am writing the Roman Catholic Church is reeling from countless allegations of sexual abuse of children by priests. We have also seen many esoteric schools set up by Hindu, Buddhist, and other mystical teachers in the '60s and '70s rocked by sexual scandals or the megalomania of their leaders. It is becoming obvious that very few so-called enlightened spiritual leaders are capable of carrying the spiritual projections of masses of followers. It may be, as one teacher I know says, that the time of spiritual teachers is over. One certainly needs to question the motivation of those who would wish to set themselves up as spiritual teachers, given the nature of the times. Yet we must ask what we are losing if, by rejecting the guidance of experienced mentors, we also dismiss the opportunity of learning the methods of consciousness transformation.

The times that I have spent learning from spiritual teachers have almost always been high points in my life. Anyone who has spent time in the presence of great teachers knows how powerful and beautiful the experience can be. Feeling states of elevated consciousness can be quite addictive in a very positive sense. These states are far easier to experience in the presence of a teacher and in the company of others who are experiencing the same thing. The sense of community and love that often pervades these gatherings is also something that I will certainly cherish for the rest of my life.

On those occasions when I have been the leader of a spiritual group, I have been aware that it was the power of the group intention that did most of the work. Sufis have a saying that "it is the students who make the teacher." This is a truth that spiritual group leaders need to remember, as it can be a heady experience to feel like a conduit of sacred knowledge. The experience of spiritual leadership may also be addictive, and not always in a positive way. True humility, which includes mastery and self-awareness, may be the greatest gift in the arena of spiritual leadership.

All of the transformations of consciousness that I have experienced are in some way related to what I have learned from my spiritual teachers, usually in the company of several other students. Much of what we are discussing in this book emerged after leaving the sphere of my teachers, but it was what I learned from them that developed my consciousness to the point where I was capable of these realizations. Understandably, I am not quite ready to dismiss the importance of teachers and spiritual groups. I am fearful of the abuses that seem to pervade spiritual groups today but cannot figure out how else we can share the wisdom of the past with a new generation.

I think one answer to this dilemma is to realize that the teacher is a bridge, not the destination. If we were to know that, like our high-school or college teachers, spiritual teachers are here to prepare us for our own individual paths, not to spend our lives with us, we could have more perspective and insight when dealing with them. The problem, not only with but also for spiritual teachers, is that those seeking guidance too easily project omnipotence, omniscience, and complete goodness upon them. They do not own such qualities, nor have any of the great spiritual teachers that have helped to guide humanity been perfect.

Authentic spiritual teachers are often wise, kind, and magnetic, and they can open incredible doors to consciousness for followers. They are also human and have human frailties just like the rest of us. Some of these failings are so large and destructive that they disqualify the person from serving as a spiritual teacher. Other teachers are basically positive and bring great blessings to their students. If we are able to understand authentic teachers as connections to spiritual energy and teachings, they can give much to us. If we look only at the superficial trappings of their roles and the quirks of their personalities, then even authentic teachers cannot help us very much.

NINE

Spiritual Freedom

SPIRITUAL FREEDOM IS central to a spirituality that moves beyond cultural dogmas and toward a spirituality of consciousness. The surprising reality is that spiritual freedom is the outcome of consciousness development and that spiritual discipline is the process by which this freedom is achieved. This may be disappointing for all of us who at some time or another may wish for an easy road to enlightenment. It takes discipline to develop, refine, and liberate consciousness. Our earlier exploration of mastery highlighted the importance of self-discipline on the spiritual path; this chapter will take the discussion a step further.

The trick to understanding spiritual freedom is not to confuse the early struggle to overcome cultural encapsulation with the outcome of the struggle, spiritual autonomy. It might be wise to label the struggle, which is the process, spiritual liberation, and the outcome of the process, spiritual freedom. We experience spiritual freedom when we have transcended our small cultural identities and are able to participate in cultural forms without being blinded by them. The Buddhist conception of the *bodhisattva,* a spiritual person who reaches enlightenment yet continues to participate in the world of human frailty for the sake of others' liberation, is a good description of spiritual freedom. Like the person in the earlier tavern story, the bodhisattva has gone beyond the

123

normal ranges of human experience. Upon attaining a certain level of spiritual realization, the individual must decide whether to remain unconnected to the human world (this is usually seen as merging with the Unity of the One Mind rather than reincarnating, but it may also refer to retiring from the world as a hermit, monk, or renunciate) or return to the world from which he or she came. The bodhisattva is the one who chooses to return in order to be of service to others.

This is spiritual freedom—being "in the world but not of the world." It is the culmination of a long and arduous path, not the beginning. As described by all the true teachers who have brought wisdom to the world, seekers first experience a sense of extinction, the loss of all that we once thought we were. At this point we are no longer cultural creatures, as we are lost in the unity of the One. Then we emerge into a new reality with an entirely different viewpoint. As bodhisattvas the consciousness of unity resides in us, and we are free of our conditioning, though we must still live by the standards of our cultures. Everything is changed, though nothing is different. Our values are the divine values, our perspective is the divine perspective, and our actions are the actions of the divine. Sufis call this transformation the shift from the *fana* stage (a process of increasing self-effacement in God, leading to the annihilation of the false ego) to that of *baka* (an advanced station where one's being is filled with the life and presence of God).

Here we come to the dilemma of all dilemmas. How do we develop self-discipline and mastery if we dismiss the dogmas of the past? It might seem that people would be attracted to this sort of spirituality as a way to avoid the structures and demands of previous religions or spiritual paths. Certainly, a portion of the young seekers of the '60s and '70s, my generation, were turned off by the perceived saturnian structure of their elders and were looking for freedom in alternative lifestyles and alternative views of reality.

My experiences of some of the first meditation seminars and camps that I attended were quite interesting. The spiritual guides, often from India or the Middle East, steeped in the discipline of their traditions, found themselves shepherding starry-eyed, undisciplined, cultural rebels who occasionally appeared at meditation sessions half-naked (or even completely naked, if we are to believe some of the stories). Some guides worked slowly to instill mastery in the well-meaning youth with their eyes on a utopian future; unfortunately, other guides joined in the fun. There are, however, no shortcuts to realization. Self-discipline and mastery are essential prerequisites to spiritual freedom.

Spiritual Liberation

Most of what is contained in this book relates to the process of spiritual liberation. We are talking about liberation from cultural forms that no longer speak to the postmodern soul. We are looking at ways to divest ourselves from perspectives that not only limit us but are also responsible for toxic ways of dealing with each other and our natural world. This is what many have called the "small ego," "the false ego," "preoccupations of the ego," or the "limited self." Spiritual liberation is about leaving these small perspectives behind and discovering our true natures; we seek to uncover the nature of the Self that is beyond the limits placed upon it by culture.

Our liberation is difficult and complex not only because we are cultural beings who know little beyond our limited cultural perspectives, but also because physically we are animals, and our cultures have helped us to transcend the purely animal state. When we become liberated from cultural constraints, we do not want to immerse ourselves in the animal state again. Rather, we wish to be able to embrace the animal in us and embrace the cultural aspects of ourselves, as we begin to discover the consciousness of unity that is growing in our hearts and minds. We then carry with us into every activity our animal vitality, our cultural capacities, and our transformed consciousness.

Institutions often become rigid, self-protective, and unable to meet the needs for which they were intended. Times change, consciousness changes, and institutions by their very nature preserve the old rather than fluidly change to accommodate new realities. The Hindu tradition shows wisdom by having a triune divinity. Brahma the creator, Vishnu the preserver, and Shiva the destroyer-transformer are good representations of the nature of reality, personal, cultural, and ultimate.

There is need for the creation of new cultural forms, there is need to preserve these new forms so that they may serve the needs of the people, and then when the forms no longer serve the needs for which they were created, it is natural that they will be destroyed or transformed to make room for the creation of new cultural forms that can fulfill the needs of the times.

Using this Hindu model we can see that it is also normal that new ways to address the development of consciousness need to emerge when the old ways are no longer useful. Cultures, however, always lag behind the emergence of new directions. The big question is now, as it always has been, how can we move beyond our culture while continuing to live within it?

It is obvious that we selectively transcend our cultures. Without culture there is no language, no family form, no group identity, no common history, and no anticipated group future. Culture gives us most of what we consider to be our humanity. Our culture provides us with the means to interact with others and to actualize ourselves. Culture also limits us to acting in culturally acceptable ways, thinking within cultural boundaries, and developing our human potential along socially approved lines.

When we have sufficient self-discipline, insight, and perspective, we can begin to sift through cultural beliefs and expectations and choose how to live within our culture and yet not be bound by it. When our hearts are open, we can avoid the cynicism, anger, paranoia, and alienation that can accompany freeing ourselves from cultural encapsulation. This is why it is so important to enter into a spiritual mentoring process and to work to develop mastery. Without an awakened heart and self-discipline, our lives would become unmanageable and bleak or even worse, exploitive and toxic to our neighbors, when we step beyond the normal ranges of understanding and belief.

As more people find that the old myths and religions are unable to bring meaning to their lives, we begin to see far too many alienated souls creating pain and suffering for those around them. An increasing number of individuals have lost a sense of depth and connectedness, because they have become alienated from their cultures without having been taught the methods of spiritual self-reliance. This is a very dangerous situation, and we may observe its ramifications in the dismal pictures from many of the world's most bleak and volatile corners.

Spiritual liberation is a systematic process that brings us to realizations beyond the cultural viewpoint and prepares us to live clear, joyful, and loving lives, in harmony with those around us. It is this life of clarity, joy, peace, love, and harmony that I call spiritual freedom.

Spiritual Freedom

"Before enlightenment, chop wood, carry water. After enlightenment, chop wood, carry water." This saying from the Buddhist tradition has been often quoted, but if you have been like me, it is just as often misunderstood. I used to believe that even though I might be doing the same things after some sort of complete consciousness shift, I would be constantly in touch with transcendent reality and would be doing my tasks in complete bliss. I don't think like that anymore. I realize now that I simply will be "chopping wood and carrying water" from a more clear and unencumbered place. There will be a quiet sense of joy in my heart in spite of all outward forces pulling and pushing me in different, less joyful directions. Clarity will, however, make it impossible for me not to see the pain, suffering, hate, and fear in the world around me.

This awareness may even lead me to become involved in some sort of social action work. I might feel called, even compelled, to be of service to those less fortunate than myself. Yet my perspective will help me to see the deeper causes of individual pain and suffering. I will see both the cultural malaise and the spiritual bankruptcy underlying the problems surrounding me. I will understand the causes of individual and societal problems, but I will also be limited by the culture in which I live. I will not be able to perform miracles and save the world; I will have risen above my cultural perspective but not above its dictates. So pain will mingle with joy in my heart, and I will feel the loneliness and occasional helplessness of those who have gained a measure of wisdom. I will find that working on inner planes of reality is often much more effective than working in the world.

I think that I will know that I am spiritually free on the day when love becomes like a fountain in my heart and continually overflows, touching everyone and everything in my environment. This may sound poetic, but I am talking of a very real, yet subtle experience. There have been moments in my life when I have experienced an almost visceral outpouring of love from the region of my heart. These were moments of bliss and ecstasy, but they were also very real and related to concrete events in my life. Spiritual freedom involves dissolving the barriers between self and others so that love can flow freely. This is not to say that we lose our ego boundaries. Although some of our barriers are lost in this process of opening up, we maintain our mastery and judgment and may choose when to allow our love to overflow and when to be cautious.

I have had the rare opportunity to know a few spiritual grown-ups in my life. A couple of qualities related to what we are discussing seem to be central to the nature of these individuals. I am talking about people who are very different from each other in many ways, so I believe these qualities are related to becoming spiritually awake and are not just coincidence. Joy, peace, and gratitude seem to be central to the lives of awakened individuals.

Joy

Joy seems to underlie the personality of individuals who are awake. This does not mean that they don't experience a full range of emotions. As a matter of fact, awakened people have access to a wider array of emotion than most, because they tend to go deep into life, and they also are tuned in to the gradations of feeling. But the basic feeling tone of these individuals is usually one of joy. Underneath everything else is quiet, all-pervading happiness that is somewhat detached from outcomes of their actions. Of course they feel grief when they experience a loss. Naturally they feel outrage at some of the actions of others, particularly injustice toward vulnerable people. Almost continually there is sorrow over the nature of the lives of many around them. But all these emotions and many more are built upon the foundation of quiet, detached joy.

Some might wonder how joy and detachment are related. Detachment is difficult for most of us to understand, because our lives are totally dependent for meaning upon our attachments. Our interests, habits, activities, and loves, as well as the attachments to people, define who we are. Imagining being detached from these things seems almost unthinkable and certainly cold, aloof, and alienated. This is not what detachment is like.

Those who have become detached as part of their spiritual progress still love, engage in their chosen activities, and are very interested in the people and things around them. They do not, however, depend for their sense of self or meaning on these outer things. Instead they draw meaning from their inner world of realization. They understand and accept one of the great mysteries of life: everything is temporary. The joy of the moment is all that there is and therefore each moment is cherished and then let go.

Peace

Peace is intimately related to joy, in the way that opposites sometimes exist paradoxically intertwined. It may be easier to see how peace and detachment are related, as detachment is one of the prerequisites of peace, just as it creates a space for joy in our lives. Creating a balance between peace and joy is a delicate and crucial task for the spiritual seeker, and it is especially relevant to the experience of spiritual freedom. Joy may be seen as the wings that lift us up in the experience of spiritual freedom, yet without a deep inner peace, that freedom may easily shift us into an imbalanced state.

Sufis often use the metaphor of the still surface of a lake when speaking of the manner in which peacefulness quiets the heart. In order to achieve this inner peace, one must learn to quiet the mind (which Sufis view as the surface of the heart). (We will address practices that help to quiet the mind in the chapter on meditative practices.) A quiet, peaceful heart and mind prepare us to enter into the silence, to experience the deeply peaceful state that mystics over the ages have yearned for. It is from this deep silence that we may be graced with the experience of

Oneness, the state called by names like samadhi, nirvana, and the "beyond the beyond."

Gratitude

It is not a great leap from joy in the fleeting moment to gratitude for each joyful moment of life. It seems to me that most of us, especially in the U.S., live our lives anticipating what is coming next and often feeling disappointed that we can't keep accumulating more things and storing up more intense experiences, always anticipating the next. We have become quite narcissistic, feeling entitled to everything we have and much of what we don't have. When we awaken from our cultural trance, we become grateful for every moment. We feel the blessing of life and realize that everything we have and all that we have done are blessings to be cherished. We become humble before the tremendous mystery of life. We recognize that forces of nature, culture, and spirit far greater than us are at work and are grateful for the opportunity to participate in the experience of life.

One of the generally unanticipated aspects of gratitude is that being in a state of gratitude puts one in harmony with the universe. When you are feeling gratitude, you not only feel intensely the abundance of blessings poured out upon you, but you also wish to pass those blessings on to others. In this way, you become part of a great circle of blessing, giving and receiving, receiving and giving. The heart is the center of all of this action, as it resonates deeply and widely with the energy of blessing.

Love

Spiritual freedom is inextricably tied to love. Love is that force which binds together and gives form. To me this means that love is the primary spiritual element in humans. When consciousness is aligned with love, we are doing what those before us have called God's will. The awakened person acts out of love in all that they do. I remember, many years ago, standing near my wife Jan, when she asked Gwin Miller, Joe

Miller's wife and spiritual partner, what was their secret, what did it take to make a marriage-spiritual partnership work. The pair were well into old age at the time, and their faces bore the creases and smile lines that distinguish the visages of those who have given much to life. Gwin visibly went deep within, and then she just smiled, chuckled, and murmured: "Love, it's all love."

That answer spoke volumes, because it was given on several levels. It was a real moment of spiritual insight. Everything is love, and when we align ourselves with love's intention we are moving in our soul's direction. So yes, as Gwin implied with her short and beautiful answer, it will take a lot of love for spiritual partners to deal with all the issues of overcoming karmic patterns, blending the spiritual with the physical and emotional, and making adamant the latent potential in the relationship. But love is also the central task in creating a meaningful life and being of benefit to those around us. When we love we are in alignment with the creative force in life. When our consciousness is sufficiently attuned to love, we are capable of the epitome of human potential, because love is the gateway from the limited to the unlimited. Love is the pathway to the consciousness of Unity.

It should be obvious that we are not speaking only of romantic and other garden varieties of loves made popular by cultural convention. We are talking about openness of heart and the removal of barriers between self and other. Love is expansive and open to the experience of others. Love "suffers with" all who suffer. Love opens horizons of possibility by expanding perspective. Love cares deeply and seeks relationship. Love sees no other, only itself in another form.

Harmony

Living in harmony with those around us seems like a simple enough thing, but is a rare commodity in our world. Individuals, unaware of unity, struggle and compete with each other for wealth, power, and position, and even try to prove our religions to be superior to our neighbors' religions. As I have been writing this book we have experienced continual cultural and religious violence. The Israelis and Palestinians continue to fight and kill each other in the so-called Holy Land. Muslim fundamentalists have committed the acts of terrorism of September 11, 2001, in the name of their religious perspective. Fundamentalists in India and Pakistan have brought their part of the world to the brink of nuclear war. These events are in addition to the ongoing genocidal movements in parts of Eastern Europe, the former Soviet republics, Northern Ireland, Guatemala, and in several African nations. Religion plays a central role in most, if not all these brutal displays of human ignorance. Cultural warfare is often religious warfare, because of the central role that religion plays in culture.

The founders of religions were most often spiritually realized people seeking to bestow upon their societies a gift of a more loving and unifying perspective. Harmony with others was often a central tenet of the teachings, although in some cases persecution of the believers brought about a more warlike perspective. The followers of the followers of the followers often destroyed the beliefs of the founders in their attempt to glorify their cultures and prove themselves superior to their neighbors. They used religion as a tool for political, economic, and military dominance, not as a means of broadening perspective and creating harmony.

Harmony is the trademark of an awakened consciousness, and those who spread disharmony are not spiritually awake! Spiritual freedom takes us out of the world of striving to prove that "we're number one" and into a state of union with the other. The difficulty is that no one is always awake. Consciousness cannot always be attuned to the highest harmonic of our being. Sometimes even the most enlightened get caught up in the world and forget unity. At those times they are not spiritually free, yet many around them may continue to expect that they are speaking and acting from only the highest perspective. It is at times like this that spiritual people can do more damage than most.

Teachings throughout the ages have urged us to "love our neighbors as ourselves" for a very good reason. Our neighbors *are* ourselves. Spiritual freedom helps us to understand that when we "do unto others as we would have them do unto us," we are indeed doing unto ourselves. This is true in the essence of things but also at the most mundane level. We are busy creating our world. We can create a world of harmony, or one of inharmony—it is up to us. Every action toward every person, place, or thing reverberates outward and builds and strengthens either planetary movement toward love and harmony or contributes to destruction and disunity. We can take our pick.

Again, the Bodhisattva

Once again we return to the contradiction of freedom. We can free ourselves from the blinders of culture, but we cannot free ourselves from the consequences of our actions. Some have tried. Those who follow Jainism attempt to become completely harmless, not even stepping on an ant or breathing in a bug. Many spiritual traditions advise vegetarianism so as not to feed off the lives of other animals.

From my perspective we cannot become harmless and still live on the planet. We can, if we wish, take on practices like the above in an attempt to become less harmful, but we must participate in our cultures to some degree, and our cultures are anything but harmless. The lesson for all of us who wish to work toward unity from a place of spiritual liberty is to take on the stance that the Buddhists call the bodhisattva. The challenge is to transcend culture but live within culture, to "render unto Caesar what is Caesar's, and render unto God what is God's." The bodhisattva lives in the world, with consciousness that touches a place beyond duality, and at the same time the bodhisattva is aware that what life is really all about is, in the words of Hazrat Inayat Khan, "to be of some little service to one's fellow man" (1982, p. 126).

PART THREE

Spiritual Practices and the Development of Consciousness

WHEN WE UNDERSTAND that a transformed consciousness underpins authentic spirituality, we discover the need for methods to help develop our consciousness. In the following chapters, we will explore the many tried-and-true methods for working with consciousness that exist in most religious and spiritual traditions. Since volumes have been and can be written about each of the methods discussed, we will undertake only an introduction to several types of practice. Yet much can be learned from even a brief examination of thinking, meditation, and creative imagination, practices with breath and sound, the retreat process, and working with nature. Go slowly through the following chapters, experimenting with the practices and contemplating their effects.

TEN

Thinking and Consciousness

"YOU CAN GET more stinking from thinking than you can from drinking, but the feel is for real" (Power, 1993: 213). That is what the iconoclastic American mystic Joe Miller had to say on the subject of thinking. But then Joe also had a deep understanding of many of the most profound thoughts of world philosophy. He was making an important point about the type of thinking in which we normally engage. He was warning us of the foolishness of trying to put the vastness of being into a box. Joe was a great fan of the powerful Buddhist sage Padma Sambhava and knew that concepts will never capture reality. Joe would no doubt agree with my premise that thinking is one of the primary spiritual practices.

Thinking is the most central of all activities related to consciousness and spirituality. How we use thought, what thoughts are personally acceptable, what thoughts are culturally acceptable, and what thoughts generally fill our minds are important issues. They serve as signs of the nature of our consciousness, and they also serve as methods of changing our consciousness. Thoughts can be used as seeds for changing, expanding, or refining our consciousness.

Our minds are amazing tools to be used in the service of consciousness. Thinking, and our minds to which we attribute the thinking process, is what sets humanity apart from the rest of the inhabitants of planet Earth. With our minds we have explored our physical world from the cosmic level down to the subatomic. We have created physical and social cultures to help us live in communities. We have sought to understand the meaning behind life and the natural world. We have plumbed the depth of our own psyches through spiritual practice and psychological disciplines. Unfortunately, we sometimes compartmentalize our thinking into either/or categories that pit knowledge and ways of thinking against each other. Each time we discover a new way of using our minds, we exclude or sometimes repress our previous ways of knowing. We have a habit of throwing our babies out with the bathwater. The most obvious example of this process is our current struggle between scientific positivism and faith. We need to examine this process and look at what we've lost along the way.

To begin this discussion, let's look at what we consider to be adult thinking. The theories we will be exploring are part of a scientific paradigm, and I feel that they are a reasonable way of viewing how adults think. Science may contribute significantly to our understanding of aspects of spiritual growth; it is only when we make it a god that the modern scientific paradigm poses problems for us.

Adult Thinking

critical thinking

What is it to think like an adult? Most experts on thinking believe that adult thinking involves what we call critical thinking. Critical thinking, to paraphrase much of the writing being done in the area, involves the capacity for receiving information, processing information through analysis, organizing information into bits of understanding, and being able to apply that information in one's everyday life. The Swiss psychologist Jean Piaget was the first to describe the process by which people develop mental maturity and become capable of critical thinking (Newman and Newman, 1984:7). More recently, the Harvard psychologist William Perry has expanded Piaget's thinking on the later stages of the cognitive developmental process (Irwin, 2002:137).

Piaget's formulation describes four distinct stages of development. The first stage, referred to as *sensorimotor,* occurs between birth and approximately age two; this is the stage of cognitive development when the infant's intelligence relies upon the senses and bodily experience for stimulation. The second stage is called *preoperational;* it lasts (according to Piaget) from about two years to seven years of age (Newman and Newman, 1984:7-9). This is a time when children know about the world primarily through their own actions. They do not necessarily generalize this knowledge or create theories about things. They simply know about their own experience. Throughout this stage they work to overcome the barriers to broader forms of knowledge, such as egocentrism until they enter the next stage, called *concrete operations* (Newman and Newman, 1984:9).

During the stage of concrete operations children begin to think with some degree of logic. They can classify things into categories and hierarchies, but this ability is fairly concrete and lacks the abstract quality, which will come in the final (according to Piaget) stage, which is referred to as *formal operations* (Newman and Newman, 1984:9). The stage of formal operations generally begins sometime around twelve years of age. At this time adolescents can explore all of the logical solutions to a problem, can imagine things contrary to fact, can think realistically about the future, form ideals, and grasp metaphors that younger children cannot comprehend. Formal operational thinking no longer needs to be tied to actual physical objects or events. It is this ability to think for one's self and reason that is at the heart of critical thinking and can often be the bane of existence for parents raising teenagers.

Many people never quite reach the stage of formal operations, or they might achieve it only in selected areas of thought. It might seem that many in our society have a hard time even reaching the stage of concrete operations, when we understand that this stage requires the ability to see from someone else's perspective. William Perry has developed a schema that looks at the development of critical or higher order thinking and outlines the process we must go through in order to fulfill the promise of formal adult thinking (1970). His schema begins with *dualism,* which involves absolutes and authorities as the arbiters of truth, and moves through several stages of dualism to *relativism.*

139

In the stage of relativism we reject the dogmatism of absolutes and find ourselves adrift in a sea of competing realities and may see everything as "relative." This is the first stage of learning to think as an adult, in that we begin to take responsibility for analyzing "truths" that we previously accepted, when we gave others the authority to impose them upon us. Relativism is an important step, but it contains a brutal trap that can keep us swimming in a sea of uncertainty for a lifetime.

Perry then leads us through a series of steps from relativism to commitment (Irwin, 2002:138). When we begin to make choices about values, knowledge, and actions, based not on external authority, but instead upon well-thought-out commitment to knowledge and belief, we have entered Perry's stage of commitment, and as Chaffee elaborates, we have become critical thinkers (1998:42). Critical thinking does not involve seeing all knowledge as equally relative, but rather weighing as much information as possible and making a commitment or choice. This is the discernment discussed in chapter 7, "Creating Personality." More recently people have been referring to this later way of thinking as *postformal* thought; at this point we are more capable of struggling with uncertainties and gray areas.

I wonder how many people may misinterpret the biblical references to believers as "sheep" to suggest absolute obedience to authority. Others may interpret injunctions to "become as a little child" to mean that we should employ childlike thinking. The deeper meaning of such references must surely point to becoming filled with the kind of joyful innocence one sees in children.

The message that we should not think in an adult fashion is a most troubling aspect of some sects of Christianity as well as of other patriarchal religions. A parallel issue relates to scientific dogmatists who suppress and ridicule those who do not conform to their faith in the infallibility of the current state of scientific thought. The sacred human ability for reason and critical thought is indeed one of the truths behind the biblical contention that "we are created in the image of God." Whether the authorities be religious or secular, the adult thinker will resist dogmatic beliefs and instead critically search for understanding and meaning within his or her own heart and mind, having first gathered as much information as humanly possible. Of course there is a time for surrender of our limited opinions in the face of the vastness of life, but if we never think critically we will never get to that point.

It is the destiny of consciousness, which from a certain spiritual perspective is the way in which the One Life can know itself, to utilize the human mind in such a way as to become what the Sufis term *Wali,* the friend of God. This state of consciousness emerges when the human mind is able to overcome man-made conceptions and align itself with the natural order (sometimes called "divine intention"). The friend of God must first unlearn much that, although considered true or right by the majority, is detrimental to conscious evolution. This process in some instances might correspond with Perry's stage of relativism.

The seeker who has reached the stage of becoming the friend of God begins slowly to make choices based upon analysis that is both rational (given that the evolving consciousness of the individual is capable of experiencing and understanding much more at this point) and in keeping with the messages continually emerging from the heart. At this point thinking becomes a divine art. The human mind becomes the mind of the One Life, and rational thought becomes the tool of consciousness.

A Brief History of a Western Dualism

Western thinkers have struggled for several millennia with the relationship between thinking and rationality on the one hand and the transcendent worlds of gods and faith on the other. It has only been recently, since the advent of behaviorist thought, that theorists like Piaget and Perry could develop perspectives that are able to gain widespread attention without addressing the ability to know God or the relationship of transcendent realms to the physical world.

This mechanistic viewpoint allows for a view of the microcosm that need not take account of the macrocosm, and in doing so theorists may concentrate exclusively on the way that things happen in physical reality. This development has been useful in our understanding of human behavior, although it deals with only a part of the puzzle of human consciousness and thought. To understand thinking from this perspective, it might be useful to take a very brief historical look at some of the ideas about thinking at the root of our Western heritage.

The history of this split in Western thought is tragic in that it has led to a strange inheritance for the modern world. It could have been very different. At points in human history, exploration of both physical reality and inner worlds could coexist without interfering with the proper pursuit of either. Temple priests in some cultures, such as the Egyptian, were the scientists of the day as well as the purveyors of religion. Even later while Christian Europe was mired in the Dark Ages, brought about in large part by religious fervor to eradicate everything that was not biblically based, the Muslim world was preserving the wisdom of the past as well as developing sciences like chemistry and astronomy. Why was it necessary to separate rational thought from religious thought?

The perspectives of Plato and his student Aristotle may be the most well-known prototypes of this split in thinking. Plato emphasized the transcendent nature of all things by stressing universal "Forms" or "Ideas" that were not provable but were the true essence behind the manifest reality. Aristotle was more of an early empiricist and saw reality in the world of concrete objects. He thought that universal truths owed their existence to objects that could be seen and experienced in the material world (Tarnas, 1991). Here we find the basic template for the divide in Western thought. Plato finds truth in the transcendent and Aristotle in the immanent. It would have made a huge difference in the evolution of the Western mind if the next great thinker to come along (and be recognized as such) had suggested that they were both right. Is it not possible that a harmony between understanding the workings of the inner world and the workings of the physical world could have saved us a lot of misery?

By the fourth century of the current era much of the classical thought of Aristotle and other great thinkers of the ancient world had been lost or repressed in Christian Europe. Gnostic, neoplatonic, and pagan thought were losing ground to the politicized Christianity of the Roman Church. Into this period came Augustine. Augustine stressed the love of God and aesthetic denial of the body. He believed the only important thing was to find God and that this had to be done in the "real" world of the mind. God could not be found in the external world (Armstrong, 1993:121). Here we see the seeds of much that plagues us today. If the only thing worth doing is seeking God, and God can only be found within, then we lose a sense of the sacred in the outer world and can condone everything from genocide to ecological disaster, since the world doesn't matter.

Luckily for us all, by the thirteenth century the philosophy of Aristotle was being rediscovered in Europe. The Muslim presence in Spain and the Crusades were bringing Western scholars into contact with classical works that had been preserved by Muslim scholars. While the Roman Church was still a repressive force to be reckoned with, Thomas Aquinas attempted a synthesis of Augustine and the philosophy of Aristotle. Aquinas listed "proofs" for the existence of God (Tarnas, 1991:181–190), which brought the objective world and human reason back into the picture. No longer were simple love and faith the only means of relating to the divine, but now the rational mind could be employed. This is a far cry from modern empirical rationalism, but it opened the door to the light of reason during a very dark time. Aquinas and the rediscovery of Aristotle paved the way for the Protestant Reformation, the scientific revolution, and the Renaissance.

Soon (if a few centuries may be considered soon), Europeans were beginning to discover a new, more self-conscious and individualistic impulse. Martin Luther, in addition to some very conservative perspectives, taught "the priesthood of all believers," which centered religious authority in the conscience and judgment of each individual Christian (Tarnas, 1991: 239).

Francis Bacon saw science as a way of fulfilling God's plan of salvation for human beings, and the pursuit of science a religious obligation (Tarnas, 1991: 273). Bacon and many of those Enlightenment thinkers who followed in his footsteps wished to replace the old religious viewpoint with empiricism, but it was often seen as a way of fulfilling a spiritual purpose. With Bacon and the Enlightenment thinkers we begin to see the opposite extreme of religious dogmatism. Science became the dogma of the time, and other more introspective ways of knowing were dismissed as no longer acceptable. A great opportunity for synthesis was missed, but of course who could blame them. It was a time when people were still burning witches, the Inquisition was still within cultural memory, and early scientists were often condemned from local pulpits.

Western thinking also began to deal with the nature of consciousness in these centuries of change. René Descartes sought to find a basis for all knowledge and with his famous "Cogito, ergo sum, I think therefore I am" found it in individual self-awareness. Immanuel Kant declared that humans could only know the phenomenal world and that any other conclusions, such as the existence of God, were unfounded. Kant saw the structures of the human mind as shaping what we can know (Tarnas, 1991:343).

It is rather delightful to speculate what our philosophical world might be like if events had taken only a slightly different course. If it were not that Kant was dismissive of metaphysical ideas, we might stretch and place Plato's world of transcendent ideas within the structure of the human mind. This might have been an early precursor of Jung's theories of the archetypes. If Kant had been able to make this leap, it could have been an interesting beginning point for a true synthesis of metaphysical and scientific thought. There is, however, one other giant of Western philosophy who went even further toward this needed synthesis.

Georg Hegel sought to unify man and nature, spirit and matter, human and divine. Hegel's evolutionary theory of the dialectic was thought to be applicable to all levels of reality. Hegel seems like a mystic when we discover that he saw the world as constantly unfolding and becoming known to itself. Hegel recognized the importance of inner and outer realities and saw the consciousness of man as central to the unfolding of the world (Tarnas 1991:381).

Unfortunately it is not Hegel, or even Kant, who informs our public dialogue about the nature of being human. Often it is the harangue of fundamentalists arguing against the "secular humanists" instead. We can also hear the empirically based folks telling us that any of our experiences that cannot be quantified or replicated should be ignored or discounted because they are not real.

In our present age the mechanistic viewpoint of pragmatic science is the primary acceptable viewpoint, with the competing voice of fundamentalist religion as a secondary viewpoint seeking dominance. Our little jaunt through the history of Western thought suggests that it might be that "the more things change, the more they stay the same." We still live in a world of competing dualistic beliefs, possibly more rigid for their having been in competition for so long. These competing belief systems no doubt have brought out the worst in each other; we often move to the extremes of our positions when confronted with a critical and vocal opponent. The scientific rejection of all concepts not supported by empirical data may relate not only to the ongoing contest for recognition of the scientific viewpoint over the religious viewpoint, but it also relates to the trauma of the not-too-distant time when scientists were being imprisoned by the Catholic Church's Inquisition for their beliefs.

It was also not long ago when any thinking that did not conform either to religious dogma or the newly emerging scientific dogma could be interpreted as heresy or witchcraft and lead to serious consequences. Because scientific thinking and religious thinking were antagonists for so long and resisted all the attempts of holistic thinkers to unite them, they continue to seem mutually exclusive. We need to remember that they could have evolved together, each modifying the other, growing together as a seamless unity.

We have a long history of either/or thinking and only a few examples (in the West) of wholistic, both/and thinking. Hegel and C. G. Jung are examples of superb minds attempting to create syntheses in Western thought. Unfortunately, these philosophers have tended to be marginalized in recent time, as the competing dualisms of science and literalist religions occupy center stage. Today we no longer try for vast schemas that encompass both empirical and divine conceptions. We have divided up our world into acceptable scientific scholarly thought and dogmatic or "fuzzy headed" religion or spirituality. There is very little expectation that these perspectives should ever be able to form a unitary whole.

A New Harmony?

While this apparent division may seem to be unfortunate, we might yet be able to salvage unity from this chaos. So long as it was expected that thinking and the gathering of knowledge belonged to one all-encompassing method, the battle over whose method was correct was destined to continue ad infinitum. Now that for the most part science has won the battle, we can declare it the victor and move on to try to understand the multitude of ways human beings think and make meaning of their existence. We can "give the devil his due" and simply understand that positivism is an exceptionally useful way of developing knowledge of the world encountered by our senses. That settles that, no more argument.

We may then go on to recognize that other means of thinking may be useful, along with science, when developing a sense of meaning in human life and in the experience of relationship with the sensory world. The inner experience of human beings can also be afforded a place in the realm of knowledge. Ways of using the mind such as creative imagination, meditation, and contemplation are useful techniques when empirical outcomes are not the desired result, but rather what is sought is meaning, relationship, or transcendence.

Perhaps there is hope that in our new, postmodern, relativistic, and yet creative and energizing intellectual world, we may recognize the importance of multiple ways of thinking and knowing. If we once understand these other modes of thinking, we will be able to make much better sense of our cultural and religious stories, since they were first told by nonscientific people with mythic intentions.

ELEVEN

Creative Imagination and Meditation

CREATIVE IMAGINATION IS the capacity for human consciousness to imbue its mental creations with meaning, psychological power, and an existence in the mind world. We should first understand that the term *creative imagination* probably would not be found in ancient texts, nor would traditional tribal elders in today's primary cultures recognize it. Creative imagination is a faculty used by shamans, gurus, elders, healers, monks, magicians, wise men and women, poets, artists, and many others seeking to plumb the depths of consciousness in order to construct meaning and understanding or intervene in the natural order of things. Creative imagination may be called journeying in one culture, meditation in another, and praying in still another. It is part of spiritual practice in almost all traditions, but may be only a small part in some traditions and the largest part in others.

Creative imagination has now worked its way into modern psychology and psychotherapy. Jung called it "active imagination." Creative imagination is an integral part of psychotherapies, where it is known as "guided imagery," "systematic desensitization," "positive imagery," and other similar labels. The use of the trained will to create images that inspire, heal, or give meaning continues to be an important part of both religious and secular life. Today, with the perspective that comes from science and cultural pluralism, we are able to isolate creative imagination and its role in the spiritual practices of religious and mystical traditions.

Poets, writers, and artists also understand the use of creative imagination. Samuel Taylor Coleridge, a poet and thinker of the early nineteenth century, formulated a theory of the imagination. He saw imagination as composed of three categories: primary imagination, secondary imagination, and fancy (Knight, 1978:4). Coleridge, like Kant, saw primary imagination as almost completely automatic. It is the way in which the mind automatically organizes reality to make it comprehensible to us. It "selects and interprets the teeming production of sense impressions into meaning and order" (Knight 1978:4).

Fancy is just the simple association of ideas. We can bring ideas together in any way we wish, but this does not imply any deeper meaning; it is just the superficial creation of an image. Secondary imagination, according to Coleridge, involves a transformation among the images. "They are not merely juxtaposed but fused, distilled or otherwise processed so as to give a meaning and experience that is a totality far greater than that with comprises their constituent parts. This is the stuff of great poetry or literature—and indeed of all the arts" (Knight, 1978:5).

Here we can see, in the fields of literature and the arts, recognition of a mental process that transcends simple mechanistic explanation and touches upon the creative potential of the human mind. Coleridge is talking about capacity known to creative artists that is one part of the broader phenomenon of creative imagination. There is no doubt that much of the great art, music, poetry, and literature in all cultures comes from the creative imagination of individuals who are in tune with the collective mind world of the culture.

Today psychotherapists, physicians, and sport psychologists use visualization, which is a form of creative imagination, to address a wide variety of needs. Psychotherapists use visualization to rehearse behaviors, to desensitize people to phobic situations, and to deal with grief, anger and guilt, and a host of other psychological needs. Physicians and others who work with people with severe pain or diseases like cancer use visualization and creative imagination as part of a holistic treatment regimen. Sport psychologists teach athletes visualization techniques and have brought a whole new dimension to athletics.

These powerful concentration devises use visualization and creative imagination to accomplish a myriad of tasks and are the modern equivalent of ancient practice used by shamans, magicians, and mystics. They accomplish much the same tasks, but do so with scientific language and explanations, and are therefore accepted by most people except for hard-core empiricists who doubt anything that they cannot touch or see.

The shamans, mystics, and seers of previous eras, as well as the few remaining practitioners of our time, generally have used creative imagination as one of their primary methods for inner work. Let us look at a few productions of the creative imagination so that we may be able to understand the pervasive use of creative imagination in creating meaning, working with psychological issues, and influencing the surrounding world. This study may help us to deduce new meanings inherent in our histories and in our religions.

I discussed my own experience in imaginal realms earlier in chapter 3, where I offered my definition of these realms as inner worlds that are created and explored through personal imagination. These realms are anchored in a reality that is not totally personal; they are vaster than that which is contained within the individual mind. We also noted that in the shamanic work called "journeying" one encounters products of a shared mind world, which are semidependent upon the shaman and also have an apparent reality of their own. They do not exist in an empirically verifiable way but inhabit the shared mental reality of the tribe, culture, or possibly humanity in general.

These realities come into existence through the creative imagination of the members of a tribal or cultural group and are slowly built up and refined over generations. Eventually they become "god realms" like Olympus, Shambala, or Hurqalya, or underworld realms related to nature's helping powers or other forces of the earth. The creative imagination of the shaman or spiritual seeker can enter these realms of consciousness and work with the content of these realms in order to bring meaning to their everyday experiences, gain psychological insight, or

Celtic influences here

149

influence the external world. This work may be effective because of the interconnectedness of the mind world with virtually all other levels of reality.

Creative imagination works with cultural images in a variety of ways. It may be employed to expand upon the insights or psychological revelations of dreams, or it may work with archetypal images for personal or group benefit. We may use creative imagination to seek insight into disease or suffering in order to do healing work for individuals or entire groups, if requested to do so. (We must be aware that we cannot simply intervene in someone's life—we must seek permission and be invited to do so.)

The idea of a shared mental reality that has a nonempirical, nonsensory basis is difficult for most modern minds to grasp; it certainly harkens back to Platonic thought. The modern reader may wish to consider, however, that this is not an attempt to displace rational critical thought, but rather to remind us of a process of thinking that is thousands of years older than our current scientific thought and has served humanity well in the creation of meaning, artistic expression, and psychological growth. This perspective honors the relationship between inner and outer realities, as well as the connections among the human, animal, plant, and mineral worlds. It is not, however, a good way in which to explore the empirical reality of the sensory world. When cultures have mixed mythos with logos, the confusion of realities has led to absurd conclusions, to adapt Karen Armstrong's terminology (2000:xiii).

Henri Corbin (1903–1978) was a scholar who did extensive study in the area of creative imagination. He was a French Islamicist who focused upon Iranian Sufism, Shi'ism, and their pre-Islamic Persian precursors (Tompkins, 2000:53). Corbin is not an easy read. He writes in a dense, scholarly fashion that requires (of me, at least) that each sentence be read over again several times, and even then I often have to revisit the material before I really understand it. I was pleased to discover in a recent copy of the journal *Lapis* a brief summary of Corbin's work on creative imagination written by Ptolemy Tompkins. Tompkins describes Corbin's approach clearly and succinctly. According to Tompkins, Corbin sees the imaginal realms as a "dimension accessible to the penetration of human imagination, but not contained by it . . . It is an 'external world,' and yet it is not a physical world. It is a world that teaches us that it is possible to emerge from measurable space without emerging from extent, and that we must abandon homogeneous chronological time in order to enter that qualitative time which is the history of the soul" (2000:54).

We certainly find ourselves in the realm of metaphysics when we encounter Henri Corbin, and it takes a courageous mind to venture into the implications of Corbin's research. Although a consummate scholar, Corbin studied with Iranian philosophers who were immersed in highly non-Western philosophical viewpoints. There is reason to question unsubstantiated prescientific perspectives, yet many of us have questions about our own experiences that have remained unanswered by Western science.

We may profit by listening to the wisdom of our ancestors as well as to those who hold non-Western perspectives; we may discover clues to our experience that have been overlooked by our current paradigm. "All humanity, Corbin's philosophers maintained, possesses this 'celestial' dimension. That was why to enter the imaginal realm was in effect not to lose one's humanity but to recover it—to become the complete creature that one always secretly remembered being before entering the limitations of the material world" (Tompkins, 2000:54–55).

The creative imagination is a vast and challenging subject. It involves us in attempting to understand the nature of the imaginal realms as well as the process of navigating these realms through the use of the creative imagination. We might tie the two together by considering one as the creation of the other; yet like all chicken-and-egg situations, this sequencing has limitations.

Let's look at one example of creative imagination that has in recent time been generally misunderstood. Many myths and stories discuss the interaction between the gods and humans, angels and humans, devils and humans, animals and humans, fairies and humans, or some such mixture of realms. One way in which this interaction sometimes plays out is in the conception and birth of cultural heroes. We have many cultural heroes who are reported to be products of intercourse between gods or angels and humans. Whether these heroes are called Hercules, Achilles, Mithra, or Jesus, we are called to understand practices involving a type of creative imagination common to our ancestors.

In some cases the claim of being conceived by a god or goddess is simply an attempt to add stature to an already recognized spiritual leader. In other cases there may have been magic at work that is unfamiliar to our modern perspectives. In these instances a highly trained and dedicated male initiate using creative imagination may have attuned himself to the god or angel desired, and in a state of deep connection to the essence of that being in the mind world, the initiate would engage in intercourse with a deeply attuned and receptive woman, generally of equal spiritual realization. Before the days of genetic engineering and when spiritual inheritance was considered as important as physical inheritance, a cultural hero conceived in this manner and raised in the proper atmosphere was seen to embody both the divine inheritance and human mortality. It is doubtful that all those to whom divine parentage was attributed were actually the product of such magical consummations, but to our ancestors it was the necessary prerequisite to be a cultural hero.

Today, having lost the knowledge of how our ancestors thought, we literalize what was never intended to be literal. For our ancestors the realm of creative imagination was often more real than the physical realm is for us. It was similar to Plato's world of ideas and was probably the precursor of his philosophy. It is important, if we are to understand much of the religion that we have inherited, that we understand the way of thinking that was employed in its creation.

Artists, poets, and writers can help us to find paths into the imaginal realms, as they commonly use the creative imagination to tap the depths of their psyches for inspiration. Writers and poets use metaphors to suggest the vastness, the subtlety, and the beauty of the realms that they have encountered through the creative imagination. Latin American writers such as Jorge Luis Borges and Gabriel Garcia Marquez are known for their early use of magical realism, which takes us deeply into the imaginal realms. Hosts of painters like Georgia

O'Keefe and Rufino Tamayo help us to see reality in numinous, fantastic ways that are evocative of inner realities.

It is also important that we become aware of our own capacity for creative imagination, not only for artistic endeavors but also for the creating of meaning and psychological growth. It is our natural inheritance from the wisdom of our ancestors, and while its application should never be confused with rational and critical thought, it can bring meaning, healing, and joy to our otherwise demythologized lives.

Meditation

Like creative imagination, which is often a part of meditative practice, some forms of meditation may be seen as introspective forms of thinking. When we are meditating we are seeking to grow or learn in relationship with energy or information gleaned from inner experience, as opposed to that obtained from the world of the senses. Forms of transcendent thinking reminiscent of Plato are relevant to meditation practice. What this inner or transcendent world actually is seen to be by those who meditate will depend upon their perspective. For some it is an inner world populated by angels, gods, ancestors, or spirit guides. For others it is the individual unconscious and/or the collective consciousness. From my perspective the nature of the inner world is created by the cultural expectations that we bring to it, but the experiences and benefits are in their essence real.

Meditation is a mental discipline, the purpose of which is to train the mind in several ways of experiencing the inner world of the mind and soul. It is also used to accomplish tasks related to seeking inner guidance and purpose in our lives, mental purification, experiencing alternative states of consciousness, and spiritual realization. What we generally call meditation actually involves three main activities: concentration, active meditation, and passive meditation. Most forms of meditation can be located in these three broad categories.

Meditative forms have developed within religions and mystery teachings and therefore carry the cultural overlays of the particular settings in which they developed. From our knowledge of core practices and

153

beliefs, we can attempt to cut through cultural trappings to begin to find the essential nature of meditation. The task involves a sort of distillation or sifting process in order to figure out what parts of meditation practice are cultural and what aspects are absolutely basic. In reality, this is a difficult undertaking, as many basic meditative techniques are in actuality fused with cultural practices. Nevertheless, simply making the attempt helps us to understand more clearly what is essential to developing a viable meditative practice.

This chapter will explore the three main types of activities generally referred to as meditation, concentration, active meditation, and passive meditation. We will relate these types of meditation to the purposes mentioned above as well as their efficacy in enhancing our lives. In addition to the purposes related to enhancing consciousness and training the mind, meditation is also effective as a potent stress reliever and psychological aide.

Concentration

All of us can relate to the phenomenon that cognitive scientists have called "roof-brain chatter." That incessant jabbering that goes on in our minds, some of which we would not want anyone else to know about, may be a severe problem for anyone wishing to achieve some degree of mastery when it comes to the development of consciousness. A mind full of clutter has little room for silence, ecstasy, or profound experience. The same is true of our mental addictions. We are so often addicted to thinking about sex, money, or a favorite activity that little time is left for contemplating meaning or even remembering our life's goals. How little time most of us take out of our busy lives just to remember who we are and where we wish to go with our lives!

When it comes to the greater questions of meaning and existence, some of us may be even lazier, as we relegate those questions to Sunday mornings (or whatever our religious day might be) and let someone who is paid to think about those things do our contemplating for us. We may go for long periods without thinking about what our life means at all. Many of us, especially men, may have to reach midlife or beyond and sometimes have a major threat to our complacency, such as a heart attack, before we begin to contemplate how we have been living and what meaning our lives have. One of the primary purposes of meditation is therefore to quiet the habitual thinking patterns within the mind and make room for the possibility of remembering who we are and how we want to live.

Breaking the unconscious trance in which we live has long-term effects that are profound. When we use meditation techniques, either of our own making or one that we have learned from others, we set in motion a discipline that, if used consistently, will gradually reduce the incessant babbling in our minds and give us more control over our mental addictions. Clearing or concentrating the mind even for a half an hour a day will, over time, provide us with more clarity of thought and depth of experience.

Concentration is a form of mental purification. When we concentrate upon one thing, we naturally make less room in the mind for other, less desirable thoughts. Beginning meditation techniques are opportunities to concentrate upon one thing in order to gradually eliminate barriers to creative imagination, silence, and the profound depths of life. Learning to concentrate is at the root of all meditation and is essential for more advanced meditation techniques.

There are many natural and contrived ways to deepen concentration. Some meditators have spent long hours staring at a nail in a wall or an intricate mandala. Along with sound, breath, and creative imagination practices, my work as a psychotherapist probably developed my concentration most profoundly. As I focused entirely upon the stories of my clients, I often lost all sense of time, place, and self. That concentration technique was indeed a joyful one, as there was a richness involved in losing myself in another human being. Most of us have opportunities in our everyday life for developing concentration. Creative projects such as gardening, making music, tending children, and painting are examples of the possibilities. We can work to turn them into meditative practice when we recognize their potential as tools for development.

Spiritual Practices to Aid Concentration

One of the most effective means of concentration is through the use of what is called mantra by the yogis and wasifa by the Sufis. The Roman Catholic Church has retained something of this technique with the repeating of the rosary. A chapter devoted to sound practices follows, so we will not spend much time discussing them at this time. Sound practices, which are an integral part of most spiritual pursuits, are amazingly effective at filling the mind with their presence; they eliminate much extraneous mental garbage. They also serve the purpose of aiding concentration by altering the vibratory field of the meditator and impressing a needed quality or idea upon the consciousness.

Another almost universal mediation technique is focusing upon the breath. Breath is one of the great mysteries of life. It serves as the foundation of all other meditative practice. The most simple meditation practice is "watching the breath," which means just paying attention to (concentrating on) each inhalation and exhalation. Watching our breath not only gives us something to concentrate upon; it also naturally slows the breath, which quiets our emotions automatically.

Breathing is a very natural rhythm and can serve as the anchor for any thoughts that we wish to place into our awareness. Try sitting under a large tree and imagining that you are drawing strength from it. As you exhale, feel your fears and vulnerabilities dropping away like the shedding of leaves. There are literally millions of these types of meditations that can be linked to the natural rhythm of our breathing.

Some of us may carry a mental picture of mediation that involves a person lost in reverie, dressed in oriental clothing and sitting cross-legged on a pillow. This is one way to meditate, but it is not the only way. The classical postures used in many forms of meditation have their purposes. The yogi's lotus position is both a discipline—it takes training and time to learn it—and a way to position the body so that there is no blocking of the energy flow. There are, however, other ways to learn discipline and other ways, sometimes more comfortable for Westerners, to avoid energy blockages. Meditation can be effective sitting in a straight-backed chair or walking, which allow one to keep the spine straight, important for energy flow. A few people can meditate lying down. The only thing absolutely necessary is concentration.

Other aids to concentration for the meditator can involve ritual, symbols, and music. Ritual can be very simple or quite elaborate. All that you truly need are environmental reminders that you are carving out an opportunity for an inner experience within an otherwise mundane outer life. Meditation at the same time and in the same place every day will eventually create a rhythm in which you will naturally be able to concentrate and enter a meditative state when presented with the ritualized outer cues of time and place. A ritualized set of activities at the beginning of meditation has the same effect. If you start each meditation by saying a brief invocation and perhaps lighting a candle or incense, it is likely that these activities will over time begin to evoke a deep and calm mental state.

Placing in the room where you meditate items that have sacred meaning, actual or symbolic, for you will evoke a calming, centering atmosphere and will also communicate with your soul in its own language. Symbols are the subconscious language to which the depths of our beings respond, so it is most effective to choose items that hold powerful meaning for you. What you choose may be quite different from what others may choose, as meditation is not a one-size-fits-all endeavor. You may love flowers, candles, and crystals, while your friend may find a special rock, seashell, or photograph more moving. You may find that the symbols that speak to your depths change from time to time, because mediation is a process that evolves with you.

Beginning meditators often use background music because it can be evocative of a desired mood. Music has a place in meditation. Music such as Gregorian chant, Native American flute music, Tibetan chant, or Turkish singing *zikr* can facilitate the use of creative imagination or simply aid relaxation. When you are seeking to concentrate, however, the best sort of music may be the songs or vocalizations that you create yourself. A devotional song that you know or create has the potential to open your heart and ease you into a sacred space.

The songs of the Dances of Universal Peace, initially developed by the American Sufi Samuel Lewis, are a wonderful example of music that you may play or sing to aid concentration and to create a meditative space. These songs originally accompanied a form of dancing meditation that has been expanded by Lewis's students over recent decades. The songs use sacred phrases and songs from around the world and are coupled with movement, typically circle dances. The repetition of sound and movement creates an atmosphere that evokes sublime states of consciousness.

These dances also have the effect of requiring a grounding concentration on the here-and-now, even as one's consciousness may be lifted to sublime states. Leaders of the Dances of Universal Peace often suggest, "Keep your feet on the ground and your head in the clouds." The concentration required to achieve this focus is useful in building a capacity for integration of spirituality into everyday life. This is, after all, what spirituality is really all about: becoming more real, more aware, and more alive in everyday life.

Active Meditation
Our discussion of the songs of the Dances of Universal Peace has already taken us into the realm of active meditation. Active meditation involves using a devise, such as sound, visualization, or a breathing practice, in order to attain a desired effect. If we wish to impress an image or quality upon ourselves, we may actively engage its symbolic representation. For instance, Sufis may use the wasifa, ya alim, to invoke the qualities of insight and wisdom. They may use ya wali to invoke the quality of mastery. A meditator may visualize a clear and sparkling stream moving from left to right before the mind's eye to promote creative thought. A Christian mystic can picture and contemplate the transfiguration of Christ as an aid to her own spiritual illumination.

One needs to develop the ability to concentrate before these types of active meditation become very powerful, but we can see that concentration and active meditation are cyclical in their development and build upon each other over time. In daily meditation it is helpful to use a set of meditative practices that strengthens your concentration, works with your psychological strengths and weaknesses, and produces deep-

158

ened states of consciousness. Good meditative practices work on all of these levels and more. That is why they have often been closely guarded secrets—these practices can be very powerful.

It is time to discuss altered states—or, more accurately, alternative states—of consciousness. Alternative states of consciousness are a vast topic that under the scientific paradigm is lumped into one small category, often dismissed as unverifiable. We have already touched on this topic when we discussed shamanic journeying and creative imagination, which require states of reverie that are different from our typical mental functioning. Meditation, however, presupposes various conditions of consciousness that differ from those underlying critical thought, reason, and sleep.

Alternative states of consciousness are achieved simply by attuning the consciousness to planes of existence beyond the physical reality we tend to focus upon in everyday life. These may be sublime states of communion with the sense of oneness and the "peace that passes all understanding" at the sixth plane, the profound experience of archetypal certainty at the fifth plane, the refined states of exalted emotion found in the fourth plane, and the flashes of illumination and intuition found on the mental plane, the third plane.

Many visionary experiences and states may be attributed to the various astral levels (the second plane) to which the consciousness can become attuned. There also exist dark levels of lower astral emotions that can be tapped into by those whose intentions are not evolution of consciousness but rather desires like domination and retribution. An experienced meditator or a person trained in shamanic practices can enter these lower planes to help others or to change his or her own emotional experience. The advanced meditator becomes capable of capable of altering the consciousness through the use of many active meditative practices in order to experience and subsequently accustom the consciousness to operate on virtually all levels which human consciousness can attain.

The ability to attain the sublime states of consciousness is a powerful tool of transformation, but it is not the transformation itself. In order to understand spiritual realization we must understand the difference between state and station. The term state refers to the forms of altered consciousness, such as the experience of sixth plane peace or fourth plane joy. When you have had such an experience, you are acquainted with a certain state of consciousness. You enter a new station when your life becomes transformed and is lived in an entirely new way, as experienced internally—it may look quite usual from the perspective of others. When your viewpoint becomes forever altered, you have entered a new station—not just an altered state.

We may experience many brief moments of realization and illumination, but a leap in spiritual realization occurs when our lives are changed by a radical shift in the way we see the world. This different viewpoint, our new station, is a result of anchoring our transcendent states of consciousness in our everyday lives. We may not look very different on the outside, but the changes in our qualitative experience will be radical. The old Zen saying "Before enlightenment, chop wood, carry water; after enlightenment, chop wood, carry water" is possibly the most accurate statement ever made concerning spiritual awakening. Often aspirants to realization ponder what it might feel like if they ever became enlightened. What is difficult to convey is that the internal transformations that preceded the experience of realization have been so profound that the personal ego that has been wondering will only barely be there to notice the change.

Passive Meditation

Passive meditation becomes far easier after one has trained the mind through concentration and active meditation. Passive meditation involves, in its most pure form, emptying and opening the mind. The goal of passive meditation is to enter a state of creative imagination, become open to inspiration and guidance, or even to enter the void of samadhi. There are techniques that are used in this process. One can passively watch the breath or stare at a blank wall in order to occupy the little part of the mind that one wishes to remain engaged.

While creative imagination can be entered into through direct intention, as in doing a soul retrieval in shamanic practice, it can also be the result of a passive opening to the unconscious process. Passive meditation opens the meditator to the creative, intuitive, and subconscious aspects of the self. It can be extremely creative and liberating, since it takes us beyond our normal expectations and limitations. Passive meditation can also be frightening for those who do not have sufficient control over their subconscious processes. People with psychological problems, poor ego boundaries, or traumatic backgrounds may be well advised to work with concentration and active meditation for quite some time before entering into the free-flow of consciousness that is the world of passive meditation.

We can see from our exploration of critical and rational thinking, creative imagination and meditation, that the mind can be used in a variety of useful ways. We are living during an era where for the first time in a long time we may be free to explore the usefulness of all of these mental activities, rather than needing to extol the virtues of one over the others. We should have no doubt that critical scientific and empirical thought is highly useful at exploring and describing the physical world around us. It is also very useful when seeking to manipulate the raw material of nature in order to make life easier for humanity, but it is less useful with regard to finding meaning in our lives.

Scientific empirical thought leaves little room for living in relationship with the planet, since it objectifies the material world and leaves no space for the existence of consciousness within nature. There can be little thought of an "I-thou" relationship with nature when it is robbed of the possibility of being a "thou." The scientific paradigm, which has helped humanity attain incredible heights of knowledge and dominance, has robbed us of relationship and isolated us from the rest of creation.

Creative imagination and meditation are alternative ways of using the human mental apparatus. They should not be seen as opposed to empirical and rational thought but rather as ways to combat the isolation and meaninglessness that emerge when nature and life are relegated to mechanical occurrences rather than joyous mysteries. There is no longer a need to submit the human spirit to the alternating dogmatisms of religion or science. We are entering a phase of human existence where freedom from the domination of such monolithic perspectives is the obvious answer.

We only need make a slight shift in our perspectives to see the inevitable answer to the dilemma of our alienated existence. The quantitative and qualitative both contain elements essential to human physical, psychological, and spiritual well-being, and we are fortunate to live in a time when the dominant myths of both religion and science are losing their grip on the human soul. A new integrated understanding of the workings of consciousness can lead to a much more meaningful life in relationship with the physical world without discounting or losing the capabilities of any of our potential ways of thinking and knowing.

TWELVE

Spiritual Practice with Breath

BREATH IS LIFE, and breath is our connection with the eternal. The mystery of breath has always been one of the most important secrets of spiritual development. Breath is not just the physical air taken in and expelled from the lungs; it is also our most tangible connection to the divine realms. The condition of our breath reflects our spiritual condition. By working with our breath we can directly influence both our spiritual and physical well-being.

From a purely physical perspective we cannot live without breathing. While we can live without food for quite a long time and water for a lesser, but still significant, period, we cannot live without breathing for more than three and a half minutes. Also from a purely physical perspective, the quality and quantity of breath we take in affects our bodies in very significant ways. Good, full, healthy breathing brings oxygen to all our vital organs, including our heart and brain, and expels toxins, such as carbon dioxide, from our bodies.

Athletes, especially martial arts practitioners, use harsh, strong breathing to mobilize energy (*ki* or *chi*), and quiet, centered, breathing to relax and concentrate. Psychotherapists may use diaphragmatic breathing techniques to help patients control stress and overcome anxiety. Breath may be used to improve performance and promote well-being in many

163

physical and psychological arenas. This chapter will focus on its paramount importance in spiritual practice.

Quality of Breath

When we discuss the quality of breath, we are referring to both the depth and the refinement of inhalations and exhalations. Deep, diaphragmatic, breathing ensures sufficient oxygen in the bloodstream and the expulsion of toxic gasses from the body. Deep breathing also quiets the body and mind. Shallow, thoracic breathing replicates stress reactions. If the breath is harsh, it mobilizes energy, and if it is weak, it leads to anxiety. Refined breathing, in other words quiet and gentle deep breathing, promotes calm, peaceful, and meditative states. In some cases, after years of meditation, all that is needed to enter a deep contemplative state is a gentle in-breath.

All types of breathing have their place in life. If we are engaging in heavy labor or a sport that requires explosions of physical power, we may breathe in an explosive way, like the grunts of tennis players when they hit the ball or the sharp screams of a black belt in karate as he breaks several boards with one punch. Other times we breathe rhythmically, as in swimming or tai chi. When we are concentrating on smaller, more detailed work, we sometimes hold our breath. In meditation we can watch or control our breathing in order to promote the quiet state we are seeking.

The most telling time to notice our breathing is when we are not doing any intensive physical activities. Pay attention to your breath when you are just sitting, watching TV, driving in your car, or sitting down for dinner. What is it like? Can you hear it rasp? Do you find yourself holding your breath? Is it irregular and uneven? Is it deep from your belly, or shallow from the upper part of your chest? All of these conditions relate to the quality of your breath.

Most of us, especially if we have not paid much attention to our breath in the past, will find that our breathing is not particularly rhythmic or deep. It will sometimes come in jerks or gasps, especially if we're a little older, and we may find ourselves holding our breath, and then having to make up for the held breath by gasping. Much of what typical members of an industrialized society experience in their day-to-day breathing is unhealthy physically, psychologically, and spiritually.

Breath and Consciousness

Before we can work effectively with consciousness, we have to heal and strengthen the vehicle of consciousness, our breath. Breath contains the etheric connection between the body and consciousness as well as that individualized portion of consciousness that is our Soul, and it is for this reason that breathing techniques have always been central to spiritual development. It is in the study of breath that we may find some of the most hidden of mysteries.

If we look at breath as not just the transfer of air between our body and our environment, but also a connection with the intangible realm of Soul, we will begin to grasp one of the mysteries of life. Consciousness doesn't exist within our brains—our brains processes conscious material. Consciousness is a level of reality that does not exist within our physical shell but is rather connected to us by our breath. When we work to deepen, strengthen, refine, and stabilize our breathing, we are deepening, strengthening, refining, and stabilizing our connection to that aspect of consciousness that is our Soul.

When we talk about consciousness, we are not talking about content, we are talking about capacity. Consciousness is the capacity to know; it is not what is known. By deepening and strengthening consciousness, we are creating more capacity to become aware. So working with breath is working with our capacity to learn and understand more about ourselves, the world, and the inner life.

Breath as Rhythm

Breathing is like the pendulum of a grandfather clock; if it swings in the proper rhythm the clock will function well. Breath can function to keep the body and mind in a healthy rhythm. Our Western culture promotes a chaotic rhythm, a rhythm that can make it nearly impossible to develop spiritually. From too long and too intense work schedules to frenetic leisure activities and the omnipresent electronic media, the rhythm of modern life is toxic to the refinement of consciousness and living in harmony with our surroundings. In the midst of this chaos, breath can provide an anchor.

It is a very difficult practice to stay in tune with our breathing as we move through everyday activities, but when we are able to watch our breath throughout the day, we can continually bring ourselves back to a quiet, masterful rhythm. The ideal breathing practice for most people would be to stay in touch with a continuous four-count inhalation and a four-count exhalation. Unless you have spent an entire lifetime doing breathing practices, it is virtually impossible to keep your attention upon your breathing all day. However, if you just bring your attention back to counting to four on your inhalation and again to four on your exhalation whenever you remember, you will make huge strides in creating a more conscious rhythm in your life. Maybe you will remember this practice ten times the first day, and then only six the second day, but if you continue watching your breath for months and years, you will be taking incredible steps toward mastering the chaos of your surroundings.

How to Use Breath in Meditation

Breathing is a natural rhythm of the body, and, along with the circulation of our blood, it is the most basic rhythm of life. Because of this we can use the natural inhalation and exhalation cycle as grounding for many meditations and visualizations. The "purification breaths" used by the Sufi Order of the West provide a good example of how we can combine the natural rhythm of breathing with visualizations to create a very beneficial spiritual practice. While the basics of this practice are always the same, the visualizations vary. I will share with you the way I normally like to do the practice.

The purification breaths are a practice given to every initiate into the Sufi Order and are also shared at many public workshops; the reader can feel comfortable in using this practice because it is suitable for all. The practice consists of four breaths, each repeated five times, each reflecting purification by a particular element.

The first breath is the earth breath, which is accomplished by breathing in through the nose and out through the nose. As you inhale you may imagine that you are a sturdy oak tree, with roots reaching deep into the earth. Your inhaled breath goes deep into your roots, where you are energized and nourished. As you exhale you draw the breath upwards, bringing nourishment throughout your body and imagining old, stale, or unwanted energy being expelled though your branches and leaves. The breath should be normal, not overly extended or held in any way. You should do this breath five times. With each breath you are working with the nourishment of the earth; allowing it to flow up through your body, carrying away impurities and stale, used energy.

The next breath is the water breath, which purifies the water element in the body. This includes our blood as well as our watery emotions. You may inhale through the nose and exhale through the mouth. As you inhale through your nose you draw your consciousness above your head and imagine a sparkling waterfall infused with sunlight. As you exhale through your mouth, you imagine the sparkling water from this waterfall descending through and over your body, washing away unwanted emotional issues and purifying the liquids of your body. You feel yourself infused with light that sparkles and cleanses. This is purification with spirit. Consciousness is filled with light, and the light washes away the stains of darkness in our being. Do this breath five times.

The fire breath is the third of the purification breaths. This breath purifies the energy of the body and the fiery emotions. With the fire breath you inhale through the mouth, with only slightly open lips, and out through the nose. As you inhale through the mouth you may imagine that your breath is a wind fanning a bonfire in your solar plexus. As you exhale through the nose, the fire turns to light as it moves upward and radiates from the heart in all directions. Your heart becomes like the sun, radiating its golden light into a growing circle around the body. This practice works to transform the passions into heart qualities and to infuse the practitioner with magnetism. This, as all breaths, is repeated five times.

The last elemental breath is the air breath. It is accomplished by breathing in through the mouth (again with only slightly open lips) and out through the mouth. As you inhale through your mouth you imagine yourself standing on a hill in a vast area of grasslands. You feel the wind blowing over your body, refreshing you and making you feel very alive. As you exhale through your mouth, you begin to identify with the wind, not your body, blowing through the waves of grass. Then upon the next inhalation you again feel your body and experience its aliveness. You should always finish the five breaths of this practice on the in-breath, to avoid getting spacey. The air breath is very useful for getting in touch with the vastness of consciousness. It is liberating, but as with all things that liberate, if not used in moderation and wisely, it can create confusion and a lack of being grounded in time and place.

The purification breaths can be done every day and are designed to bring balance into our lives. They have impact upon our bodies, minds, emotions, and spiritual development. There are those who say that by doing this practice every day, we can avoid colds, the flu, and many other nuisance illnesses. While I have found that there are exceptions to this statement, I believe that I have been physically and emotionally more healthy over the years, in part because of this practice.

The Breath "Swing"

A common way to use breath in meditation is to anchor key visualizations or thoughts in the inhalation and exhalation "swing" of breathing. Any key thought or insight can be linked to this natural rhythm and thereby locked into a concentration that can be done throughout the day. Let's look at a few examples.

Mystics often work with light. You can imagine drawing white light down from above your head as you inhale and exhaling golden light from your heart as you exhale. You could also imagine light of differing colors in the various energy centers. (The energy centers or chakras are generally seen as centers of the subtle body that are related to the body's nervous and glandular systems. They are explained more fully in chapter 13 on practices with sound.) You may inhale red light through the center at the base of the spine and exhale orange light from the center just below the navel. You may inhale blue light in and out through the throat center and violet light in and out through the third eye center.

There are many options when working with light and also many different perspectives on what colors belong to what centers. It is wise to be open to various schemas until you find one that works for you. Caution is also recommended when working with light and the breath, since these are very powerful practices and unbalanced flooding of light to certain centers can be harmful. It is important to strengthen heart qualities and to be well grounded before trying to develop power or psychic abilities.

Guided imagery, as discussed in chapter 11, can also be linked to the breath. Early in my career as a psychotherapist I learned to use guided imagery in various psychotherapeutic modalities. It was very useful in working with anxieties and in teaching people to relax. I was not taught to link the visualizations to the breath when I first learned these techniques. Later as I worked more with breathing practices in my own consciousness development, I began to link guided imagery to the breath and found that it was a far more powerful technique that way. Now whenever I lead people through a visualization exercise of any sort, I anchor it to the breath. It seldom fails to produce profound results.

We need not always learn specific visualizations with the breath from teachers or books. Some of the most helpful practices I have done came either spontaneously or as the result of very individual insights. At one point I felt a very profound connection with two historical figures, one male and one female. I found that by visualizing the man above my head to the right and the woman above my head to the left as I inhaled, then drawing them together in my heart as I exhaled, I was able to combine their central qualities into my vision for future growth. This conscious creation of the alchemical marriage of male and female was a powerful spur for my own deeper work with masculine and feminine energy.

The possibilities for using imagery with the swing of breath are unlimited. You will find unique images that speak to you, and you will be able to create highly individualized practice to propel you toward further growth.

Breath and Intuition

Breath is the part of us that is not exclusively located in our bodies; it flows and connects us with the subtle, spiritual worlds that exist around us as well as with other people. Breath may be used to explore the inner realities of the natural world around us, and it can help us to stay connected with loved ones. Mystics use the breath to intuit answers to questions; one notes which nostril is dominant at the moment and bases the answer on that. This method requires considerable knowledge and practice.

Refining the breath makes a person more intuitive, and when guiding a person either through therapy or spiritual guidance, it is useful to refine the breath as much as possible in order to be open to intuitions. This refinement of the breath helps one to become empathically tuned to another person. As a psychotherapist and as a spiritual guide, I have often used the attunement with a person's breath to receive guidance regarding the condition and the needs of that person. Each of us is unique and has different gifts, so it is best to find what works for you and use it, rather than to try to follow a set of instructions.

Alternate Nostril Breathing

Alternate nostril breathing is used in the Yogic tradition extensively; it is important in the Sufi tradition as well. Alternate nostril breathing involves alternately closing one nostril and breathing through the other in a sequential order. For example, one may take five breaths in through the right nostril and out through the left, then five breaths in through the left nostril and out through the right, and then five breaths in through both and out through both. This sequence is coupled with the holding of the breath for double the count of the inhalation

170

between the inhalation and the exhalation. This practice, as taught by the Sufi Order of the West, is known as *kasab*.

Alternate nostril breathing practices work to refine consciousness and open the energy passageways in the body. We need to be cautious with breathing practices such as these, since they are quite powerful and can evoke kundalini-related symptoms that can be quite disturbing. It is best to work with alternate nostril breathing in conjunction with a guide who is knowledgeable and skilled regarding breathing practices.

Breath is our connection to the infinite. Through breath we have a direct link to the inner realms. We can make significant gains in spiritual growth by being aware of the quality of our breath and by working to understand the meaning of our breath in its various conditions. It is not an exaggeration to state that if we continually stayed in touch with our breathing, we could know all that we need to know about life.

THIRTEEN

Spiritual Practice with Sound

"*IN THE BEGINNING was the Word, and the Word was with God, and the Word was God*" (John 1:1). Translation: everything is vibration and has its roots in undifferentiated Oneness. "*He was in the beginning with God; all things were made through him, and without him was not anything made that was made*" (John 1:3). Translation: the vast latent potential of undifferentiated vibration began to develop form, and all things came into existence in the field of time.

The wisdom contained in the above quotation from the Revised Standard Version of the Christian Bible is something that modern science has begun to understand, while mystics have spoken of it for thousands of years. At its root everything is vibration. What the mystic understands that most other people don't know is that the sounds that we make allow us to create new realities in very direct ways. The sounds in our lives affect us in powerful ways.

Whether we passively absorb the sounds of the world around us, or actively work to place certain types of sounds in our lives, our bodies, minds, emotions, and spirits are influenced by sound. Evidently this knowledge has been discovered by many cultures, as sound practices have been a part of almost all spiritual traditions around the world. Sound is the medium through which we all have the opportunity to act as the *Brahma*, the creative principle in our own lives. We can create the vibratory climate for the growth of our consciousness.

A second aspect of sound is meaning. I remember very early in my use of the Sufi sound practice of wasifa (mantra), I asked a more experienced practitioner, "Does this stuff work?" I could not quite comprehend how saying an Arabic word over and over would help my spiritual development. The answer that I got was, "Would you like to go sit in a corner someplace and repeat the word 'hate' over and over?" Then it made perfect sense to me.

Filling my mind with a word that means wisdom, mastery, healing, or light is certainly preferable to what is usually going through my mind. Even if vibration were not a factor in sound practices, meaning would be. If we look at what is normally filling our minds, anger with someone or something, habitual desires for bigger and better stuff (what I call the "wanting beast"), and of course doubts and fears, it becomes obvious that a positive thought would be a real relief.

In chapter 6, "Mastery," we discussed "roof-brain chatter," which is that constant monologue going on in our minds. Replacing that useless, often negative chatter with something more constructive often involves audibly creating sounds that over time impress themselves upon the mind and replace the chatter with what Sufis call *fikr*, the silent repetition of a sacred phrase. This is one of the secrets of repetition: once begun, it continues to go on of its own accord, replacing the less useful thoughts. Here we see a third use of sound, to impress the mind with an alternative, more useful habit.

Using Vibration to Change Consciousness

Chanting, singing, and repeating sacred words or phrases have long been used by religions and spiritual schools as part of their rituals, ceremonies, and contemplative traditions. If you were to ask a Christian minister, Jewish rabbi, Muslim mulla, or Hindu priest, you would get a variety of different answers to the question of why sound practices are so useful. They might discuss a sense of community that emerges from singing together, a sacred space that is created by chanting or singing together, or the creation of an emotional atmosphere involving joy, holiness, or love.

All of these answers would be true because all involve a change from the normal range of consciousness into a higher (more refined) or wider (more communal) range. There are reasons for these changes in consciousness that involve sound and group participation. These reasons involve the effect of vibrations on the energy centers of the body and the intention of the individuals and the group.

Sound and the Subtle Bodies

From an esoteric perspective, the repetition of various vowel sounds affects different energy centers in the etheric body of the individual. As we discuss the energy centers, it will be helpful for you to remember that there are several different systems for conceptualizing them. The Sufis most often refer to five centers, and the Yogis talk of seven; these traditions also recognize several additional lesser centers throughout the body. The system of sounds related to the centers that we will be exploring is one that I learned early in my studies and have found no reason to modify, even though there are others that are quite different than this one. The important thing is that you feel free to experiment in order to find the system that works best for you. This system has worked well for me.

Beginning at the second center, an inch or two below the navel, and moving upward to the crown center at the top of the head, certain sounds will tune and energize each center. People sometimes ask about the sound of the root *chakra* (center) at the base of the spine. Teachers have assigned various sounds to this center (the *muladhara chakra*), but there is little agreement about this center. I believe that the sound of the root center may be the inaudible sound of the body's functions, or possibly the sound of the earth rotating. Since we cannot reproduce these sounds intentionally, we must leave it up to the natural world to help with the center at the base of the spine. A wonderful practice is finding a quiet natural place in our environment and retreating to it briefly each day in order to bring this center, which relates to our physical existence, into harmony and health.

The sound that affects the second center, the *swadhisthana chakra,* is a sound often heard in Tibetan chanting. It is a low "ooo" sound. This center relates to sexuality and creativity in worldly activities. When this center is unhealthy we may have difficulty regulating our sexuality or may find it difficult to find creative outlets for our physical energies. Tuning the navel center allows us to move beyond preoccupations with sex and accomplishment, because we are comfortable in these areas of life. Western traditions don't use this sound often in their practices, presumably because the patriarchal traditions are uncomfortable with sexuality and worldly activities.

If you would like to work with this sound, there are some good chants from the Buddhist tradition. Try chanting *"Om mani padmi hum"* at the lowest pitch you can use. It literally means "jewel in the lotus" and refers to the sacred space at the center of the heart. There are many other sounds in this practice, like the "eee" sound of the third eye, the "ahhh" sound of the heart center, and the "mmm" of the crown, but the emphasis that we are discussing here involves a low "ooo" (as in hope) sound that occurs with the opening *Om* and runs underneath the rest of the sounds.

As we examine various practices, don't be overly concerned about "doing it right," but rather concentrate on letting the proper sound and the deeper meanings emerge. Experiment, listen to CDs of Tibetan monks chanting, and contemplate what the jewel of wisdom in your heart might be like. The practices will emerge through you as they are done and will be more effective than they would be if you tried to impose the perfect sound or meaning upon them. (One of my Sufi teachers used to say, "Let the practices 'do you.'") Seek the sound and meaning within.

The next center to work with is the solar plexus center, called the *manipura chakra* in yoga. The sound to work with this center is an approximation of "aiiee," as in a boisterous "Hi!" The third center is the power center. Power is a complicated quality, and power is needed to make anything happen in our lives. Yet power is also used to dominate others. Problems in this center can involve being unable to exert one's own power, being at the mercy of the energy of those around us, or having the need to dominate.

A practice related to the manipura chakra that you may want to work with is the Sufi wasifa "Ya Hayy." The Arabic words mean "Oh Thou Life" and are an affirmation of the One Life that lives within us all. Ya Hayy is one of the 99 Names of God in the Islamic religion. It is important to say "Ya Hayy" with a sense of love and the thought that you are creating within yourself an accommodation for the divine quality. This orientation applies to the use of all of the wasifas, and it will greatly increase the meaning of your practice. Many persons also find it powerful to know that these names have been used by Sufis for centuries to strengthen particular divine qualities in aspirants.

The heart center responds to the sound "aaahh" as in "Allah." In the Yogic tradition the heart center is referred to as the *anahata chakra*. As discussed in an earlier chapter, the heart is of crucial importance for spiritual progress. The heart center needs not only to be kept tuned, but it is a center that needs continual expansion and strengthening. Qualities like love, compassion, kindness, sympathy, empathy, and magnanimity are heart qualities.

There are many good practices to do that emphasize the "aahh" sound. Most names for the divinity involve this sound—think of God, Allah, and Brahma. Most mantras and sound practices from a wide variety of traditions use the "aahh" sound at some point in the practice. A good starting place is to intone the syllable "sa" over and over, just to stimulate the heart and work with feeling the sound in the center of the chest. Chanting the *Ramnam* might be the next step.

The Ramnam is the phrase *"Om, Sri Ram, Jai Ram, Jai, Jai, Ram."* It means "Victory to Rama" or as a Christian might say, "Glory to God." It has its roots in the Hindu epic poem, the Ramayana. Rama carries the meaning of a strong, good, and loving being whose power came from the heart, so saying "Victory to Rama" actually suggests that one is focusing on the strengthening of one's own heart qualities. When chanting the Ramnam, it is helpful to place emphasis on the "aahh" sound in the heart and to concentrate on the heart space.

When chanting the Ramnam you are also participating in a great modern tradition. Papa Ramdas and Mother Krishnabai kept this mantra going in their ashram in southern India as an attempt to ameliorate the troubles of the world for many years. When Papa Ramdas died, Mother Krishnabai kept the practice going at the ashram for at least another thirty years until she died in the early 1990s. Although we never had the opportunity to meet Papa Ramdas or Mother Krishnabai, Jan and I feel an affinity for them and their quiet, loving work.

The fifth energy center, the *vissudha chakra,* responds to the "uuu" sound, as in the word "food." The fifth center, located in the throat, relates to communication, self-expression, creativity, and receiving nurturing from the universe. This is a troublesome center in our Western society; many of us have difficulties in the areas of communication, self-expression, creativity, and higher forms of receptivity. This may not seem true until we understand that much of our self-expression is narcissistic and our communication, stifled, manipulative, or in service of only our image.

We may live in the communication age, but that does not mean that our communications is healthy. There is just a lot of it. This center is also involved in states involving feelings of holiness and reverence, which relate to the ability to tune into higher energies and to receive the nurturing of the universe. The vissudha chakra is often represented in mystical drawings as a cup or chalice, the receptacle of the sacred.

You may want to use the practice *Ya Hu,* which means "the divine presence." *Ya* means roughly "O Thou," and *Hu* means "divine presence," so that when you speak, chant, or sing these words you are saying, "O Thou, Divine Presence." You are calling the ineffable presence into your life. This is a powerful practice and should be done with a sense of awe. Start by singing the words sweetly. Allow the feeling of sweetness to grow, and pay attention to what other, possibly more subtle emotions begin to emerge. Later, once you have worked with sweetness for a while, you can begin to work with the overtones, which can open up another new realm of experience. Working this way with the "uuu" sound can also have a strong purification effect, since another important aspect of the fifth center is purification.

The sixth center has often been called the *third eye* because of its location between the brows, above the eyes. In India it is called the *ajna chakra*. Another way to describe it is as the wisdom center. The sound that corresponds to the ajna chakra is "eee" as in "tea." Tuning the sixth center increases insight, intuition, discernment, clarity, and understanding. It is a center that cuts through illusion like a laser, opening inner vision to what is hidden. This sort of knowledge is beyond sentiment and is therefore not fooled by emotional subterfuge. The third eye can clearly see when the emperor has no new clothes, even though all around us are remarking about how beautiful they are.

Because of this emotionally detached clarity, working with the sixth center can promote an insufferable sense of superior knowledge, unless we also engage the heart qualities of compassion, sympathy, and love. That is why practices for awakening the third eye are often given in tandem with practices to strengthen heart qualities. Without engaging the heart, an awakened third eye may lead one to an aloof attitude and a lonely existence.

A very good tandem practice for working with the wisdom center and strengthening the heart at the same time is the wasifa, Ya Alim, pronounced "aleem," which means "O Thou, Wisdom," followed by Ya Wali, pronounced "walee," which means "O Thou, Mastery." This was the first practice that I received when I was initiated into the Sufi Order of the West many years ago, and it continues to be important to me. If you would like to use these practices, you could begin by repeating Ya Alim thirty-three times. Then you repeat Ya Wali thirty-three times, and finally you repeat them together thirty-four times for a total of 100 repetitions. (This is a gentle way to begin; there are many variations of these practices.)

The "eee" sound in each of the words, if pronounced correctly, can be felt from the pallet of the mouth up into the forehead. It is preceded in each word by the "ahh" sound, which evokes heart qualities; the "mmm" sound at the end of the word, *Alim,* vibrates in the crown, adding a transcendent quality. The transcendent quality helps us remain somewhat detached from what we see, and believe me, once we begin to see more clearly there is far more need for detachment.

179

I have done the above practice, in addition to many others, for well over twenty years, and it continues to unfold new layers of meaning. The sound also continues to unfold. I started doing the practice by following my teacher's example and using a falsetto singing of the "eee" sound. Soon I discovered the sound wanted to occur on my pallet with more of an "ng" component to it, and soon I was concentrating primarily on the overtones I was creating. (The overtones tend to deepen or lift the consciousness and also have an impact on the physical body.)

After several years of doing and teaching the practice, I began to be able to create an internal buzz as I closed the "mmm" in "Alim." The soft buzz seems to occur at a point directly behind my eyes, at about the middle of my head, which is the position of the pineal gland, which many say is directly related to the sixth energy center. If you choose to experiment with this practice, you should have patience, experiment with the sounds, and make sure you work with the heart as well.

At this point it you may be noticing that the "mmm" in the crown center seems to have a close relationship with the "eee" in the third eye. In my experience, the sixth and seventh centers are closely related. They may even be seen as two aspects of one phenomenon. The heart and solar plexus have a similar relationship. It appears that when properly tuned, the solar plexus draws and stores energy from the environment that is used by the heart in the forms of giving, loving, caring, courage, and similar heart qualities.

When the heart and solar plexus are not properly connected and tuned, people act from the energy of the solar plexus, devoid of heart qualities. At this point the heart is starved of energy and cannot function properly. In the case of the third eye and crown centers, it appears that the crown touches vast perspective, and the third eye channels the perspective into our perceptions of daily life. I see these two centers as performing the one function of wisdom. It is even possible to look at each of these pairs of centers as one center with points of intake and outflow. With that in mind we can look at the seventh center.

The crown center, or *sahasrara chakra,* is located at the top of the head. It relates to transcendence and consciousness beyond the limited. The crown center also relates to spiritual freedom. It is detached from the cultural and worldly aspects of the personality and is the point at which we open to consciousness of eternity. As we noted before, the "mmm" sound is helpful in attuning to the crown center energies. In addition to Ya Alim, another good practice is the Sanskrit word *aum*. This is a word that includes the heart sound, "ahh," the throat sound, "uuu," and the sound that tunes the crown center, "mmm." According to the Hindu tradition, aum is the seed sound, the essential vibration behind all others.

Receiving and Doing Sound Practices

Sound practices have always been an important part of spiritual training. Aspirants are given a particular practice in order to concentrate on a seed thought or quality, as well as to attune to a vibratory pattern beneficial to certain changes in consciousness. The key to working with sound involves receiving the correct guidance about what practices to do. If we were to choose our own practices, most of us would pick practices to strengthen certain qualities that interest us or that we think would benefit us in some way. It is often the case that these are not the best practices to help us reach our goals. Our blind spots are usually what hold us back more than anything, and it is often a blind spot that can be seen by a spiritual guide. The spiritual guide can suggest practices that can help students move past their blind spots.

What if you don't have a spiritual guide? There are some basic sound practices that won't get you in trouble but will be of help until you can find a nonexploitive relationship with someone who can help you with choosing practices. These are some practices from the Hindu tradition:

Aum—The seed sound.

Om nama shivaya—Invoking the Shiva (divine) within (a strong purification practice).

Om sri ram jai ram jai jai ram—Victory (or glory) to the Rama (divine) within.

Practices from the Buddhist tradition include:

Gate, gate, paragate, parasamgate, bodhi, svaha—Gone, gone, gone beyond. Gone beyond the beyond. Awakening.

Om mani padme hum—Hail to the jewel in the heart of the lotus.

Namo Amida Bhutsu—Invoking the Amida Buddha.

Basic practices from the Sufi tradition that you might try are:

Ya Faz'l—O Blessings.

Ya Hadi—O Divine Guide.

Ya Alim—O Wisdom.

Ya Vakil—O Guardian Angel.

Practices from the Christian tradition include:

Alleluia—Praise be to God.

Kyrie Eleison—God have mercy.

Any of these practices, and more, can be repeated to begin the process of using the vibration and meaning of sound to transform the psyche. Remember that meaning is like an iceberg—most of it is below the surface, waiting to be discovered. Both sound and meaning are latent potentials seeking to be brought to the surface. The more you work with them the more they will emerge and modify your consciousness.

When I first started using sound practices, I doubted that they would be of any use at all. It did not take long for me to realize just how effective sound practices are. After working with my first sound practices for several months, I began to notice a qualitative change in my thought patterns, emotions, and receptivity to inspiration. Since ancient times priests, healers, saints, contemplatives, shamans, magicians, and sorcerers have used sacred or "power words" to focus their consciousness on the changes they wished to make in themselves or their environment.

When doing sound practices we should repeat the word or phrase consciously. The biblical injunction to avoid "vain repetitions" refers to a trap we need to attempt to avoid. We are attempting to replace our normal vibratory level with one that is consciously chosen. We are wishing to place a seed thought at the center of our mental activity. Imagine a year when the primary thought at the center of your consciousness, when at rest from other activities, is a quality like mastery or wisdom. What an incredible change from the usual! The ultimate intention when we are working with sound is that eventually the practices will do themselves; we may discover that whenever we free our minds, the practices are humming along.

Experimenting with Sound

Whenever we work with sound we need to forget about doing it "right" and just play with the sounds. Experiment with creating vibrations in different parts of your body and creating overtones if possible. Meditation and spirituality is experiential, not theoretical. It is important to pay attention to how sounds affect you. You might ask yourself, "What changes do I notice in my emotions and consciousness as I perform the practices?" Some practices produce changes that are noticeable quickly, perhaps within two or three weeks. Other practices take longer and produce more subtle changes.

One of the givens on the spiritual journey is that other people generally notice the changes in us before we are aware of them. You may find people asking you what you are doing to become more peaceful, more assertive, more gentle, or more compassionate. That may be the first time you realize that you really are changing. The best approach is simply to do the practices with patience and with an open heart; the changes will follow.

FOURTEEN

Spiritual Retreat

PROGRESS ALONG THE path of consciousness is difficult, if not impossible, without time-out from our often far too busy lives. We who live lives in the world, not in the protected spaces of monasteries or *ashrams,* are constantly being pulled into out-of-balance, unconscious living conditions. We often work longer hours under more hectic conditions than is healthy for us. The technology of our time keeps our minds preoccupied with trivial matters and leaves little time for quiet reflection. Societal expectations leave no room for wandering mendicants or holy people, supported by alms. Time for thinking, reflecting, and meditating is an increasingly precious commodity.

Periodically we must make time work for us, rather than continually being subject to its dictates. This can happen during spiritual retreat. Retreat is the setting aside of an extended period of time, usually from three to forty days, to devote entirely to spiritual practice. Practices with sound, breath, and light, as well as meditation and the experience of the natural world are the primary activities during retreat. Simply relaxing the overworked mind and body is a vital aspect of a meaningful retreat.

There are many different methods of conducting retreats, depending upon the tradition the retreatant is following, but all require solitude and meditation. I have heard some members of the exoteric clergy talk about getaways where they golfed or played tennis as a retreat, but from my perspective this is a vacation and not a retreat. Sometimes, however, after one has done many retreats, just getting away creates a retreat space, even when it is not intended. This has happened to Jan and me fairly often. While it may sometimes be inconvenient, it is evidence of the truth that our lives follow the dictates of our deepest intentions, whether or minds know what is happening or not!

Retreats generally follow a pattern, in spite of the fact that they are conducted in a variety of ways, using many different techniques. Change has a pattern, and because retreat is about creating the conditions for change and growth, there are certain constants that will be found. For those who are seeking profound change through spiritual practice, retreat is a balm for the soul. Retreats are essential for growth at key points along the path. Some steps are hard to take until we can withdraw from our everyday experiences sufficiently to make room for profound change. Taking time for a retreat interrupts the usual patterns of our lives and allows new energies to enter to create the beginnings of change and renewal.

Withdrawal from the Mundane

The act of intending to do a retreat begins the process of the retreat. Sometimes you begin to experience changes in your consciousness a week or two before you actually begin the official retreat. For instance you may find yourself more sensitive to external stimuli, or you may find that your dreams begin to change. Once you arrive at your retreat site (it is essential to do your retreat away from your normal surroundings, if at all possible), you will accelerate the process of disengaging from your everyday experiences, but it will take a while.

Depending on how long a retreat you are doing, you can allow the process of disengagement to develop slowly and profoundly, or you may need to accelerate the process with selected spiritual practices. As you take time to reflect upon your life, you will often find yourself dwelling upon ways in which you have failed to live up to your expectations of yourself. It is often necessary to work with forgiveness (of self as well as others) and letting go during this phase. This phase is sometimes called the "examination of conscience." It may be a profound experience.

In addition to withdrawing from your usual surroundings, you will also have to disengage from the typical rhythm of your life. Retreat will pull you into a natural rhythm, or it will not be a retreat. Most of us normally have no idea of what a natural rhythm is, and therefore we may resist our natural rhythm as it begins to emerge. It is this natural rhythm that will do the most profound work of the retreat; it must be accepted eventually if you are to attain the most profound results.

Immersion in the Retreat Process

The next step in the typical retreat process is to become fully involved in the rhythm and activities of the retreat. This may sound a bit contradictory, as a retreat is truly about letting go of wanting to make things happen. It is about placing ourselves in the hands of the process of spiritual growth and accepting what happens. Any hint of striving or need for accomplishment destroys the purpose of the retreat. Surrender to the process and acceptance of whatever emerges is the hallmark of immersion in the retreat.

Spiritual practices used while immersing ourselves in the retreat are the types of practices that clear the mind. The immersion phase is a time when we withdraw from the social world and enter the quiet inner world of the psyche. During this phase the mind is cleared of mundane thinking and becomes involved in meditative themes and practices. Depending upon the length of the retreat, many hours or days may be spent clearing the mind, the emotions, and even the body of impediments to spiritual growth.

Exploring Heights and Depths

After clearing out and letting go of excess baggage, you move toward the apex of the retreat. This takes energy, so practices that create spiritual energy are useful in propelling the consciousness forward. Sufis use various forms of the *zikr* to deepen and speed up the process, and there are many other means to achieve this movement. As you go deeper into the retreat, you begin to enter rarified states of consciousness that provide you with perspective and insight into the workings of both the outer and inner worlds. This does not necessarily refer to the altered states of consciousness related to visions or knowledge of unseen worlds, although that is possible. Often the most rarified states of consciousness feel quite normal; it is only the perspective that is very different from usual.

During my thirty-day retreat in Bali I spent a couple of weeks in one of the most profoundly normal states I have ever experienced, and yet I have never been so "high" in my life. These states of consciousness are hard to explain; while you are immersed in them, even the very unusual seems quite normal. The heights of consciousness and the depths of consciousness are profoundly normal states, when the psyche has been properly prepared.

Some spiritual practitioners, especially those from monotheistic paths, talk about getting high. Other practitioners, such as those involved with natural religions or the Jungian perspective, talk about going deep. What is the difference between high and deep? Some of the difference depends upon a person's concepts, like seeing the spiritual as being above and the demonic as being below. Some of the difference also depends upon one's inner experience of the worlds of the depths and the heights.

For me, the higher experiences are those where we experience liberation from biocultural restraints and can allow our consciousness access to wisdom and understanding that transcend our bodies, emotions, and cultures. We may experience realms of light and glory, great joy, deep peace, vast understanding, the boundless ocean of consciousness, and other glimpses of the nature of Reality.

At the summit of the retreat, some may experience an almost total detachment from the emotions and even the ordinary workings of the mind. While "going up" or "coming down" from the high place, many people experience visions, dreams, or simply a deep knowing about their purposes in life. A sense of profound connectedness with both the Oneness and the multiplicity of life is usually part of the experience. We *know* that we are connected with everything and everyone, as the wave is part of the ocean.

Depth experiences generally involve deep understanding of self and others and the natural world. These experiences may be even harder to describe than the height experiences, as they may be felt on a level completely beyond words. We may experience the depth of our souls, or we may feel a powerful kind of "realness." In my experience neither of these worlds is better than the other. Fullness of understanding and wisdom involves both the heights and depths of experience, and some of these experiences are inaccessible except during times of spiritual retreat.

Grounding Insight in Your Life

After probing the heights and depths of consciousness you have the potential to return to your life with a vast, new perspective. The next stage of the retreat process involves applying the insights gained during the retreat to your everyday life. It is a time for looking at your life and evaluating it from your newly emerging perspective. If you see that there is an issue that is plaguing you that could be changed by a different way of approaching it, it is at this point that you can plan and visualize how you might solve the problem. If you see that your priorities are out of sync with your spiritual nature, you can plan ways to make your life more congruent. You may be able to identify a latent quality that you may be able to develop in order to move forward with your life.

This phase of the retreat is about perspective. At this point you are closest to your true nature, and from this place you can bring the perspective of your true nature to bear upon any life issue you wish. You can ground your new insights in your everyday life, making them solid and real. This process marks the beginning of personal transformation.

The Pledge and Integration

The goal of a spiritual retreat, like the goal of the spiritual journey, is to become more fully human. The purpose of life is not to leave it but rather to become more fully alive and conscious. Retreat is the process of taking some time to order our priorities, explore our consciousness, and harmonize with the rhythm of life. The ultimate purpose is to return to your life more fully yourself than before, better able to keep your consciousness in tune.

As I end a retreat I like to make a pledge to myself that I will make certain significant changes based upon insights gained during the retreat. I usually use two practices that have significance for me. The first practice I use comes from the Zoroastrian tradition. As I have learned it, the early Zoroastrians pledged each day to fight for light over darkness, wisdom over ignorance, good over evil. The pledge involved saying "I will!" The "I will" means that "I will fight for light over darkness, I will fight for wisdom over ignorance, I will fight for good over evil." At the end of a retreat I often say "I will" 101 times, indicating that I will make the changes in my life needed to make the realizations of my retreat part of my everyday existence.

A parallel practice often used in Sufi retreats is the Arabic phrase *Ya Fatah,* which means, "O Opener of the Way." Using this phrase is asking for the way to be opened in order to make the needed changes in your life. You need to be careful with the timing of this practice, however, as it is powerful and can have the effect of opening doors prematurely. The best time to use Ya Fatah is when you sense that you are just on the brink of a new beginning in your life, and you need a little push to finish opening the door to that new phase. The practice is often said with a concentration on the heart center, with the thought of opening the heart to the next chapter in your life.

When to Do a Retreat

Doing a retreat is a powerful message to the self. It tells our entire being that we will not settle for business as usual. Choosing to do a retreat is choosing to change our life. Retreats are spiritual markers;

they initiate and mark major leaps forward in the development of our consciousness. The question then becomes when we should do a retreat. How do we know the time is right to initiate growth?

In my case I did three-day to six-day individual guided retreats each of my first three years as an initiate and then alternated individual and group retreats about every other year over the next ten years. For about two years toward the end of this period, I belonged to a study group that met about six times a year to delve deeply into the teachings of the Sufi Order in a retreat-style format. This series was capped by a thirty-day retreat in a coconut grove overlooking the Indian Ocean in Bali, Indonesia.

This long retreat was done with Jan and was dedicated not only to individual growth but also to our spiritual partnership. My last formal retreat was a Sufi Order leaders' retreat, held in the California Sierras, at which time we decided to take a sabbatical from Sufi Order activities and pursue our own realizations. That was about two years after the Bali retreat. Since that time Jan and I have done several less formal retreats, typically in the mountains of Colorado, Wyoming, or Montana. Many people on spiritual paths do not have the opportunity to do retreats as often as I have had, and I consider it a great gift that I have been able to devote as much time as I have to the retreat process. I am certain that these opportunities have had the effect of accelerating the changes that have occurred in my consciousness.

I have shared the timing of my retreats because it shows the sort of pattern that works for many. Doing several early retreats was an effective way to put a halt to some of my old patterns and open new vistas for personality growth. Having grown up in a family of mystics, I have always sought spiritual insight, but I had become quite immersed in physical preoccupations by the time I committed to a spiritual path. I could have easily continued my way of life, which was fine on the surface but devoid of depth.

The early retreats shattered my complacency and forced me to grow. As I look back at where I was going before my initiation and retreats I shudder, because it is not at all who and where I wanted to be. It was initiation that set me on the road to where I am today, but the early retreats were what broke the old habits and created new possibilities.

The later retreats were useful in several ways. They provided respite from the artificial ways of living that too easily become habitual in everyday life. Later retreats allowed me to explore more deeply the vastness of consciousness as well as my own psyche. Especially important was the periodic tuning of my consciousness. It seems that change in consciousness often happens in a lightning-like way. First there is a dramatic leap forward, often while on retreat; then over time consciousness loses some of its gains and becomes a bit more gross. It never quite falls back to its previous state, however, so the starting point for the next leap forward is a little farther along than the last.

My last two retreats while in the Sufi Order, thirty days in Bali and the leaders' retreat in California, brought about a depth and clarity that showed me an entirely new aspect of consciousness and spirituality. Retreats never end when we simply go home. They play themselves out for months and even years afterward. I am certain that this book is the culmination of those retreats done over ten years ago.

The answer to when we should do a retreat is both simple and complex. If you have good inner guidance, then the answer is, anytime you can. The synchronicity of opportunity combined with the intention to change is all you need. There are some pivotal points in our lives when all of us need a boost to the next level of consciousness, and this, too, is a sign that a retreat might be needed. The only warning needed here is that if you are seeking to do a retreat in order to run from issues your life is presenting you, or if you are continually going on retreat rather than living a life, you need to take care of your life first and then go on retreat.

Who Leads Retreats?

One of the most difficult aspects of making a retreat is finding a place to do it and someone to help lead the process. Typically by the time individuals are ready to do a retreat they have committed to a path and have avenues open for finding guides who lead retreats in the traditions they are following. However, as people begin to seek spiritual growth outside the traditional schools tied to dying patriarchal traditions, there will be a need for more generic retreat possibilities to be developed.

There are currently esoteric traditions that are quite capable of providing deep inner experiences that are either not tied to patriarchal traditions or are fairly progressive in their approaches. I feel comfortable in suggesting that anyone interested in doing a retreat should discuss the possibility with a recognized teacher or guide associated with any of the following groups. These groups have proven both their integrity and their depth of knowledge of the retreat process. It is still important, however, to check the credentials and references for any retreat guide and to follow your own intuition regarding the individual's suitability as a guide for your retreat.

The Sufi Order of the West has developed the *alchemical retreat* process. This retreat process follows the *solve et coagula* alchemical pattern. This means that we dissolve our old nature and are then put back together in a new way. Most of my retreats have been with the Sufi Order and have followed this pattern. There is a branch of the Sufi Order that is charged with developing and leading retreats, so there are always people available to lead retreats.

The retreat process, however, is one that not everybody should undertake. People who grapple with certain types of serious psychological problems might find their problems becoming worse during the process of a retreat. For this reason a good retreat guide will want to get to know you before being willing to lead your retreat. As a matter of fact, if guides don't check you out, you should be concerned about their credentials.

One way to get to know a guide is to take a weekend workshop with her or him. Not only will you have an opportunity to see whether this is a guide that you can trust, but the teacher will also be able to evaluate the possibility of guiding an individual retreat for you, or they may recommend someone who will. The weekend workshops led by Sufi teachers often provide benefits similar to a retreat, but they are a little less intense. These workshops might be a good way to begin.

The Foundation for Shamanic Studies does intensive workshops that are similar to retreats. A weekend workshop on shamanism could be a reasonable alternative or precursor to a longer retreat for individuals who are deeply attuned to nature as a spiritual path. Foundation teachers do longer workshops, which may involve a retreat-like process; their Basic Shamanism course is a prerequisite to all their other offerings. I have found the workshops I have done with teachers from the Foundation for Shamanic Studies very helpful and suggest that people who have spent a lot of time studying the patriarchal sky gods could balance their understanding with a course in shamanism. If the two teachers that I studied with are good examples of the type of leadership found at the Foundation, they are also ethical and trustworthy.

My suggestion to most people would be to start with the above sources, simply because I know firsthand of their trustworthiness. If you are attuned to a more cerebral path, you might look into the possibility of finding a Buddhist retreat center or guide. I have not done a Buddhist retreat myself (although I did the Kalachakra Initiation with the Dalai Llama), but I respect the tradition. Buddhists have for the most part avoided the "our god is better than your god" dualism of the West and have preserved a strong inner tradition. If I were going to do a Buddhist retreat, however, I would get to know some local teachers, and then when I was ready to do a retreat I might hop on a plane for Katmandu, Bangkok, or Dharmsala. Many Westerners do retreats at centers and monasteries near these cities, and while life can be hard in these places, the retreats can be transforming. There are a number of Buddhist centers in other areas as well that are known to offer fine retreats.

Another place that has offered a marvelous variety of retreats from many different traditions is the Lama Foundation, located near Taos, New Mexico. The Lama Foundation has been in existence for over thirty years and has a track record of providing quality retreats with respected and powerful spiritual teachers. I have visited Lama, and Jan has attended several fine retreats there.

Many Christian monasteries and retreat centers also offer individual retreats. Scattered around the country, these groups sometimes offer guided retreats, and sometimes they simply provide a quiet, peaceful place where you may create your own retreat. Most of these retreats are not designed to take the individual as deep as those described earlier, but they tend to be more easily accessible for many people.

There are many other excellent retreat opportunities not mentioned here, but these suggestions will give readers who are not in contact with spiritual groups that offer retreats a place to start. We need to remember that the time for blind faith in gurus, lamas, murshids, and priests is over, but people who have walked the inner paths before us are still important when it comes to teaching us the ABCs of transforming consciousness. Once you have done several retreats, you may find that inner-world sources begin to lead you and outer guides are no longer necessary, but in the meantime it is helpful to find elder brothers and sisters who can show the way.

FIFTEEN

Nature and the Natural Rhythm of Life

"IMAGINE NOT, THINK not, analyze not, meditate not, reflect not, keep in the Natural State" (Power, 1993: 56). These six rules of Tilopa may make little sense to today's Western mind, but they contain some of the most hidden (and rejected) of truths. We are not able to live by these words in the modern world, and because of the changes in human consciousness during the last several hundred years, we would not expect ourselves to. Yet, this stillness of mind and harmony with nature is a part of our human potential and needs not to be lost. We have great need of deep communion with the natural world and also of finding our natural rhythm, which are just two of the many nuances of Tilopa's words.

These essential but rapidly fading aspects of consciousness need to be integrated into our full potential and not relegated to memories of past, supposedly more primitive, human experience. Consciousness evolves not in order to forget the past, but rather to build the human of the future upon the foundation of previous understanding. We need not relinquish our intuitive, holistic, natural minds in order to add the rational analytic mind; we can have both. The concept that we are either one or the other is misleading. We need to begin remembering that nature is the greatest teacher and contains the keys to wisdom. Without an attunement to nature and the ability to quiet our

197

rhythm, we keep ourselves estranged from nature, the most important source of wisdom.

Nature and Consciousness

The most problematic of all the patriarchal perspectives is the divorcing of spirituality from nature. The idea that an invisible otherworld is more important, and indeed more pure, than the natural world is not only destructive of our ability to grow, but it is also simply untrue. The natural world is the source of our physical life and a tonic for our heart, mind, and soul. Nature is a world of balance, harmony, and beauty, sometimes an awesome and terrible beauty, but beauty nonetheless. When we spend time in nature, especially "wild" nature, our bodies, minds, and souls can become balanced and harmonious with our surroundings.

Some who live or spend a lot of time in natural surroundings can become attuned to the harshness of nature, and for this reason we often find some fairly rough-edged people living in natural environments. Others can live or visit the same natural environments and resonate with the vastness and beauty of the environment. Like often attracts like, and rough-edged people harmonize with the survival-of-the-fittest aspects of nature, whereas more sensitive individuals harmonize with the beauty and interrelatedness of life.

Nature contains all that is needed for any temperament. Whatever we seek we can find in nature. The survivalist will find independence and self-reliance in the wilderness, while the environmentalist will see the interrelatedness of Gaia, and the mystic will encounter the Divine. Nature, like all real things, does not have an opinion; it simply is. This is what makes it so difficult for patriarchal adherents to understand the sacredness of nature, as they want only goodness or that which agrees with their definition of good. They want a conception of reality that agrees with their perspective—not a neutral conception. Nature supports life but is neutral when it comes to our values and opinions, and that is not tolerated well by some.

Nature is more than just physical objects like trees, grasses, bushes, animals, and birds. Nature is the web of conscious life that connects the entire natural world. When I am in the wilderness I not only enjoy the beauty, I also feel the inner life of all that surrounds me. It is the energy and inner life of nature that nurtures my soul, just as the beauty nurtures my heart. Some places, where there have been relatively few unconscious people tramping around, still feel full of natural energy. Other places, though still beautiful, have endured the never-ending visits of people who have disregarded the spirits of the natural world; these sad places now feel depleted and dead. It is up to us who visit forests, wild areas, beaches, and national parks, to treat them with respect. These places are certainly as sacred as any cathedral, temple, or mosque and need to be approached with equal regard if they are to retain the power that naturally belongs there.

Practices in Nature

Nature is its own practice, and so we do not necessarily need to do special spiritual practices when in nature. Sometimes, though, it is helpful to do some practices just to get ourselves in the proper mind set to receive the bounty that nature has to offer. We may enhance our experience by preparing our consciousness to receive the more subtle and mysterious aspects of the natural world. This kind of preparation is a way of declaring our intention to partake in the beauty and inter-connectedness of our surroundings, instead of concentrating upon the survival issues.

Key to Success

I often do the purification breaths discussed in chapter 12 when embarking upon a short stroll or a day hike in the wilderness. I usually can find a large tree to aid my concentration for the earth breath. Then a stream or pool of water, or possibly even a waterfall will help my concentration on the water breath. Sunlight filtered through the trees or reflecting off a lake is a wonderful stimulus for the fire breath, and the air breath is very appropriate in a meadow, on a hill, or by a vista point on a trail. After doing this practice I feel better tuned to the elements and the elementals that infuse the natural environment with life.

The best practice to do in nature, however, is to be quiet and watch and listen with a sense of love and connectedness. From my experience

199

there is always a resonance between the inner processes and the natural environment. What I need to know about life is often answered by synchronicity through nature. Maybe more important is that my deepest identity and the rhythm of life I need to adopt can be communicated in natural places, if I will only slow down and watch and listen.

Many of my most profound spiritual experiences have happened in natural settings and were often heralded or punctuated by natural events. It is not surprising that transformations of consciousness are often associated with wanderings in the wilderness. The Buddha gained enlightenment while sitting under a tree, and Jesus' forty-day retreat in the wilderness preceded his ministry. These stories recognize that human teachings can only take us so far; the most profound growth often happens while in relationship with the natural world.

While nature is always instructive, my strongest experiences in nature usually occur with the sudden appearance of an animal or bird. Eagles or hawks fly over at just the right time, usually right after I have said or thought something that needs an exclamation point from nature. Animals that represent certain qualities sometimes appear to herald the development of a needed quality.

Over twenty-five years ago, a wonderful fourteen-point stag appeared while I was leading a meditation walk for the public at a nature preserve. We were in a meadow of tall grasses when the large stag leaped out of the dense forest about ten feet in front of me, looked me in the eyes for a couple of seconds, and then bounded off in the opposite direction. It was a startling and awe-inspiring experience and one (although I didn't know it at the time) that announced a leap forward for me in the development of my heart qualities.

My list of these synchronistic experiences is too long to recount, but a few more might be useful. A series of these experiences seem to have been tied to the desperate need for us humans to notice and to do something about the tragic condition of the natural world, even though they also have meaning on a host of other levels. There was the coyote, either stunned or in an altered state of consciousness, walking down the middle of a high pass on Trail Ridge Road in the Colorado Rockies. He headed directly toward the place where Jan and I were standing, just when we were sadly noticing the way in which the multitude of tourists was devastating the high alpine meadows. There was the emaciated fox that we kept running into while walking on the outskirts of our small town. His presence in that area seemed unnatural; too many humans had been invading his territory.

One late summer a peacock, apparently escaped from confinement somewhere, kept looking into and pecking at the sliding screen door of our house in the Midwest countryside. The most interesting creature may have been a seemingly possessed ground squirrel that invaded our campsite in the Jemez Mountains west of Los Alamos, New Mexico. This fellow kept us entertained for hours, but his demeanor suggested a problem; later we learned of the serious environmental issues in the area.

Dozens of hawks, deer, wild turkeys, stray cats and dogs, snakes, hummingbirds, butterflies, dolphins, bears, and other marvelous creatures have entered our lives to bring messages and have left just as quickly. Nature is infinitely creative in both its messages and messengers. Obviously the meaning of these events is imputed by our own consciousness, but when we are aware of the interconnectedness between our inner worlds and the outer world, synchronistic events may become our most reliable teachers

The Rhythm of Life

The most unnatural aspect of our lives is not necessarily living in cities, working in offices, and living separately from our communities. These contribute to artificial lives of isolation and despair, but it is the rhythm and pace of our lives that does the most damage. First of all, we humans function best when there is a balance in our lives. Second, we each have a pace that is good for us, and we cease to function well when we stray from that pace.

Balance

It does us little good to meditate if the rest of our life is out of balance. Finding a reasonable balance of activity and rest, accomplishment and surrender, and time devoted to physical, emotional, mental, and spiritual well-being is what is required to develop a balanced life. Balance may be the ultimate spiritual practice. If we have sufficient mastery to create a balanced life in the middle of our chaotic postmodern world, we can certainly become self-realized and conscious individuals. That, however, is a very big *if.*

What do we need to do in order to bring balance to our lives? First of all, we must recognize our needs. We need rest as well as activity. We need to let go sometimes and recognize our limitations, just as we sometimes need to persevere to accomplish our desires. We need to honor the needs of our bodies, minds, and souls. When we recognize who we are and what we need, we are in a better position to ensure a balance among our needs. The first obstacle to overcome is a lack of self-awareness. Our lack of self-awareness is aided, abetted, and in reality promoted by cultural institutions; realigning our lives to focus on our true needs might not be perceived as being good for the economy or the politicians.

Second, we need to understand the nature of the pressures based upon cultural expectations that we must endure. Even when we know what we need, the familial, professional, or financial demands of our lives may require us to make very difficult decisions about what we will consider important. Life is full of choices, and some choices seem patently unfair, but if we are seeking spiritual growth we will be required to make choices based upon our deepest desires. All of our choices have repercussions for what rises to the top of our priorities. In a very real sense, we become our priorities. If a balanced life is not one of our major priorities, we will have great difficulty in working deeply with consciousness.

Pace

A judge that I used to work with had a little sign in his chambers that said, "The hurrieder I go, the behinder I get." This is about the size of it. In today's postindustrial Western societies we are constantly hurrying and always behind. This kind of pace is toxic to consciousness. We humans need time to think and to make choices. We too often live in societies that expect us to be more like cattle, herded and prodded from point A to point B. Modern capitalistic societies function best when people are asleep and willing to hurry and not think. Our environment promotes a fast-paced, thoughtless approach to life. Consumer-based, acquisitive values promote blindness to the consciousness-dulling monotony of most workplaces; in order to feel alive we buy the latest clothing style or useless gadget.

The electronic media keep our minds active, when they would be far better off resting. The media also manipulate our emotions to promote everything from buying the latest fashion to voting for the right candidate or hating the right enemy. If we make the mistake of getting too hooked on the pace of world news and entertainment hype, we may be kept in a constant turmoil of manipulated emotions, without much chance of developing inner quiet.

This crazy pace is now begun in childhood, with children's overly orchestrated lives of both learning and play. Young children are kept busy with scheduled activities, rather than being lovingly parented. Children are overtaught and overorganized, rather than allowed to find the natural rhythm of childhood. No wonder we grow into adults who have no idea about a healthy pace of life. I remember a supervisor in a mental health center where I was a psychotherapist; he told me I needed to walk faster so I would get more done. I moved on from that rather pathological environment fairly quickly and found a mental health center that appreciated my non-neurotic pace.

Individuals have different rhythms. A fast pace may be natural for one person and a slow pace natural for another. We are not and should not be expected to be all the same. Activities also determine a proper pace. I enjoy playing golf, and one thing that every golfer must come to understand is that pace, in this case called tempo, is crucial to the golf swing. A good golf swing is built upon a good tempo, and although everyone's tempo is different, there seems to be a workable range. Anything too much faster or slower causes problems. Life is similar to golf in this way. In order to be successful at life, whatever we consider successful, we will need to tune in to our natural rhythm and pace and follow it. It is upon this natural rhythm that we can build our capabilities and knowledge.

Acknowledging the Natural

What all of this boils down to is rediscovering nature and a more natural way of life. As the quotation from Tilopa at the beginning of the chapter exhorts us to do, it is possible for us to "be in the natural state." We have objectified nature to the point where a relationship with it is nearly impossible for many individuals, and we have even lost the relationship with our own natural being. We need to discover that the only viable way of living on this planet is by being *in relationship with* the natural environment, which includes our bodies.

Developing a natural life does not mean that we must reject modern conveniences, move to remote areas, and live as hermits or in communes. This sort of solution is neither viable nor advisable. Rather it is the great opportunity of our time that we can learn to live in relationship with nature while maintaining the benefits of technology. Too often we can only see either/or solutions to issues of this sort, rather than recognizing the opportunity for both/and solutions. We humans have great capacities; we are just acting as if we do not. We can reclaim our natural minds and bodies while still creating and living in a technologically comfortable world. Our vision and concepts have been far too small.

SIXTEEN

An Authentic Spirituality for the Future

WHAT IS IT that is required of a spirituality capable of carrying us into the temporal future and beyond, into the future of the human species? Human beings contain the hidden treasure that seeks to be known, and we need a spiritual perspective that can recognize the divinity seeking to emerge from the human heart. An authentic spirituality is anchored in the *Divine Real*. It is not about rejection of the world in favor of an anticipated afterlife; instead, it embraces the mysterious grandeur of the depth of everyday life, while developing a relationship with the more subtle realms of existence. An authentic spirituality transcends cultural and historical aspects of any group of people and instead invites all of humanity to transform consciousness, regardless of ethnicity, culture, race, or gender.

There was a point at which I toyed with calling this chapter "On the Consequences of Not Knowing These Things." There are very real consequences that go along with continuing to equate spirituality with historical and cultural religious institutions. We will continue to impute wisdom and holiness to those who represent the static, patriarchal religions that perpetuate much of what is wrong with the world today. With consciousness rather than culture at the center of spirituality, wisdom could instead be associated with those who have done the most to transform their consciousness and open their hearts. Love, compassion, and connectedness would be central to holiness or a sense of the sacred. This could create an incredible change in how we might view wise decisionmaking and moral choice in a future society.

This book has its direct roots in the vision I had at the medicine wheel in the Big Horn Mountains, described in chapter 3. The powerful need for reconciliation between the masculine sky gods and the feminine earth spirits is the crying need of the day. Harmony between nature and humans, feminine and masculine, earth and sky, is central to authentic spirituality. However, if we know anything about power, the followers of the sky gods will need to lose some of their privileged position in order to be amenable to cooperation.

To some it might seem that it is "godless materialists" that are doing the most damage on the planet, but I think the rise of materialism is directly related to blind adherence to outdated, untenable religions. The inability of these religions to address the crying needs of humanity creates a sense of meaninglessness that opens the door for materialism. When our societal versions of what should provide meaning for us are absurd, one of the more common responses is to drown ourselves in materialism. My perspective is that much of the responsibility for the sorry state of human consciousness and the environmental peril we face today lies with the patriarchal religions that have dominated the West for the last several thousand years. The dual pathologies of religious fundamentalism and scientific materialism are directly related to the decline in the capacity of these patriarchal religions to provide meaning in an ever-changing world.

During the time I have been writing this book a very powerful event has made us all even more acutely aware of the divide between the two pathologies of fundamentalism and materialism. On September 11, 2001, Muslim terrorists flew two airliners into the World Trade Center in New York City and another into the Pentagon in Washington, D.C. All of a sudden Americans were asking why, and needed to be given a quick lesson not only in global politics, but also Islam and fundamentalist Islam. We became suddenly aware that our Judeo-Christian cultural perspective, along with the blatant materialism and political imperialism that accompany it, was not admired by all and that our freedom-loving and democratic political perspective was an aberration to religious fundamentalists. If people paid very close attention, they would realize that this division between democratic principles and religious fundamentalism is not only true of Islam, but also all fundamentalists. Christian fundamentalists may not be blowing up buildings, but they are hard at work trying to dismantle the Bill of Rights of the American Constitution. If we are to learn the lessons of September 11, we need to recognize the basis of our own cultural perspective and understand the insidious nature of religious intolerance.

The wide chasm between those in our world who are deeply immersed in a literalist faith system and those who are of a more scientific, modern bent is only now emerging into our public consciousness. This chasm can only grow deeper unless we can understand spirituality as consciousness transformation and becoming *real* and begin to recognize the potential for being both postmodern and spiritual people. It is only our definition of spirituality that needs to change. We need to ask ourselves, what are the consequences of maintaining the present perspective?

Business as Usual?

The continuing Middle East crisis in which Jewish and Muslim literalists and fundamentalists have gained the upper hand and have made resolution of the crisis nearly impossible, is a good example of the frightening direction our patriarchal cultural myths continue to take us. When your religion tells you that your inflexible sense of entitlement is justified and the fundamentalists in your religion argue that atrocities are acceptable when done in the name of your god, there is a very good possibility that you will destroy the world around you.

An incredible example of the evil that can take hold in fundamentalist circles is the mulla who recently said that Allah wants us (fundamentalist Muslims) to have nuclear weapons in order to destroy our enemies. We will undoubtedly create humanitarian catastrophes when we have a cultural perspective that may have made sense a millennium or two ago, but makes no sense today. The idea that an anthropomorphized God is on your side is not only foolish, but it is also extremely dangerous to the world around you. The Middle East is only one of the larger of many such conflicts around the world. A spirituality of consciousness would help defuse some of these conflicts or at least would not provide further fuel for cultural warfare.

The potential for environmental catastrophe is another example of how current perspectives need to change. As I have mentioned many times in this book, the denigration of the Earth and the peoples who are in tune with the Earth in the name of patriarchal religions has been like a cancer for nature and humanity. Out of our Western religious teachings about subduing and dominating the world has not only grown the technology and scientific perspective of the modern world, but also the subjugation of indigenous people, destruction of species, pollution of earth, water, and air, and global climate change. If we can't turn this around we will discover that this is not a sustainable trade-off.

The World Wildlife Fund has reported in their "Living Planet Report 2002" that unless human beings drastically decrease their use of natural resources, global standards of living will plummet by mid-century. The main culprits, according to the Wildlife Federation, are the United States, Canada, Japan, and most of Western Europe. Most of these areas carry the bias of Western patriarchy and the earth-devouring materialism currently associated with it. A spirituality of consciousness could weaken the basis for patriarchal control.

The oppression of women has been part of the cultural bias of Western patriarchal religions, but can be found around the world wherever warlike male-dominated cultures have gained ascendancy. It is related to denigration of nature, but deserves to be viewed separately. Wherever scientific thought and universal education gain the upper hand, the oppression of women declines, although its vestiges generally remain. In other, more premodern societies where the patriarchal religions or particularly warlike male-dominated traditions control the population, women are subject to slave-like conditions.

Recently a story has been in the news about a Pakistani woman who was gang-raped as a punishment because her brother was seen in public with a woman not of his class. We in the industrialized West may look at this story with a sense of superiority, and yet we forget that it was not long ago that we were burning witches for no better reason. Patriarchal religions seem to provide men with a sense of privilege that makes almost incomprehensible behavior possible. It seems that the development of consciousness through education, travel, and the fruits of freedom often works to modify patriarchal hubris. Authentic spirituality would be free of the cultural biases of patriarchy. Consciousness dwells equally in women and men, and spiritual development can occur equally in women and men.

There are many other issues where outdated spiritual perspectives create problems for individuals and societies. The population of the world is growing in an unsustainable way, and some religions, such as Catholicism, continue to oppose birth control. The world now has six billion human inhabitants, and is expected to grow by another billion in about ten more years. The reason for us to "be fruitful and multiply" has long since passed, and yet Catholicism and conservative Protestant Christians continue to fear changes to anything related to sex.

Christianity, and (to a lesser degree) Islam, claim to be the sole road to salvation, seeing everyone else as condemned to eternal damnation or at least estrangement from the Divine. How people can see themselves as compassionate, evolved, or even human, while seeing the rest of humanity as condemned to an eternity of suffering, is a puzzle to me, and yet this is the strange state of affairs we have inherited from our ancestors. The wisdom of reviewing the true nature of spirituality has never been more obvious.

Cultural Loss or Cultural Change

The music, art, and literature of cultures are often centered on historical-religious themes. The characters, events, and lessons of our mythic and religious stories are so infused in our cultural productions that it seems that it might be an incredible loss if we suddenly stopped believing literally in the stories from the Torah, Bible, or Qu'ran. This is not likely for two very important reasons.

We do not lose the past by moving into the future. Our past beliefs continue to infuse our culture; we just realize that they are teaching stories and not literally the way things happened. The power of a story is not destroyed by understanding it, as a matter of fact it can become greater. Stories of Zeus, Jupiter, Hercules, Oedipus, Odin, Loki, Merlin, the Lady of the Lake, and King Arthur have not lost their capacity to inspire our souls and our art. Why should the powerful stories of Jesus, Mary, Moses, Solomon, Muhammad, Fatima, and Ali not continue to inspire human consciousness through art, music, and literature? The primary difference is that we have moved away from small, highly competitive tribal cultures, and therefore we need to develop an authentic spirituality that serves the global, multicultural context of modern life. We need not leave our important cultural stories behind; we simply need to understand their roles in our lives.

The other reason why moving beyond literal belief systems would not lead to great loss is that consciousness needs symbols to help it grow and change. There is every reason to keep our transformative symbols alive and active in our culture, even as we disengage from literal understandings of them. Cultures are continually creating new symbols that speak to the deeper nature, but it would make no sense to completely discard entire interrelated sets of symbols contained in teaching stories that have become deeply engrained in our culture. These stories, if seen as symbolic and related to the depths of the psyche, can still be extremely important to us all. If they change, it will happen slowly over time. If they recede, other, newly energized symbol systems in tune with the contemporary needs will emerge and grow to become complex and fully developed.

Incorporating Authentic Spirituality

There are many things that we can do to incorporate a spirituality of consciousness into our lives. At the very least, these ideas will help all of us understand our own religions better. We can seek to understand the symbolism of our religions, and because of our understanding we can allow it to change with the times. We can take more personal responsibility for figuring out how to apply the teachings of our religions to our everyday lives. We can develop the tools to make our own choices, rather than simply having to rely upon priests, ministers, rabbis, or mullas to interpret spiritual and moral issues for us.

Our mainstream religions can, if they want, incorporate techniques for transforming consciousness into what they provide members, although they will have to learn them first. By changing from being completely culture-based to including a consciousness-based spirituality, religions can keep their history and culture but also incorporate consciousness-transforming techniques into their teachings. This would be a huge step for mainstream religions, since there has been so much pressure exerted on them to become more literalistic in recent times.

Mainstream religions have resisted the rush toward literalism as best they could by stressing social themes, but people are seeking more, and the personal relationship with God that is offered by fundamentalism has great appeal for many. Mainstream faiths could recognize and accept the significance of individual spiritual growth and compete with fundamentalist sects for the hearts of those seeking transformation.

With this possibility arises the question: is it better to promote incremental change away from rigid patriarchal perspectives that have already begun to die in the mainstream of the three large Western religions, or is it better to seek new forms without their tainted history? My answer seems always to involve the middle road of *both/and*. Some will need new religions and spiritual schools, and others will be quite happy to work on the evolution of the traditions they belong to into more balanced religions.

For those who have found religion as well as other mystical or New Age spiritualities to be too corrupt, irrelevant, or ungrounded to fit their needs, an authentic spirituality of consciousness provides techniques for developing their spiritual faculties. There are those who have a more pragmatic leaning and seek meaning, but want it to make sense and not require the suspension of reason. Faith can give us the gift of moving from our heads to our hearts, and yet it is reasonable to think that we should not always be required to do so. We need to learn to balance the head and the heart.

Sometimes reason and discernment uproot the false. Some of those who find it difficult to accept deeper or unseen realities simply on faith will, with a spirituality based upon consciousness, have the opportunity to work with their own experience. Authentic spirituality does not require belief in a specific cultural reality or revealed message; it is simply an approach to developing consciousness and becoming *real*.

The people that will probably be most drawn to authentic spirituality will be those of a mystical bent. There are always a few people who desire to go beyond the culturally recognized range of spiritual exploration. They typically seek spiritual freedom and a truth that they intuit is beyond the ken of those around them. These people are often drawn to mystical paths. There are always mystical paths available that can teach the aspirant how to develop their consciousness, and yet they are often hidden; they go about their great work quietly. The ones that come out into the open can easily be corrupted by the prevailing religions of the culture. Corruption can take the forms of intimidation and extermination, such as those done to the mystics (Sufis) in Iran in recent times, or it may creep in insidiously through modern materialism that seeks to impress potential students or make the teacher wealthy, as has happened to some schools in the United States.

A good portion of our discussion of the spirituality of consciousness contains descriptions of some central tenets of mysticism. What I call *authentic spirituality* is a repackaging of some mystical perspectives and practices. The primary difference is that I separate authentic spirituality from cultural history and myth. This is a major difference from much of what we would find until the very end of a course of study in the typical mystical school.

This difference is significant. In the path of authentic spirituality, the seeker with a mystical nature who wishes to explore reality beyond the range of cultural belief systems can be aware from the beginning that it is not necessary to buy into literal cultural stories or lifestyles in order to benefit from techniques to transform consciousness. People can continue to benefit from those stories and myths that call them and to which they resonate. Mystics can work with an understanding of a map of the spiritual growth process, while participating in whatever symbol system feels best for them, including science.

Conclusion

We have explored much territory in this book, but we have just barely touched the surface. Our human search to understand and find meaning in our lives, our deaths, our relationships, our communities, and our world is vast and never-ending. I have attempted to challenge the prevailing perspectives and offer alternatives from the perspective of a lifelong mystic. Some of the same issues that puzzled me as a child listening to my grandma and her friends discuss life and the nature of the soul still intrigue me today, over fifty years later. This is how consciousness evolves, by exploration, contemplation, and spiritual discussion.

Some readers may find much to argue with in the pages of this book, especially if they are fond of one of the patriarchal religions. No one should be deprived of a religious viewpoint that confers meaning upon his or her life, and I would hope that those who need the prevailing literalist perspectives would put this book down and continue their sleep. It is not good to awaken too soon. Some, however, may have mixed feelings. They may have a strong allegiance to a faith, but also know that some of what they are seeking is addressed in these pages. The only reason why one religious friend of mine can allow himself to read some of my work is because he believes this is precisely what his Protestant denomination needs to become complete. He may be right, though I am skeptical that I'll ever be invited to do a workshop at his church.

I hope this book will be a call to those who seek to explore and discuss beyond the parameters of what is normally acceptable, not only in church or synagogue, but even in schools of inner study and New Age communities. Wherever there are people trapped by those who would limit the range of consciousness exploration because of culturally created religious doctrines or worldviews that are constrained by cultural encapsulation, I hope this book will be a call to courage. Whenever people seek to explore beyond the mainstream, but need an understanding of the basics of spiritual growth, I hope this book will shed some light. It is not a comprehensive exploration of spirituality, it just opens a few doors. Hopefully those open doors will let in fresh, clean air, so sorely needed today.

Finally, and possibly most important, I hope that this book will find its way into the hands of many young people from their late teens to their middle thirties. This group of people seems more than most generations to be caught in a void of meaning. They are a group of often bright and energetic young people caught on the cusp of change. The old ways often seem incomprehensibly outdated to them, and yet there are few alternatives offered.

These young people watch the world around them disintegrating into religious and ethnic fratricide, and they find it hard to relate to the motivations behind such destruction. They know that life needs to be explored in order to find its deeper meaning, but the only options that are not dependent upon old, patriarchal perspectives seem to be the new extreme testing of their bodies. Little is available to challenge them to think in new, extreme ways, or to feel more fully—or most importantly, to explore the extremes of authenticity and connectedness.

In recent years, my heart has felt as if it would break when looking at the paucity of choices offered my children and my students. If this book can offer even the smallest hope for this generation to find opportunities to move beyond the old, dying ways and into a future open to possibilities for the development of a real and authentic spirituality of consciousness, I will feel fulfilled.

GLOSSARY

Ashram: A center for contemplative activities related to the Hindu Religion; similar to a monastery.

Balanced Path: A spiritual path that seeks truth along traditional lines and stays within the wide parameters of a religious tradition.

Consciousness: The faculty of awareness.

Darshan: An in-depth spiritual interview in which the teacher serves as a mirror for the inner reality of the student.

Dhikr (*also* **Zikr**): Repetition of the Arabic phrase La Illaha illa la (hu) which literally means "there is no god but God." When repeating Dhikr the meaning evolves as does the Zakir (the doer of Dhikr).

Direct Path: A spiritual path which eventually pulls the aspirant out of all cultural religious forms. The person on the direct path must then integrate a non-cultural transcendent realization into their everyday cultural existence.

God Ideal: A way of looking at the concept of god or gods that sees the concept of god that is held by an individual or culture as the highest ideal to which their consciousness can reach. With this perspective we can see that different understandings of god can be useful for different individuals and cultures. The god ideal becomes an evolutionary tug upon human consciousness. It must, however, evolve or it can become a weight that holds consciousness down.

Karma: A Sanskrit word referring to the spiritual law of cause and effect. The belief is that we get back what we give out. Therefore both good and evil actions will eventually rebound and we will experience their effects in our lives. It is also Karma that holds us in the wheel of life. Hindu renunciates believe that if one can refrain from action, either good or bad, one will eventually step off the wheel of samsara and no longer need to incarnate.

Mantra: A Sanskrit word for the repetition of a sacred phrase.

Modernity: The perspective that began with what has been termed the "Enlightenment" in Europe and characterizes the predominant worldview in Europe and North America. Modernity has certain core beliefs such as secularization, individualism, democracy, a utopian view of science, and a belief that modernity is the most advanced state of human evolution to date.

Morality of Consciousness: Proposed ethical framework based upon the effect of a situation or action upon consciousness.

Morality of Contract: Ethical framework based upon one's culture. The tried and true practices that promote harmony among individuals living in a particular place and time.

Postmodernism: A broad emerging social theory and philosophical base that rejects some of the primary perspectives of modernity. Postmodernists doubt the existence of one Truth and look to understand and give voice to the multitude of competing cultural truths. Deconstruction of the dominant belief systems central to science and religion and looking at alternative possibilities lies at the heart of postmodern theory-making.

Sufism: A mystical path often associated with Islam. There are many schools of Sufism throughout the world but predominantly in the Middle East and Central Asia. There is debate over the origins of Sufism, but the best description of Sufism's beginnings that I have heard involves a confluence of Neoplatonic, heretical Christian, and Jewish influences that found resonance with the emerging message of the Prophet Mohammed and his son-in-law Ali. Later, as Sufism spread along with Islam, influences from Hinduism and Buddhism also found their way into the eclectic mysticism of the Sufis. Sufis have a long history of persecution whenever governments find their openness and focus on the personal experience of God to be a threat to the state.

Synchronicity: Meaningful coincidence; the pairing of two events in a meaningful way.

Wali: One of the 99 Beautiful Names of God. Muslims place a special emphasis on the various names used for the divine in the Koran. Wali refers to the quality of mastery. It can also mean the "friend of God." The Arabic language has layer upon layer of meaning. Each word stems from a "root" word and depending upon various additions to the root the word will take on deeper and deeper meaning. I do not claim to truly understand the meaning of "wali," but can only share the little that I have been taught.

Wasifa: A sound practice used by Sufis typically repeating one of the 99 Beautiful Names of God from the Koran.

WORKS CITED

Arasteh, Resa. 1973. *Rumi the Persian: Rebirth in Creativity and Love.* Tuscan: Omen Press.

Armstrong, Karen. 1993. *A History of God: The 4,000 Year Quest of Judaism, Christianity, and Islam.* New York: Ballantine Books.

———. 2000. *The Battle for God.* New York: Alfred A. Knopf.

Bailey, Jim. 1994. *Sailing to Paradise: The Discovery of the Americas by 7000 B.C.* New York: Simon and Shuster.

Campbell, Joseph. 1999. *The Hero's Journey.* Edited by Phil Cousineau. Boston: Element.

Chaffee, John. 1998. *The Thinker's Way.* Boston: Back Bay Books.

Crow, John A. 1992. *The Epic of Latin America.* Fourth Ed. Berkeley, CA: University of California Press.

Dandaneau, Steven P. 2001. *Taking It Big: Developing Sociological Consciousness in Postmodern Times.* Thousand Oaks, CA: Pine Forge.

Edinger, Edward F. 1984. *The Creation of Consciousness: Jung's Myth for Modern Man.* Toronto: Inner City Books.

Evans-Wentz, W.Y. 1968. *The Tibetan Book of the Great Liberation.* London: Oxford University Press.

Inayat, Taj. 1978. *The Crystal Chalice: Spiritual Themes for Women.* New Lebanon, NY: Sufi Order Publications.

Irwin, Ronald R. 2002. *Human Development and Spiritual Life: How Consciousness Grows Toward Transformation.* New York: Kluwer Academic/Plenum Publishers.

Johnson, Robert. 1974. *He: Understanding Masculine Psychology.* New York: Perennial Library.

Jung, C. G. 1973. *Synchronicity.* New York: Bollengen.

Khan, Inayat. 1978. *The Complete Sayings of Hazrat Inayat Khan.* New Lebanon, NY: Sufi Order Publications.

———. 1978-1982. *The Sufi Message of Hazrat Inayat Khan:* 12 volumes. Katwijk, Holland: Servire.

Knight, Gareth. 1978. *A History of White Magic.* New York: Samuel Weiser.

Newman, Barbara M., and Philip R. Newman. 1984. *Development Through Life: A Psychosocial Approach.* Homewood, IL: Dorsey Press.

Perry, William. 1970. *Forms of Intellectual and Ethical Development During the College Years.* New York: Holt, Rinehart, and Winston.

Power, Richard, editor. 1993. *Great Song: The Life and Teachings of Joe Miller.* Athens, GA: Maypop.

Ritzer, George. 1993. *The McDonaldization of Society.* Thousand Oaks, CA: Pine Forge.

Segal, Elizabeth A., and Layne K. Stromwall. 2000. "Social Work Practice Issues Related to Poverty and Homelessness." In *The Handbook of Direct Social Work Practice.* Thousand Oaks, CA: Sage.

Tarnas, Richard. 1991. *The Passion of the Western Mind: Understanding the Ideas that Have Shaped Our Worldview.* New York: Ballantine Books.

Tompkins, Ptolemy. 2000. "Recovering a Visionary Geography: Henry Corbin and the Missing Ingredient in Our Culture of Images." *Lapis.* 11. 53-55.

von Franz, Marie-Louise. 1982. *Interpretation of Fairy Tales.* Dallas, TX: Spring Publications.

SELECTED BIBLIOGRAPHY

Armstrong, Karen. 1993. *A History of God*. New York: Ballantine Books.

———. 2000. *The Battle for God*. New York: Alfred A. Knopf.

———. 1997. Jerusalem: *One City, Three Faiths*. New York: Ballantine Books.

Bly, Robert. 1988. *A Little Book on the Human Shadow*. San Francisco: Harper and Row.

Bradley, Marion Zimmer. 1982. *The Mists of Avalon*. New York: Del Rey.

Byrom, Thomas, trans. 1976. *The Dhammapada: Sayings of the Buddha*. New York: Vintage Books.

———. 1990. *The Heart of Awareness: A Translation of the Ashtavakra Gita*. Boston, MA: Shambhala.

Campbell, Joseph. 1968. *The Hero with a Thousand Faces*. Princeton, NJ: Bollingen Series, Princeton University Press.

———. 2001. *Thou Art That.* Novato, CA: New World Library.

———. 1990. *Transformations of Myth Through Time.* New York: Harper and Row.

Chittick, William C. 1994. *Imaginal Worlds: Ibn al 'Arabi and the Problem of Religious Diversity.* Albany, NY: State University of New York Press.

Corbin, Henry. 1971. *The Man of Light in Iranian Sufism.* Boulder, CO: Shambhala.

———. 1969. *Creative Imagination in the Sufism of Ibn 'Arabi.* Princeton, NJ: Princeton University Press.

DeMallie, Raymond J., ed. 1984. *The Sixth Grandfather: Black Elk's Teachings Given to John G. Neihardt.* Lincoln, NE: University of Nebraska Press.

Edinger, Edward F. 1984. *The Creation of Consciousness: Jung's Myth for Modern Man.* Toronto: Inner City Books.

Eisler, Raine. 1988. *The Chalice and the Blade.* San Francisco: Harper.

Evans-Wentz, W.Y. 1968. *The Tibetan Book of the Great Liberation.* Oxford: Oxford University Press.

Gergen, Kenneth J. 1991. *The Saturated Self: Dilemmas of Identity in Contemporary Life.* New York: Basic Books.

Gimbutas, Marija. 1991. *The Civilization of the Goddess: The World of Old Europe.* San Francisco: Harper.

Hancock, Graham. 1995. *Fingerprints of the Gods.* New York: Crown Trade Paperbacks.

Harman, Willis and Jane Clark, eds. 1994. *New Metaphysical Foundations of Modern Science.* Sausalito, CA: Institute of Noetic Sciences.

Harner, Michael. 1990. *The Way of the Shaman.* San Francisco: Harper and Row.

Inayat, Taj. 1978. *The Crystal Chalice: Spiritual Themes for Women.* New Lebanon, New York: Sufi Order Publications.

Ingerman, Sandra. 1991. *Soul Retrieval: Mending the Fragmented Self.* San Francisco: Harper. 1991

Johnson, Robert A. 1991. *Transformation: Understanding the Three Levels of Masculine Consciousness.* San Francisco: Harper.

Jung, Carl G. 1965. *Memories, Dreams, Reflections.* New York: Vintage Books.

———. 1973. *Synchronicity.* Princeton, NJ: Bolligen Series/Princeton University Press.

Knight, Christopher, and Robert Lomas. 1997. *The Hiram Key.* Shaftsbury, Dorset: Element.

Knight, Gareth. 1965. *A Practical Guide to Qabalistic Symbolism.* York Beach, MA: Samuel Wiser.

———. 1968. *A History of White Magic.* New York: Samuel Wiser.

Khan, Inayat. 1979. *The Sufi Message of Hazrat Inayat Khan:* 12 volumes. Katwijk, Holland: Servire.

———. 1983. *The Music of Life.* Santa Fe, NM: Omega Press.

Khan, Vilayat I. 1978. *The Message in Our Time.* San Francisco. Harper Row.

————. 1994. *That Which Transpires Behind That Which Appears.* New Lebanon, NY: Omega Press.

Lao Tsu. 1972. *Tao Te Ching.* Translated by Gia-Fu Feng and Jane English. New York: Vintage Books.

Matthews, John and Caitlin. 1985. *The Western Way: A Practical Guide to the Western Mystery Tradition.* London: Arkana.

Meade, Michael. 1993. *Men and the Water of Life.* San Francisco: Harper.

Mehta, Gita. 1993. *A River Sutra.* New York: Vintage Books.

Muktananda, Swami. 1978. *Play of Consciousness.* San Francisco: Harper and Row.

Pinkola-Estes, Clarissa. 1992. *Women Who Run With the Wolves.* New York: Ballantine.

Power, Richard, ed. 1993. *Great Song: The Life and Teachings of Joe Miller.* Athens, GA: Maypop.

Quinn, Daniel. 1997. *The Story of B.* New York: Bantam.

Rahda, Swami Sivananda. 1998. *Kundalini Yoga for the West.* Boulder, CO: Shambhala.

Rama, Swami, Rudolph Ballentine, and Swami Ajaya. 1976. *Yoga and Psychotherapy: The Evolution of Consciousness.* Glenview, IL: Himalayan Institute.

Richardson, Alan. 1990. *Earth God Rising: The Return of the Male Mysteries.* St. Paul, MN: Llewellyn.

Tarnas, Richard. 1991. *The Passion of the Western Mind: Understanding the Ideas That Have Shaped Our Worldview.* New York: Ballantine Books.

Thompson, William Irwin. 1981. *The Time Falling Bodies Take to Light.* New York: St. Martin's Press.

Trungpa, Chogyam. 1984. *Shambhala: The Sacred Path of the Warrior.* Boulder, CO: Shambahala.

von Franz, Marie-Louise. 1982. *Interpretation of Fairy Tales.* Dallas, TX: Spring Publications.

Wilson, A. N. 1999. *God's Funeral.* New York: W. W. Norton.

INDEX

Black Elk, 42–43
Bodhisattva, 9, 105, 123–124, 133
Borges, Jorge Luis, 152
boundaries, 5, 52, 70, 81, 99, 102, 126, 128, 161
Brahma, 125, 174, 177
breath, 8, 37, 45, 74, 87, 133, 135, 155–156, 158, 160, 163–171, 185, 199
breathing practices, 87, 166, 169, 171
Buddha, 27, 96, 107, 182, 200

Campbell, Joseph, xv, 13, 114
Cathers, 62
chakra(s), 69–70, 74, 168, 175–180
character, 13, 88–89, 97
Christ, 27, 62, 158
Christian(s), ix, 9, 24, 47, 57, 59–61, 63, 65, 87, 119, 142–143, 158, 173–174,
    177, 182, 194, 207, 209, 217
cognitive development, 100, 139
Coleridge, Samuel, 148
commitment, 15, 45, 116, 140
community, 3–4, 9, 17, 40, 49, 51, 54, 56–57, 61, 66, 93, 120, 174
compassion, 60, 71, 74, 77, 84, 86, 94, 96, 105, 107–109, 177, 179, 183, 206,
    209
concentration, 47, 89, 103, 141, 149, 153–158, 160–161, 163, 168, 176–177,
    181, 190, 199
conjunctio oppositorium, 15
consciousness, x, xvi–xviii, 3, 6, 11–14, 19–28, 30, 34, 37–40, 43, 46, 48,
    50–56, 59–61, 65–67, 69, 71–72, 74–75, 77, 80, 83, 85–88, 91, 95, 97,
    102–104, 111, 113, 115, 118–121, 123–127, 130–133, 135, 137, 139,
    141–145, 147, 149, 153–154, 156, 158–162, 165–169, 171, 174–175,
    180–183, 185–186, 188–192, 195, 197–202, 205–216
Constantine, 60, 62
Corbin, Henri, 150–151
Council of Nicaea, 62
creativity, 3, 6, 10, 12, 16, 20, 22–27, 30, 32, 37–38, 40, 47, 52, 54–57, 63–64,
    67, 73, 86, 95, 97, 99, 101, 103–105, 107, 109, 111, 126, 129, 131–132,
    139–140, 145, 147–153, 157–158, 161, 165–166, 168–170, 173–178,
    180, 183, 186, 195, 202, 204, 206–207, 209–210
critical thinking, 98, 100, 138–140, 161
cultural encapsulation, 5, 123, 126, 213

☾ ORDER LLEWELLYN BOOKS TODAY!

Llewellyn publishes hundreds of books on your favorite subjects! To get these exciting books, including the ones on the following pages, check your local bookstore or order them directly from Llewellyn.

Order Online:
Visit our website at www.llewellyn.com, select your books, and order them on our secure server.

Order by Phone:
- Call toll-free within the U.S. at 1-877-NEW-WRLD (1-877-639-9753)
  Call toll-free within Canada at 1-866-NEW-WRLD (1-866-639-9753)
- We accept VISA, MasterCard, and American Express

Order by Mail:
Send the full price of your order (MN residents add 7% sales tax) in U.S. funds, plus postage & handling to:

Llewellyn Worldwide
P.O. Box 64383, Dept. 0-7387-0442-3
St. Paul, MN 55164-0383, U.S.A.

Postage & Handling:
Standard (U.S., Mexico, & Canada). If your order is:
Up to $25.00, add $3.50
$25.01 - $48.99, add $4.00
$49.00 and over, FREE STANDARD SHIPPING
(Continental U.S. orders ship UPS. AK, HI, PR, & P.O. Boxes ship USPS 1st class. Mex. & Can. ship PMB.)

International Orders:
Surface Mail: For orders of $20.00 or less, add $5 plus $1 per item ordered. For orders of $20.01 and over, add $6 plus $1 per item ordered.

Air Mail:
Books: Postage & Handling is equal to the total retail price of all books in the order.
Non-book items: Add $5 for each item.

Orders are processed within 2 business days. Please allow for normal shipping time.
Postage and handling rates subject to change.

Discover Your Spiritual Life

Illuminate Your Soul's Path

Elizabeth Owens

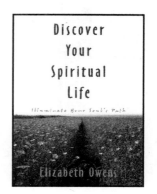

Some are led to the spiritual path by a mystical experience, by a tragic life circumstance, or by nagging feelings of discontent. Whatever the reason, you need a road map or guide to assist you along the way. Spiritualist medium Elizabeth Owens gives you the tools to connect with that higher guidance that, she says, already resides within yourself.

Learn a life-changing method for handling problems and disappointments. Discover effective ways to meditate, pray, create affirmations, forgive those who have hurt you, and practice gratitude. Process painful emotions and thoughts quickly through the art of becoming a balanced observer.

0-7387-0423-7, 264 pp., 5 ³/₁₆ x 8   **$12.95**

To order by phone call 1-877-NEW WRLD
Prices subject to change without notice

Transformative Meditation

Personal & Group Practice to
Access Realms of Consciousness

Gayle Clayton

Never underestimate the power of a small group of conscious, committed individuals to change the world. As humanity grows ever more complex, we need to balance technological advances with an evolution of higher consciousness. One way to do that is through group or collective meditation.

This system of meditation creates a single identity that transforms the individuals, the group, and later, the world. Select groups and teachers have already incorporated collective meditation into successful practice. Now, *Transformative Meditation* introduces this system to everyone. It presents an overview of meditation systems, explores the various levels of transformative meditation, and teaches you how to move the group to upper astral planes, how to chant to create a higher identity, and how to increase moments of mystical awareness.

0-7387-0502-0, 216 pp., 6 x 9   **$12.95**